# KATANGA
# 1960–63

# KATANGA
# 1960–63

## MERCENARIES, SPIES AND THE AFRICAN NATION THAT WAGED WAR ON THE WORLD

## CHRISTOPHER OTHEN

For my parents

Cover illustration © Tommy Nilsson

First published 2015
This paperback edition first published 2018

The History Press
The Mill, Brimscombe Port
Stroud, Gloucestershire, GL5 2QG
www.thehistorypress.co.uk

© Christopher Othen, 2015, 2018

The right of Christopher Othen to be identified as the Author
of this work has been asserted in accordance with the
Copyright, Designs and Patents Act 1988.

British Library Cataloguing in Publication Data.
A catalogue record for this book is available from the British Library.

ISBN 978 0 7509 8916 9

Typesetting in Bembo 11/13pt by The History Press
Printed and bound in Great Britain by TJ International Ltd

# CONTENTS

# KATANGA CONFIDENTIAL

## An Introduction

**Bruges, October 1999**

Somewhere in this Belgian city of canals and rain and gothic spires, 84-year-old Gérard Soete is finally ready to tell the truth about a murder.

A crew from French-language television station RTBF are in Soete's home to catch the moment on film. Cameras, cables and tripod lights crowd his living room. An interviewer makes notes on a clipboard. The crew huddle around a monitor.

Leathery and bald, the former colonial police commissioner shows the camera a small wooden box and spills its contents on the coffee table. Two off-white cubes, like eroded dice, roll around.

'They believe that he will come back from the dead,' he says.[1]

Soete laughs.

'If he does, he'll have to do it without these.'

The off-white cubes are human teeth.

***

The Democratic Republic of the Congo is an artificial state, created by Europeans drawing lines on a map in the nineteenth century.

Almost all modern African nations are the same. Only a few bear any resemblance to their pre-colonial existence. Rwanda's mountain borders have maintained continuity between its ancient kingdoms and current republic. Ethiopia was occupied only briefly by outsiders and its territory has changed little since the days of Emperor Menelik II. The rest of the continent got diced up by Europe's nineteenth-century land grab like an onion on a chopping board.

In February 1885, King Léopold II of Belgium helped himself to a chunk of Central Africa. The Congo Free State's 900,000 square miles made it the largest country on the continent and twelfth largest in the world. It stretched from the Mountains of the Moon in the north-east, down to the red dirt of Katanga's southern copper belt, and as far west as the narrow snout of land where the River Congo poured into the Atlantic Ocean with such force it carved a 100-mile long trench in the seabed.

Over 250 tribes called this territory home when Léopold created the Free State. The new nation's borders sliced some tribes in half, bisecting the Bakongo along the Angolan frontier and stranding many Lunda in Rhodesia. It fenced together others who had been enemies for centuries. Léopold did not care about ancient feuds between Lunda and Baluba, Baluba and Lulua, Lulua and Basongye. The hatred remained, old hands reaching for old throats.

Europeans, who put nationality above everything, never appreciated the importance of tribal loyalty. For many Congolese, it governed marriage, morality, friendships and war. If a Lulua asked another Lulua for money he would get it, even if they were strangers. If a Lulua were stupid enough to ask a Baluba, the *panga* machetes would swing.

The spilt blood would have meant nothing to the Belgian king. His Congo Free State was a moneymaking machine, rich in natural resources. Its most disposable parts were human. Léopold's soldiers worked the Congolese like slaves and crushed any resistance by burning villages and killing families.

In 1908, international outrage forced Léopold to hand over the country to professionals in the Belgian government. Their rule was less violent but more paternalistic. They treated the natives like children, justifying it with the phrase *dominer pour servir* (dominate to serve).[2] The new administrators held the Congo together for fifty-two more years, milking its assets and telling themselves they were helping Africa, until Brussels reluctantly granted independence in June 1960.

When the Congo fell apart in a pandemic of army mutinies and gang rape a week after going solo, Europeans blamed the unwieldy size of the new nation and its warring tribes. The July secession of Katanga, a rich mining province in the south, seemed proof that the Congo was too big to function as a country. Africans had a simpler explanation. They accused Belgium of masterminding the break-up to protect its investments. The term 'neo-colonialism', a continuation of empire through intrigue and espionage, was born.

Also in the mix were Soviet technicians at the controls of Ilyushin Il-14 transport planes, CIA agents hiding behind dark glasses, United Nations peace-keepers from a hundred countries and air-conditioned Swiss bank vaults that swallowed up diamonds and francs, no questions asked.

And one thing more dangerous than the rest put together: white men with guns.

\*\*\*

If you were thirsty in Brussels, perhaps in the mid 1980s, there was always 42 rue du Marché au Charbon. Officially called La Renaissance, regulars knew it as Bar Simba, the only place outside Katanga you could get a Simba beer, straight from the Elisabethville brewery.

Today it is a gay bar, but Bar Simba used to be a military pub famous for giving free drinks to any soldier who donated his cap badge. Green Berets, SAS and Navy SEALs had all dropped by to take advantage of the offer.

Not every customer was a career soldier. If you limited yourself to a few Simbas and stayed off the Chimay Trappiste, a lethally strong black beer, you might notice the map of Katanga province on the wall. You might see the similarity between Charles Masy, the bald and moustached owner, and the slim, crop-haired young man in the photographs hanging by the bar. You might overhear some of the regulars talking about their adventures in Angola, Biafra, the Congo and Yemen, throwing around words like '*Les Affreux*' and '*Les Mercenaires*'.

It would not take you long to realise that Bar Simba doubled as a hangout for old mercenaries. No fighting for them any more, but a lot of talking. Veterans of Africa, like Masy, argued bitterly about the United Nations, the USA, the USSR. Old grudges from Congo politics lived on: the settlers versus the merchants, the Walloons versus the Flemish, the Belgians versus the French, the British versus the rest.

As the evening came in and Masy helped himself to a Simba or two, he would tell his patrons about the time he was arrested by the Rhodesians in '63 and questioned about his adventures in Katanga.

'Finally, they asked me: How many did you kill? I was fed up with their games so I said: Not enough!'[3]

And through the rest of the night, the refrain from drunken, middle-aged men. *Les Mercenaires*. *Les Affreux*. We could have won. You understand? We could have won. If it hadn't been for the UN bastards. For the American bastards. For the bastards in Brussels. For the African bastards. We could have done it. We could have made a new country.

That new country was Katanga. The man who hired them was Moïse Tshombe, a Congolese politician. To some, a hero of national self-determination; to others, a villain, responsible for those unplugged teeth Gérard Soete kept in a wooden box.

\*\*\*

Moïse Tshombe was born to be a businessman. Just not a very good one. The son of a tough-minded Congolese capitalist, Tshombe went bankrupt so often before independence that people in his home province of Katanga stopped counting. Short, happy, with a face as round as a dinner plate, the millionaire's son always tried to bounce back. Import and export, a chain of general stores: his father had to bail him out every time. It was not until the 1950s that Tshombe discovered his real talent lay in politics. Katangese politics.

Katanga had always been different. Rich in copper, tin and uranium, the vital ingredient in atomic weapons, the Congo's southern province only joined the rest of the country six years before the Second World War. It felt separate, with its 32,000 white immigrants (more than any other province), its massive mineral wealth and its social services provided by Union Minière, the mining corporation that had built modern Katanga from the ground up and had no love for the government in the national capital Léopoldville. It even looked different. Where the rest of the country was covered in lush jungle, Katanga had red dirt roads, scrappy patches of vegetation and parched baobab trees.

Tshombe's Conakat party agitated for secession before the Congo's independence. The men in Brussels humoured him, because secessionist threats were useful for keeping other Congolese politicians in line, but most never expected him to go through with it. The Rhodesians held secret meetings with Conakat in Salisbury hotel rooms, but their African federation was already falling apart. When Tshombe made a new country out of Katanga in July 1960 he had to do it himself.

A man alone. Except for Union Minière, which preferred a stable secession to the chaos that ripped apart the Congo when it sailed from Belgium. And except for the white mercenaries who came pouring into Katanga, drawn by the smell of money like starving dogs to the back door of a restaurant kitchen. And except for the Belgian 'ultras' in Elisabethville, the Katangese capital, who saw communism everywhere: in the Congo's new leaders, in Washington, even in their own government, despite the military advisors Brussels sent to help Tshombe when it realised he was serious about independence.

Western Europe tried to stay neutral in the conflict. Everyone else from America to the Soviet bloc lined up to condemn the secession. They saw Tshombe as a puppet of the Belgians.

'I simply prefer the support of little Belgium,' said Tshombe, 'to that of big America or big Russia.'[4]

It was the Cold War. The men in Washington and Moscow did not think Tshombe should get to choose who supported him.

But Katanga's chief opponent was the United Nations, the peacekeeping organisation that drew support from around the world. Under Dag Hammarskjöld, a Swedish civil servant who had become Secretary General in

1953, the UN entered the Congo to stop the post-independence chaos. It found itself knee-deep in blood when a mission to protect the Baluba of northern Katanga, who had remained loyal to Léopoldville, mutated into a crusade to end Tshombe's secession. Katanga was not the UN's first shooting war (Korea had that honour), but it became the most controversial.

Tshombe's new nation went toe to toe with the UN's multinational troops. His gendarmes in camouflage gear, helped by grass-skirted jungle guerrillas and led by Belgian advisors, directed on the ground by truckloads of mercenaries, declared themselves willing to die for an independent Katanga.

Over the next two and a half years many would die. The UN claimed it acted only in self-defence. But to the outnumbered Katangese and their small gang of international supporters, it seemed the organisation had become the enforcer of a new world order, crushing anything in its path. Jet fighters over Elisabethville, mortar shells dropping in the streets, shock waves blowing in hospital windows, bodies buried in unmarked graves.

The backlash from the conflict was so strong that the United Nations would not go to war again until Yugoslavia at the end of the century. And it lost Hammarskjöld, the UN's brightest star, in mysterious circumstances near the Rhodesian border, an event some believed to be conspiracy rather than accident.

Tshombe's country is now dirt beneath the fingernails of history, but while it lived the Katangese cause divided the world. Even now it divides the Congo from Europe. If you want to see an African diplomat rage, praise Tshombe. Want to start a bar fight in Kinshasa? Wave a Katangese flag. The events of 1960 are the ground zero of CIA-sponsored African dictatorships, private military contractors, conflict diamonds and global corporations picking clean the bones of Third World countries.

The arguments continue. Neo-colonialism or independence. Imperialist power games or secession. Murder or necessary measure.

Those off-white cubes on Gérard Soete's coffee table? They once belonged in the mouth of Patrice Lumumba, the independent Congo's first prime minister and arch-enemy of Tshombe.

'He had good, strong teeth,' Soete told the television interviewer.[5]

So he kept them as a souvenir.

***

This book would not have been possible without Nicholas Bołtuć, Agnieszka Egeman, Rebecca Lewis, my brother Phillip and nephew Jacob, Tron and Tristian Tyrie, and Peter Wood. Very special thanks to Rysiu, Lilly, Jazz and Bella. And, above all, to Magdalena Wywiałek.

Invaluable help came from Interviewee A, an anonymous former member of the Compagnie Internationale, who provided first-hand information about this short-lived but important mercenary group; Terry Aspinall, founder of www.mercenary-wars.net, who smoothed introductions to former soldiers of fortune; Hans Bloemendaal who sent useful documents, including a rare Katangese pamphlet picked up during a long career in the province; Leif Hellström, a Swedish writer and expert on Congo mercenaries, who shared information and photographs from his own research; Denis Kurashko and Thomas Mrett provided some otherwise inaccessible books; Tommy Nilsson, former Swedish UN soldier and Malmö police detective, was generous with his time, memories and photographs; Victor Rosez shared his experiences of fighting with the Katangese gendarmes as a teenage schoolboy; Jacques Saquet talked about being a radio operator in Elisabethville's Belgian consulate; J.P. Sonck, an expert on the secession, answered many questions and provided background on the lesser-known characters involved; John Trevelyn (a *nom de guerre*), Welsh veteran of the Katangese forces, spoke in depth about his time as a volunteer in Tshombe's army.

If you have further information about Katanga or the Congo in the period 1960–67, please contact me via my website: www.brightreview.co.uk.

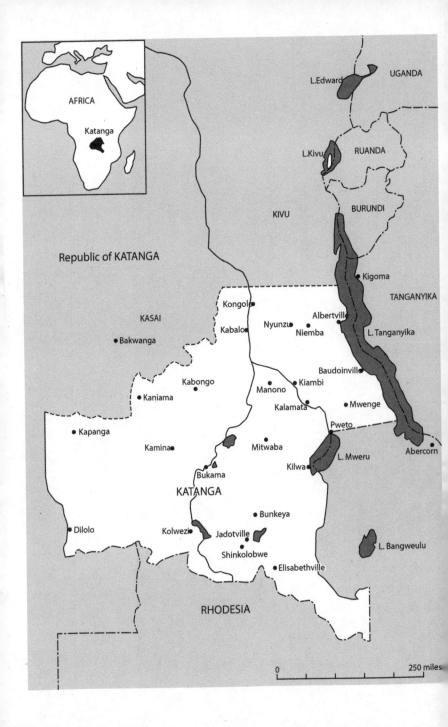

# DAWN

# 1

# A SLICE OF AFRICAN CAKE

## The Birth and Death of the Belgian Congo

Today it is Kinshasa, capital of the Democratic Republic of the Congo. But it used to be Léopoldville, a port city with 4 miles of quays and jetties poking into the black water of the River Congo, hundreds of boats tied up and bobbing on the tide. If you watched the river long enough, said the locals, you would see the bodies of your enemies float past.

Léopoldville's Ndjili airport, a cross-hatch of runways and white modernist terminals, lay on the eastern outskirts of the city. On Thursday 30 June 1960, it was thick with crowds watching the skies for a royal visitor.

The DC-6 airliner carrying the king of the Belgians touched down with a squeal of tyres in mid-morning. Reporters jostled for position as the aeroplane door opened and Baudouin I, wearing a white dress uniform with gold buttons, emerged into the grey-sky, oppressive humidity of the Congo.

'*Vive le Roi!*' shouted Belgians in the crowd, faces glossy with sweat.[1]

The 29-year-old Baudouin I had been doing this for nearly a decade. He was a veteran of the parades, state visits and official occasions that made up the daily life of a ceremonial monarch. The young king looked good in his uniform – even if the glasses and neat black hair gave the impression of a bookworm – had a strong speaking voice and could be relied upon by the Belgian government not to do anything embarrassing.

Gravitas and statesmanship mattered to a country still split over the wartime decision by Baudouin's father, King Léopold III, to remain in Nazi-occupied Brussels when he could have fled to London. Léopold believed he was standing by his people but some Belgians, and the country's Allied liberators, thought it closer to collaboration.

After the war, Léopold exiled himself to Geneva. When he returned home in 1950, strikes and riots tore the country apart. French speakers in the south pulled down the Belgian *tricolore* and replaced it with a strutting Wallonian rooster. Poorer, Dutch-speaking Flanders remained loyal. Civil war loomed. Léopold bought peace by passing the throne to his son Baudouin and retreated into his hobby of entomology, spending his days netting rare insects in exotic places.

The royal house survived but a guillotine blade hung over its neck, ready to drop at the first jolt. Baudouin I understood this and had proved himself a talented royal workhorse capable of looking regal and avoiding controversy.

Today, more than any other, he would need those qualities.

The jewel in Baudouin's inherited crown was the Belgian Congo, close to a million square miles of steaming jungle that hid huge reserves of cobalt, copper and diamonds. White settlers had lived here since the nineteenth century, chopping out roads, building factories and digging mineshafts. The Congo had made Belgium rich.

A piece of prime real estate in the heart of Africa, the colony bordered Rhodesia, Angola, the French Congo, the Central African Republic, Sudan, Uganda and Tanganyika. It divided into six provinces: Équateur in the north-west, Orientale in the north-east, Léopoldville to the east and Kivu to the west, with Kasaï wedged in between, and Katanga hanging down to the south. Baudouin ruled a land that dominated the world copper and cobalt markets, had supplied the uranium that built the first atomic bombs, owned a decent share of the industrial diamond traffic and had profitable interests in palm oil and other sectors.

But now all that was at an end. The Second World War had showed Africans their colonial rulers were not invincible. Nationalist movements formed and demanded self-government. When European powers ignored them they experimented with civil disobedience, then violent revolt.

By the late 1950s, British soldiers were fighting dreadlocked Mau Mau guerrillas in Kenya, Portuguese forces battled Movimento Popular de Libertação de Angola (Popular Movement for the Liberation of Angola – MPLA) partisans in their flagship colony and France was in a bitter war with Algerian independence fighters.

'The wind of change is blowing right through this continent,' said British Prime Minister Harold Macmillan to an unenthusiastic white audience in South Africa, 'and whether we like it or not, this growth of national consciousness is a political fact. We must all accept it as a fact, and our national policies must take account of it.'[2]

Slowly and reluctantly, western nations disengaged from their colonies. Today was Belgium's turn to say goodbye. After seventy-five years, the Belgian Congo had been granted self-government and Baudouin I was in Léopoldville for the official handover ceremony.

It was Independence Day.

King Baudouin was greeted on the runway by Joseph Kasa-Vubu, the new Congolese president, surrounded by his ministers. Patrice Lumumba, both Prime Minister and Minister of Defence, towered over them, a gangly praying mantis of a man with goatee, glasses and a neat side parting razored into his hair. Then there was an inspection of Congolese troops and their Belgian officers before Baudouin and his entourage were guided into a convoy of black limousines. The king placed his ceremonial sword, all polished steel and dark hilt, on the seat behind him.

The cars set off along boulevard Albert I, towards the city centre. The Congo's new flag, dark blue with seven yellow stars, flew from lamp posts. A few Belgian *tricolores* snapped in the wind high on official buildings. The king had visited Léopoldville before. In 1955, huge crowds of Africans and Europeans had cheered him. Four years later, Congolese nationalists heckled his speeches.

Today, the sweaty crowds were thinner and whiter. Women in pastel outfits and elaborate hats waved as the convoy drove past. Men with a filterless cigarette hanging from a lower lip lifted up children to see over the fence of Congolese soldiers lining the pavements. The newsreels caught them all in sweeping shots then panned back to the king standing next to President Kasa-Vubu in the back of an open limousine.

The new president, a short and fat-cheeked 50-year-old with some Chinese blood in him thanks to a long-dead labourer on the Léopoldville–Matadi railway, was leader of the Alliance des Bakongo (Bakongo Alliance – Abako) party. Belgian officials had once considered Kasa-Vubu too introverted to be an effective politician; his supporters preferred to see him as aloofly dignified. In 1957, he surprised everyone by campaigning for mayor in Léopoldville's Dendale district elections wearing a leopard skin and waving a sword. He won. Three years later, he was president.

As the convoy rolled towards the Palais de la Nation, Baudouin made a good show of listening to Kasa-Vubu's commentary on the sights of the Congolese capital. The Congolese president was pointing out office blocks in the distance when an African man in jacket and tie ran out of the crowd on the right side of the avenue. He dodged the motorcycle outriders and ran up behind the limousine.

The outriders went for their guns as he reached for the king.

Léopoldville was founded in 1881 as a trading post on the banks of the River Congo, the waterway that winds like a giant snake through the country. Thirty-five years later, the trading post had grown big enough to replace Boma, a port town in the far west, as national capital.

The city was named after the man who created the Congo: Léopold II, Baudouin's great-grand-uncle. The old king, who had eyes like black olives and a waterfall of white beard down his chest, first heard about the jungles of Central Africa in 1878 from his morning newspaper, crisply ironed by the royal butler. It was full of the exploits of a man called Stanley.

Nine years previously, the *New York Herald* had sent Henry Morton Stanley, a Welsh journalist with a bad temper, in search of a missionary lost in Central Africa for three years. The missing man, Dr David Livingstone, was a Scot determined to save Africans from Arab slavers, find the source of the White Nile and shine the light of Christian capitalism on the jungle. These were the days when so little was known about the heart of Africa that cartographers left the region blank on their maps. Livingstone's disappearance was headline news.

'Draw £1,000 now, and when you have gone through that, draw another £1,000,' the *Herald*'s owner told Stanley, 'and when that is spent, draw another £1,000, and when you have finished that, draw another £1,000, and so on – but find Livingstone!'[3]

Stanley found him near Lake Tanganyika. The missionary was so short of supplies he had been eating lunch in a roped-off enclosure to entertain the locals in exchange for food. Sick but determined to complete his expedition, Livingstone refused to be rescued. Stanley turned defeat into victory with some self-mythologising despatches and a snappy one-liner ('Doctor Livingstone, I presume?').[4] He returned home a celebrity with a taste for African adventure. Three years later, Livingstone was dead of dysentery near Lake Bangweulu and Stanley had a new quest following the River Congo to the sea.

The *Herald* journalist was the first to map the twisting river. It nearly killed him. Of the 356 men who started the expedition, hacking through jungle so dark that day and night melted together, more than half died on the way. Stanley was the only European to survive.

Léopold II read about the Welshman's adventures at the royal breakfast table. The future suddenly seemed clear. He would create a new country out of that blank space in the African interior. And Stanley would help him.

European powers had been gobbling up Africa since the 1870s, turning vast areas into colonies and protectorates. They convinced themselves they were stopping cannibalism, introducing the rule of law, freeing slaves and teaching the true word of God. But the driving force was always money. Africa provided materials unavailable at home, like diamonds, palm oil and rubber, and opened up new markets for European goods.

Belgium had been sidelined in the land grab. The government in Brussels did not share Léopold's enthusiasm for empire building and refused to finance any overseas projects. The king would have to use his own money. He considered Fiji or part of Argentina, but Africa remained his dream.

On 10 June 1878, Léopold invited Stanley to his palace overlooking the Parc de Bruxelles. After tea and flattery, the king made his offer. To put together a colony he needed Central Africa's emperors, headmen and warlords to sign up with the Association Internationale Africaine (International African Association – AIA), an organisation Léopold had created to bring Europe's version of civilisation to the continent. It was a front group: the king had no interest in civilising anyone. The small print would give Léopold absolute power over the other party's territory.

Stanley, a social climber from the wrong end of the class system, was happy to do the king's dirty work. Back in Africa, he persuaded 500 chiefs to sign shaky crosses on contracts they could not read. He returned home to find that quarrels over the division of Africa's wealth had brought Western Europe to the verge of war.

'We don't want war because whoever will win the natives will suffer through the struggle,' Stanley wrote to a friend, forgetting all the Congolese porters he had shot when they tried to desert his expeditions. 'Why should the natives suffer? What have they done?'[5]

The 1884 Conference of Berlin calmed the situation by establishing rules for European powers seeking a place in the sun. Behind the scenes, Léopold hustled the participants into agreeing that Stanley's treaties gave him rights to Central Africa.

Foreigners had been nibbling at the fringes of the Congo for centuries. In 1482, the Portuguese explorer Diogo Cão made contact with the Kingdom of Kongo, a trading nation on the shores of West Africa. The Bakongo people who lived there worked iron and copper but had failed to invent the wheel. They opened up to gifts and Catholicism. In 1518, the son of Emperor Afonso Mvemba a Nzinga became a bishop.

Slave trade disputes ended the Portuguese connection in the seventeenth century but other foreigners had more luck. While Léopold lobbied in Berlin, a blind Afro-Arab slaver from Zanzibar called Tippu Tip ruled parts of the eastern Congo.

A year after it began, the Conference gave Léopold II his territory. The Belgian king became the private owner of 900,000 square miles of jungle. He bought off Tippu Tip and called his new country the 'Congo Free State'.

'A slice of this magnificent African cake,' said the king. He ate until he was sick.[6]

It took five years for the world to realise that something had gone badly wrong in the Free State. George Washington Williams, a black American lawyer and journalist, visited the country in 1890, where he saw women in chains, men with stumps in place of hands. He had hoped to lead black Americans back to Africa. Instead he wrote an open letter to Léopold about the abuse. Other whistleblowers followed, like Edmund Morel, a Liverpool-based shipping clerk who did business with companies in Antwerp, and Roger Casement, British consul to the Congo.

Léopold II had turned the Free State into a ruthless meeting between the capitalist hammer and the imperialist anvil. His agents toured the country, offering natives European goods in exchange for ivory and rubber. At first, the Congolese were happy with the arrangement but soon discovered that the king had a limitless appetite. Léopold imposed quotas when demand exceeded supply and sent in native bosses called *capitas* to terrorise the locals.

If the *capitas* failed, they were replaced by the Force Publique, an army of native conscripts under white officers. The soldiers amputated villagers' hands, burned down their huts and killed anyone who resisted.

'Don't take this to heart so much,' a Force Publique soldier told a horrified Danish missionary. 'They kill us if we don't bring the rubber. The Commissioner has promised us if we have plenty of hands he will shorten our service.'[7]

In twenty-three years, millions of Congolese died from violence or disease. In a country without a census, accurate figures are difficult to establish but the population dropped by somewhere between 15 and 50 per cent.

International outcry at the bloodshed ended Léopold II's African dream. Williams's open letter shocked Europe. Morel founded the *West Africa Mail* to expose Léopold's activities and wrote *Red Rubber*, an indictment of the Free State. Casement's lectures, full of graphic first-hand accounts, appalled British audiences. The king claimed ignorance and offered reform but in 1908, under pressure from socialist politician Émile Vandervelde, handed control of the Free State to the Belgian government. Léopold could not understand why his subjects had not supported him.

'Small country, small people,' he said. He died the next year.[8]

A more benevolent, but still imperialist, rule began. Belgium deflected responsibility for the Free State onto excesses by sub-contracted Congolese and promised a new dawn.

Baudouin I was proud that his great-grand-uncle had carved out a new country in the jungle. He was even prouder of Belgium's subsequent role in the Congo. But the Congolese never forgave Léopold.

The new Belgian colonial regime imported medicine, industry and advanced agriculture. Civil servants taught hygiene, opened schools and inoculated the Congolese against diseases that had decimated their ancestors. Roads and railways were cut through the jungle. Land was cleared and cultivated. Cities rose into the sky.

The Belgians laid 3,256 miles of railroad transporting 9,000 freight cars; put down 121,299 miles of road for 60,000 vehicles and 800,000 bicycles; sailed 1,400 ships along 9,057 miles of waterways; built 6,000 hospitals and medical centres with 86,000 beds; and ran a powerhouse economy that increased the Congo's gross national product by nearly 5 per cent every year from 1920 onward.[9]

The official information service, Inforcongo, pumped out press releases telling the world that, thanks to colonialism, the Congolese were becoming more like Europeans every day. The idea took literal form in Hergé's 1930 comic strip *Tintin in the Congo*, where the boy reporter gives grateful natives a geography lesson about their homeland: Belgium. Hergé was embarrassed about it later.

'I only knew things about these countries that people said at the time: "Africans were great big children ... Thank goodness for them that we were there!" etcetera,' he said. 'And I portrayed these Africans according to such criteria, in the purely paternalistic spirit which existed then in Belgium.'[10]

Life outside the comic strip was less idyllic. The Congolese remained low-level drones in the hive, taught just enough to do their jobs, and were rarely promoted. Whites kept them at arm's length. In big towns, Africans lived in native districts, aureoles of mud huts and brick bungalows known as *la cité*, and risked arrest if they broke curfew. A few Congolese achieved success (Moïse Tshombe's father became a dollar millionaire in Katanga) but a wall of racial preference held back the rest.

'The white man is good!' sang Congolese workers in Léopoldville. 'The white man is kind! The white man is generous!'[11] In the mosquito dusk, as they trudged home and left the capital to Europeans sipping Primus beer outside cafés, they sang another verse:

But the work is hard!
And the pay is small!
Ai Brothers! All together!

Belgians boasted that their laws banned racial discrimination but everyone knew the police looked the other way when bars and businesses refused to serve Africans. Other laws were equally toothless. Whites who used the racist insult *sale macaque* (dirty monkey) rarely received a fine. Congolese risked jail if they said *sale Flamand*, an insult that cut deeper by reminding the Flemish that in Africa, as in Belgium, they took orders from Wallonian bosses.

Prison time was harsh. The 10 per cent of Congolese men who found themselves behind bars every year were at the mercy of their jailers.[12]

'Seven days of jail meant seven times four strokes of the whip,' said an anonymous Belgian warder. 'I always managed to find an excuse to give the whip to the prisoners. Maybe you find this shocking, but it was like that.'[13]

Settlers also tried a spiritual lash to keep the Congolese in line. Belgian Catholic missionaries had been martyring themselves in remote mission stations since the days of the Congo Free State, bringing the word of God to a people who preferred jungle spirits and ancestral ghosts. Priests achieved some influence over their flock, helped by church management of schools and hospitals, but even outwardly devout natives clung to a belief in magic. The most Christian Congolese could be driven into a state of terror by a fetish made by the local witchdoctor.

'It doesn't matter what diplomas you give them,' said an unhappy priest. 'A native can get good marks in his exams, complete his courses, become a teacher, even a lawyer or a doctor. Underneath he's still a savage.'[14]

Where Christianity did take root, it twisted into strange shapes, entwined with magic and politics. Simon Kimbangu was an African Baptist preacher who claimed to heal the sick and raise the dead. He told his followers that independence one day would come to the Congo.

'And the white will become black,' he said, 'and the black will become white.'[15]

In 1921, the Belgians charged him with sedition, gave him 120 lashes with a hippopotamus-skin whip and jailed him for life. He died behind bars thirty years later. But the Église de Jésus-Christ sur la Terre par le Prophète Simon Kimbangu (Church of Jesus Christ on Earth by the Prophet Simon Kimbangu) kept growing, and when the Belgians finally legalised it, thousands of Kimbangists rushed to worship openly.

Brussels caged Kimbangu because he threatened its control of the Congo's natural wealth. The rubber market had collapsed before the First World War but Belgian corporations still got fat on copper, diamonds, cobalt, uranium, gold, manganese, cotton, coffee and palm oil.

'An investors' paradise,' claimed a 1952 issue of America's *Fortune* magazine.[16] Belgian settlers raised a Primus to the prosperity they thought would never end.

In the mid-fifties, Antoine Van Bilsen, a university professor in Antwerp, took a risk and wrote a speculative article about independence for the Congo. Van Bilsen, a pre-war member of Verdinaso (a far-right Flemish separatist group) and no liberal, endorsed a handover of power sometime in the 1980s under UN supervision. The reaction to his article revealed the discontent boiling beneath the Congo's calm surface.

'An irresponsible strategy,' said Colonial Minister Auguste Buisseret of the Parti Libéral (Liberal party),'which sets dates that show he knows nothing and understands nothing about Africa.'[17]

The Belgian establishment thought Van Bilsen a dangerous radical. The growing Congolese nationalist movement, led by Kasa-Vubu's Abako, saw him as a reactionary imperialist. Abako masqueraded as a language preservation society to get around a ban on home-grown political parties and wanted immediate self-rule.

'Rather than postponing emancipation for another thirty years', said Kasa-Vubu,'we should be granted self-government today.'[18]

Buisseret had no time for Congolese nationalism but was smart enough to understand that something had to be done to calm the storm. He legalised native political parties and allowed some low-level democracy. Hundreds of groups came to life, bubbling up, dividing and recombining like bacteria under a microscope.

The British and French were already decolonising across Africa. Morocco and Tunisia in 1956. Sudan and Ghana in 1957. Guinea in 1958. In 1959, Congolese nationalists rioted in Léopoldville, angry that their turn had not yet come. Fifty died. Kasa-Vubu, Lumumba and other rising stars of Congolese politics demanded the right to govern themselves.

Belgian Prime Minister Gaston Eyskens could see the colony turning into another French Algeria, where a lengthy guerrilla war was bleeding men and morale from the mother country. His coalition of Parti Social Chrétien (Christian Social party) and Libéral politicians agreed to free the Congo.

Independence was fixed for 30 June 1960. Baudouin I flew to Léopoldville for the official ceremony. His bodyguards finalised security precautions.

The royal motorcade rolled through the streets of the capital towards the Palais de la Nation.

Kasa-Vubu was pointing over the trees to the tall office blocks, usually crewed by Belgian administrators who commuted in from suburban bungalows far bigger than anything they could have afforded in Europe, when a Congolese man in black jacket and tie ran up behind Baudouin, hands reaching out.

The man dipped into the back of the limousine and pulled the king's ceremonial sword off the back seat. As the car moved on, he danced around the road, pumping the sword in the air over his head with both hands. Africans in the crowd laughed; Europeans scowled. The king continued to wave. Officers of the Force Publique wrestled the sword back and arrested the thief.

Independence Day had started badly for Baudouin I. Things were about to get worse.

# 2

# KEYS TO THE CONGO

## Independence Day in Léopoldville

Patrice Lumumba took the microphone in the Palais de la Nation. The words poured out in a lava flow of rage.

> We have known ironies, insults, blows that we endured morning, noon, and evening, because we are Negroes. Who will forget that to a black one said 'tu', certainly not as to a friend, but because the more honourable 'vous' was reserved for whites alone?[1]

European diplomats listened, their faces smooth masks of polite interest. Belgian Prime Minister Gaston Eyskens, black hair slicked back on his head and teeth like an Angler fish, looked discouraged. Yesterday he had presented Lumumba with the Order of the Crown, Belgium's highest decoration.

> We have seen our lands seized in the name of allegedly legal laws which in fact recognized only that might is right. We have seen that the law was not the same for a white and for a black, accommodating for the first, cruel and inhuman for the other.[2]

The independence ceremony was almost over. The king and President Kasa-Vubu had given their speeches and were preparing to leave. Baudouin still had a cemetery to visit and a 500-strong open-air lunch before the flight home. Kasa-Vubu and the new Léopoldville establishment needed time to prepare for that evening's Independence Day party. Philippa Schuyler, the famous bi-racial American pianist, had been booked to entertain them. The Force Publique had returned Baudouin's sword. Everything was on schedule.

Then Lumumba began his impromptu speech.

We have seen that in the towns there were magnificent houses for the whites and crumbling shanties for the blacks, that a black was not admitted in the motion-picture houses, in the restaurants, in the stores of the Europeans; that a black travelled in the holds, at the feet of the whites in their luxury cabins.[3]

The circular hall's air conditioning vents hummed. Lumumba's finger wagged up and down as he spoke. He seemed to be conducting an imaginary orchestra.

We have known the atrocious sufferings of those who were imprisoned for their political opinions or religious beliefs and of those exiled in their own country. Their fate was worse than death itself.[4]

The king sat tight-lipped as Congolese politicians applauded around him. Some wore western suits and ties, others beaded caps dangling animal horns. A few whose skulls had been bound as babies had pointed heads.

Who will forget the rifle-fire from which so many of our brothers perished, or the jails in to which were brutally thrown those who did not want to submit to a regime of injustice, oppression and exploitation which were the means the colonialists employed to dominate us?[5]

The Congolese prime minister's words were being broadcast live to the country by radio. Lumumba's finger rose and fell as he talked, rose and fell.

Patrice Émery Lumumba would tell anyone willing to listen that his struggle with Belgium began one afternoon in the early 1950s as he walked through Léopoldville with a freshly minted Carte du Merité Civique (Civil Merit Card) in his pocket. The card officially made Lumumba an *évolué*, the term used in Belgian to denote educated Congolese. *Évolués* saw themselves as the green shoots of a Congolese intelligentsia; Brussels saw them as filler material for low-level teaching and civil service jobs.

The Congo had the best literacy rate in sub-Saharan Africa, with a quarter of its 13 million population able to read and write. Education ended abruptly when students became teenagers. Too much schooling, thought the men in Brussels, would spoil them. Of the 1.6 million native children who passed through primary school, less than 4 per cent would go on to further education. Only Africans with very good connections made it into the Congo's two universities: Léopoldville's University of Lovanium, opened in 1954 with a working nuclear reactor in its basement, and the University of Elisabethville, whose half-finished campus sat north of the Katangese capital. Most of the 763 students were white.

The authorities made grudging concessions to Congolese who climbed the educational rock face. In 1948, Brussels introduced the Carte du Merité Civique for any native who could prove he was 'living in a state of civilisation'.[6] The card offered mild legal benefits but failed to impress the Congolese. Ten years later, only 1,557 had been given out.

'Those who get it are disappointed,' said a Belgian lawyer in Elisabethville. 'Those who don't get it are bitter.'[7]

Lumumba applied. Despite only four years of primary school while growing up in Kasaï province, he had achieved good grades at a government training college that prepped workers for the post office. In Léopoldville, the Carte du Merité Civique officials checked his education, his skill with a knife and fork, and that he had only one wife. Lumumba lied about the wives (he had four) and passed. He was now, in the eyes of Belgium, officially civilised. The day he collected the card, a white woman passed him on the street. Their eyes met.

'*Sale macaque*,' she said.[8] Dirty monkey.

That was the moment Lumumba decided Belgian rule had to end in the Congo. He was two days away from his thirty-fifth birthday when he made his speech at the Palais de la Nation. He had been to prison twice, once for politics and once for embezzling money. He liked bow ties and brandy, rhetoric and weed, and wanted freedom for his country above everything.

As independence approached, Belgian men put furniture into storage and sent their families back home. In smoky bars they talked about government betrayal over a tableload of Primus beer. Brasserie de Léopoldville; the Only Beer for Sportsmen. They were afraid the Congolese would rise up and boil them down for glue.

'You see pantomimes of throat cutting and menacing gestures,' said a young Belgian colonial policeman. 'It is the ingratitude of the blacks. Look at all we have done for them – why, there is not a city like Léopoldville in the whole of Africa.'[9]

They swapped stories about what independence meant out in the bush. One tribe waited by the graves of their ancestors, expecting the dead to rise on 30 June. Another, remote in the jungle of Orientale province, turned cargo cult and built a wooden mock-up of an aeroplane.[10] Their witchdoctor had prophesied that independence would bring a flood. The tribe climbed inside and refused to leave. Soon they were up to their ankles in piss and dysentery.

Only Jan Vansina, a balding 30-year-old lecturer in African history at the University of Lovanium, had anything positive to say about independence. He had watched his black students moved to quasi-religious ecstasy by the thought of freedom.

'They were dazzled by the vision of a grand future, tinged with millenarian fervour,' said Vansina. 'They saw before them a new Jerusalem in which they were to be the new priesthood, idealistically offering all their talents to raise the splendour of the future nation, while also basking in the kind of prestige accorded Catholic saints: confessors or martyrs.'[11]

Few Belgians shared Vansina's optimism, but after another round of beers, the older ones admitted they were prepared to stay and work for Africans they had previously employed. Younger drinkers felt sick at the thought.

But going back home was not easy. Congolese whites had a reputation as arrogant racists in the motherland. No one wanted to hear them complain about a *planton* (office boy) dodging work or a *zamu* (watchman) sleeping through his shift, or listen to yet another story about the domestic help stealing from the kitchen. A few Brussels shops had signs in their windows: 'No Colonials'. Someone in the bar remembered a story about a friend of a friend who had stones thrown at him in the Wallonian countryside because his car number plate was Congolese.

Young or old, Belgian drinkers agreed on one thing: their problems had started with Patrice Lumumba.

Lumumba's journey to prime minister began a few years after his epiphany on a Léopoldville street. Now a postal clerk with wives and children to support, he moved to Stanleyville and made a name for himself in the city's *cercles* (discussion groups), the closest Congolese could get to nationalist activism. In 1955, a local representative of Belgium's Parti Libéral, unusually sympathetic to anti-colonialism, took notice of the fiery young debater and arranged a three-week study trip to Brussels.

When Lumumba returned home, horizons widened, Stanleyville police arrested him for embezzling 126,000 Belgian francs from post office funds. He got twelve months in prison. He had been arrested for similar offences on two previous occasions but this time his post office bosses refused to squash the charges.

Lumumba left prison in July 1956 to discover that Auguste Buisseret had legalised political parties. The plans Lumumba dreamed up in jail for his future had not involved democracy; he believed many Congolese were 'dull-witted illiterates'.[12] But he was too smart to swim against the current. In 1958, employed as publicity director of a Léopoldville brewery, Lumumba took over journalist Joseph Ileo's Mouvement National Congolais (National Congolese Movement – MNC) with the help of his old Kasaï friend Albert Kalonji, a balding accountant with a Hitler moustache, and veteran trade unionist Cyrille Adoula.

The MNC was a 2-year-old party with Congo-wide ambitions and no time for tribal politics. It polled best in Kasaï and Stanleyville, where Lumumba remained well known. To boost support, the MNC formed an alliance with Antoine Gizenga's Parti Solidaire Africain (African Solidarity Party – PSA), a group from the north-east with big ideas about pan-African unity. The Congo's other political parties preferred to target tribe and province.

Joseph Kasa-Vubu's Abako, the oldest independence movement, represented the Bakongo people from Léopoldville province. Abako had been around since 1950 as a vehicle to preserve the Kikongo language; original leader Edmond Nzeza Nlandu was obsessed with the idea of his mother tongue being swamped by the growing number of Lingala-speakers. Kasa-Vubu took over in 1954 and steered the party in a more political direction.

The Van Bilsen controversy made Abako the loudest voice on the Congolese scene but its politics confused voters. Sometimes Kasa-Vubu hinted at resurrecting the fifteenth-century Kongo kingdom for a future in which the rest of the country had only a vague role; in other speeches, he offered the Bakongo people as leaders of a united Congo. Neither path had much support outside Léopoldville province.

A nebula of other parties hung around the political stars. Down in Katanga, Moïse Tshombe's Confédération des Associations Tribales du Katanga (Confederation of Katanga Tribal Associations – Conakat) represented tribes from the south of the province; Jason Sendwe's Association des Baluba du Katanga (Baluba Association of Katanga – Balubakat), a split from Tshombe's party, gathered together those from the north. In the rest of the country, the Union des Mongo, Alliance des Bayanzi, Centre de Regroupement Africain and over a hundred others had their share of supporters. Out in the bush, tribal chiefs exercised their own kind of power through subordinate chiefs, regional heads and village elders.

In December 1958, Lumumba broke away from the pack when he got an invitation to the All-African People's Conference in Accra, capital of newly independent Ghana. Lumumba made friends with Kwame Nkrumah, the conference host and Ghana's prime minister. A former lecturer in political science, the big nosed and balding Nkrumah was a leftist who believed he could steer a course between Western Europe and the Soviets.

'The only colonialist or imperialist I trust,' said Ghana's leader, 'is a dead one.'[13]

Lumumba got home in the last days of 1958, radicalised. Thousands heard him call for independence at an MNC rally in Léopoldville.

Kasa-Vubu's Abako organised its own rally for Sunday 4 January to snatch back the spotlight. Thousands of Abako supporters turned up at a Léopoldville YMCA to find that the authorities had banned the event. The crowd turned violent, burning cars and stoning policemen in two days of rioting. The Force

Publique cleared the streets with live ammunition. Fifty protestors lay dead when the gun smoke drifted away. Blood pooled on the pavements. Force Publique commander, Lieutenant General Émile Janssens, a 58-year-old Belgian usually seen in shorts and knee-high socks, did not apologise.

'This must serve as a warning,' he said, 'to those lucky enough to escape our bullets'.[14]

Janssens's words made things worse. Black workers of the Huileries du Congo Belge (Oil Mills of the Belgian Congo) rioted in Leverville, sparking rolling demonstrations in Luluabourg, Matadi and Stanleyville through the first half of the year.

In June 1959, the political landscape was shaken further. Kasa-Vubu announced that he wanted a secessionist Bakongo state. Then the MNC split over Kalonji's enthusiasm for a federal Congo. Lumumba remained a nationalist. A leadership struggle divided the MNC into two factions, each hanging onto the name. The Congo seemed about to fragment before it achieved its independence.

That summer, the Belgians, overwhelmed by popular feeling against them, announced self-rule in five years. The Congolese refused to wait that long. Under Abako influence, parts of Léopoldville province stopped paying taxes. Baluba and Lulua tribes clashed in Kasaï. In October 1959, police arrested Lumumba when a riot killed twenty people at an MNC conference in Stanleyville. By the time of his January trial, the Belgians had caved in and agreed to independence later that year. They flew the Congo's forty-three most important political leaders to Brussels for a round table conference and freed Lumumba from prison to join them.

The top hotels, talented chefs, obsequious whites and pretty girls asking for autographs failed to smooth over disagreements between the different factions. Kalonji's MNC and Tshombe's Katangese wanted a federalist system with autonomy for the provinces; Kasa-Vubu was still talking about an independent Bakongo state but was prepared to compromise for a juicy political job; Lumumba and the Belgians wanted the country in one piece. Lumumba quickly fell out with the Katangese delegation.

The MNC leader mocked Tshombe's white advisors, all right-wingers, but made excuses for his own Serge Michel, a 50-year-old Frenchman sentenced to death by Paris for helping Algerian rebels and widely believed to be a Soviet agent.

'He has a white skin,' said Lumumba, 'but a black heart'.[15]

The tame Belgian leftists advising Abako and Gizenga's PSA ran for cover as Conakat and the MNC threw threats at each other.

'If you spend one day in Katanga', one of Tshombe's cronies told Lumumba, 'you will piss blood.'[16]

The issues were buried but not solved when Lumumba used every scrap of charisma to negotiate a consensus on May elections with independence the next month. Federalism was not on the menu. Congolese men would cast their votes for Provincial Assemblies and a national Chamber of Representatives, then the Provincial Assemblies would elect eighty-seven members to a national Upper Senate. The electorate would not include prisoners, black women, the insane or whites.

Lumumba had avenged the insult from the woman who passed him on a Léopoldville street. *Sale macaque.* The Belgians had agreed to hand over the keys to the Congo.

There were strange signs as the elections approached. In Katanga, Colonel Remy Van Lierde, a Second World War fighter ace in charge of Kamina military base, claimed to have seen a 50ft-long giant snake while on a helicopter trip.

'It was very dark green with his belly white,' he said. 'It could easily have eaten up a man.'[17]

He produced a fuzzy black and white photograph as proof. In neighbouring Kasaï, the Bushong people, descendants of the once-great Kuba Empire, were overrun by witches. They resurrected ordeal by poison, with survival proving innocence, and tried 500 old women before police stepped in. A story circulated in Orientale province that pygmies near Lake Tele had speared to death and eaten a 'Mokele-mbembe', a small brontosaurus the size of an elephant. None of that stopped the men of the Congo going to the polls for the first time in their history. May's results reflected the fragmented political scene.

Lumumba's MNC, which used a cow emblem to guide illiterate supporters to the right spot on the ballot paper, emerged the biggest party but had only 26.6 per cent of the vote, winning thirty-six of the available 137 seats in the Chamber of Representatives. Antoine Gizenga's PSA got 12.6 per cent of the vote and thirteen seats. Kasa-Vubu's Abako took 9.5 per cent of the vote and twelve seats. Albert Kalonji's MNC faction got eight seats, Moïse Tshombe's Conakat the same. Jason Sendwe's Balubakat got seven. A galaxy of other parties divided the remainder.

The Belgians asked Lumumba to form a government. After weeks of haggling, including some drama when Kasa-Vubu announced that his Bakongo people were seceding and marched on the Léopoldville Provincial Assembly only to be sent home by a policeman, Lumumba formed a coalition. Kasa-Vubu agreed to forget secession if he was made president. He got the job.

The political trade-offs to create the Congo's first government broke friendships, squashed some dreams and hurt a lot of feelings. Lumumba's enemies took consolation in the fact that he had agreed not give a speech at the Independence Day ceremony in the Palais de la Nation. But the temptation to make his mark, with the whole country listening in by radio, was too great to ignore. As the ceremony ended, he climbed on stage and began to speak.

When Lumumba gave up the microphone, Baudouin I marched out of the Palais and directed the royal entourage to the airport. Kasa-Vubu caught up and urged him to stay. An hour of angry discussion followed. Kasa-Vubu pointed out that Baudouin's own speech at the ceremony had been undiplomatic.

The king had called independence *un don* (a gift). He had advised the Congolese not to risk their new freedom with reforms.

'It is your job, gentlemen,' Baudouin said, 'to show that we were right in trusting you.'[18] Then he called Léopold II a genius.

Baudouin preferred to believe Lumumba's speech was a premeditated insult rather than an angry ad lib, but was persuaded to stay. He attended an independence mass at the church of St Maria and visited a local cemetery. At lunch under open tents overlooking the river, Lumumba gave another speech, this time not broadcast nationally:

> At the moment when the Congo reaches independence, the whole Government wishes to pay solemn homage to the king of the Belgians and to the noble people he represents for the work done here over three quarters of a century. For I would not wish my feelings to be wrongly interpreted.[19]

Baudouin I smiled politely.

That afternoon, Force Publique soldiers, youth groups and phalanxes of sportsmen paraded through Léopoldville. By the time Baudouin flew out in the early evening, the streets were a stomping whirl of cha-cha songs under a skyburst of fireworks.

The street noise came in through the windows of a Léopoldville house where Philippa Schuyler, in a purple silk dress, ran her hands over imaginary piano keys in preparation for tonight's performance. The five-finger exercises helped block out memories of the man who had attacked her a few days before.

Celebrations took place across the country: Stanleyville, Luluabourg, Coquilhatville, Bukavu. In Elisabethville, capital of Katanga, new Provincial President Moïse Tshombe attended mass at St Pierre et Paul cathedral before going on to a service at a nearby Protestant church. On the way to a final stop at the city's synagogue, he laughed off questions from reporters about a political scandal local police had uncovered in the last days of colonial rule.

The Congo's new leaders in Léopoldville had less spiritual plans. They had a party to attend this evening in the grounds of the Palais. Lots of food and drink. Good music. No whites allowed. They intended to enjoy it.

It would be the last party anyone in the Congo would enjoy for a long time. Within a week, the country would fall apart and Belgian paracommandos would come floating out of the sky to take back their colony.

# 3

# THE PIANO PLAYER

Philippa Schuyler Confronts Rape and Murder in the Congo

Philippa Schuyler, 28-years-old and scared, stood in the hallway of the apartment while the Congolese man explained his plans for Independence Day.

'Me and my friends', said the man, 'we have made a list of all the European women in the neighbourhood we are going to rape.'[1]

It was late at night. Schuyler had only opened the door because she thought it might be Victor Vanderlinden, the Belgian owner of the apartment, come to check on her. The half-built block on avenue Joséphine Charlotte had no lights, no telephone, no working toilets. The alternative had been sharing a houseboat with five male journalists. Schuyler took the apartment. It seemed safer.

The Congolese man had a knife. He explained that Schuyler was not on his list because she had only just moved into Kalina suburb. And she was not European. The man looked her up and down. The classical pianist from New York liked knee-length dresses in floral patterns, tied back her long, wavy black hair and had skin the colour of milky coffee. He was going to rape her anyway. He had fallen in love with her. That was why he had come to the apartment on his own. He had been watching her for days. He was going to rape her without his friends to show his love.

'Please leave,' said Schuyler.[2]

'Yes!' he said. 'I am going to do! I will do!'

He did not move.

Philippa Schuyler grew up on Edgecombe Avenue, an upscale part of New York's Harlem home to a constellation of famous African-Americans. Called 'Sugar Hill' by the locals, its smart rows of houses provided shelter from American bigotry for stars like jazz legend Duke Ellington and historian William Du Bois.

And bigotry was everywhere. Southern states used Jim Crow laws to segregate the races. Every town had 'Whites Only' drinking fountains and seats for blacks at the back of the bus. North of the Mason-Dixon Line, whites relied on property prices to corral African-Americans into ghettos.

'Down South white folks don't care how close I get as long as I don't get too big,' said comedian Dick Gregory. 'Up North white folks don't care how big I get as long as I don't get too close.'[3]

Philippa Schuyler's parents were one of the Hill's rare mixed-race couples. George was a journalist and former soldier, handsome and sad-eyed, from a middle-class African-American home in Syracuse. He married Josephine Lewis Cogdell, a full-faced white blonde from a rich Texan family, the year after they met in the offices of New York newspaper *The Messenger*. The couple would later describe the marriage as a sociopolitical experiment, a smashing down of racial barriers that bred a superior child. But their relationship was more than a meeting of minds.

'He is a marvellous lover and possesses the most gigantic anatomy,' Josephine told an old boyfriend.[4]

Philippa was born in 1931 on the fourth floor of the Park Lincoln apartment building, overlooking the maple trees of Colonial Park. The Schuylers believed their baby was full of 'hybrid vigor'.[5] To prove it they gave her piano lessons every day, talked frankly about sex, read Proust aloud in French, fed her on raw vegetables and vetoed friends her own age.

Philippa Schuyler was playing Mozart by the time she was 4. Fame blossomed as a child prodigy pianist, first within the African-American community, then white America. She performed in concert halls, on the radio and in person for New York Mayor Fiorello La Guardia.

'The Shirley Temple of American negroes', said *Look* magazine.[6]

The transition from child prodigy to adult musician was hard. Professional invitations dried up. Equally damaging was her mother's desire to keep her young forever. Schuyler never lost the look of an uncertain schoolgirl, pretty but awkward, smile always too wide, posture too self-conscious. She turned her back on the US and toured abroad, making a new home in Brussels, where she stood glamorously exotic among the wives and elephant-legged mothers-in-law nagging beak-nosed men to church every Sunday. A world away from Sugar Hill. Schuyler liked it.

In 1955, she played her first African tour, performing for Haile Selassie in Ethiopia, Kwame Nkrumah in Ghana and to the white establishment of the Belgian Congo. Schuyler admired newly independent Africa but the continent's sexism shocked her. Female circumcision was common in Ethiopia and fathers married off their daughters without telling them. Ghana's buses carried public information signs: 'Never Trust a Woman.'[7]

Congolese women had an equally rough time. In the bush, many men found it a sign of weakness that whites allowed their wives to eat at the same table.

'They wouldn't even let us talk,' said Beatrice Mohana, rare feminist and wife of a Katangese politician. 'If we tried to express an opinion they would say "Shut up! You're only a woman"!'[8]

Henriette Cardon-Sips, a darkly attractive 40-year-old Flamand whose husband Willy was chief engineer at the Elisabethville Simba brewery, claimed she heard worse than that when she sneaked into a Lumumba speech before the elections.

'You've got to kill all the white men but keep the white women,' was how she remembered Lumumba's words. 'You can have all their houses and all their cars. When the men are dead you can marry the white women.'[9]

MNC supporters derided Cardon-Sips as a racist with a rape fantasy. Belgians were less sure. Across the Congo, sharp natives were making good money conning dumber compatriots; for 1,500 francs, the mark would get a certificate that allegedly gave them rights to a European's house and either the wife or daughter, whoever was prettier. In Léopoldville, a tailor casually remarked to his white employer that he had spent his life savings buying her and her sewing machine from a man who lived in his village.

Following the tour, Schuyler's views moved further to the right, following her father, whose natural scepticism had hardened into far-right conservatism. Both joined America's anti-communist John Birch Society.

Philippa performed in Japan, Korea, Taiwan. She wrote occasional journalism and had affairs with unsuitable Belgian men. She played for the Dowager Queen Elisabeth of Belgium, a performance that persuaded the Congolese to book her for their Independence Day celebrations. By the time Philippa Schuyler touched down in Elisabethville on 7 June 1960 and boarded an internal flight to Léopoldville, she was a well-travelled 29-year-old right-wing musician and journalist, troubled by her identity and career, fond of tarot cards and men who treated her badly.

You could fly over the Congo for hours and see nothing man-made except an occasional dirt track and a few huts. The population averaged six people per square kilometre. Sometimes the only sign of life from the air were old boats ploughing through the hyacinth lilies on the River Congo. These Victorian relics, painted the colour of rust to hide their age, looked like a ferry mated with a Ferris wheel, smaller boats roped to them like remora on a shark.

Railway lines took cargo were the rivers did not flow. They said that one Chinese worker died for every sleeper and a white engineer for every kilometre of track. No one counted the dead Congolese. Sometimes the connection

between river and rail was a port, sometimes only needle-nosed canoes bobbing in the water hinted at a station behind the trees. Passengers disembarked
from the riverboat, scrambled up a bank, waded through elephant grass and
found a steam train waiting on the tracks, all panelled wood, brass fittings and
white-uniformed attendants.

The railways and rivers vanished on the approach to Ndjili airport. Then
it was a bumpy touchdown and surly officials in the terminal. Lumumba had
asked Belgian administrators, army officers, bureaucrats, engineers and other
professionals to remain in the Congo until locals could be trained to take over.
The Congolese resented working for their old masters. In Léopoldville, the
dockers were on strike and public transport sporadic. Domestic staff did the
bare minimum as they counted the days until independence.

A civil servant called Victor Vanderlinden was waiting at the airport with the
choice of a houseboat or an unfinished apartment block.


The man in Schuyler's hallway would not leave. He pulled a fetish covered in
animal hide from his pocket and waved the knife. He wanted her blood to feed
the fetish. Schuyler ran for the door. He grabbed her arm. She pulled away
and ran into the street, shouting for help. The man ran off in another direction.

Schuyler returned that evening to sleep on a bare mattress in the bedroom. She woke when the man tried to break in through a window. She
screamed, nearby dogs barked and the man ran away. She moved out to stay
with Belgian friends.

On the afternoon of 30 June, a shaken Schuyler put on a purple silk evening
gown and waited for the official car. After three hours, she made her own way
to the Palais and arrived at 10 p.m. Pavilions had been set up in the gardens.
Congolese politicians drank under a cloud of dagga smoke. Guitar players,
samba bands and cha-cha acts drifted on and off the stage. Schuyler was pointed
towards a battered upright piano on a pontoon floating in a swimming pool.
A brief announcement on the microphone introduced Schuyler's programme
of Chopin, Gershwin and Schubert. The badly tuned piano bobbed about and
her arm ached where the man had grabbed her. A fountain sprayed her with
water. Two Congolese men leant on the piano and argued with each other.

In the early hours of the morning, a drunk politician drove Philippa
Schuyler home.


The parties continued all weekend. Music, dancing, drinking. A depressed
Schuyler spent time with white friends, seeing bad omens in everything. The
tired, angry faces of Force Publique soldiers policing the celebrations. The

biting mosquitoes flourishing now that the Belgian pilots who sprayed DDT over the city had gone back to Europe.

'Congo's independence will be tragic,' Schuyler thought.'All the whites and many of the educated blacks know this already … But all seem powerless to stop the coming holocaust … How can good come of all this? … The Congo will collapse like a house of cards after June 30 …'[10]

On Friday, Bayakas and Bakongos fought each other in Léopoldville a few blocks from joyous street parties. The radio announced renewed violence between Baluba and Lulua in Kasaï province. Later that day, celebrations in Coquilhatville, Equateur province went sour. Locals demonstrated about the economy and demanded provincial self-rule. The new government sent in Force Publique troops, who opened fire and killed ten people.

On 2 July, there were riots in Orientale province. In Léopoldville, music kept playing and people kept drinking. International guests departed, leaving only United Nations observer Ralph Bunce, a light-skinned African-American with kind eyes and a cigarette habit, famous for brokering the ceasefire between Israel and the Arabs in 1949. Lumumba made a radio broadcast encouraging young Belgians to come out to the Congo and make careers. He assured investors their money was safe.

'Belgium should be the first country to take the Congo's outstretched hand of friendship,' Lumumba said.[11]

The partying wound down on Sunday. The country had work the next day.

On Monday 4 July, normal life began in the independent Congo. Parliament's first act was to raise its members' salary from 100,000 francs a year to half a million. Lumumba was one of the few to object. Politicians squeezed lemon juice into the wound by promising all government employees, apart from the army, a pay rise. They had not forgiven the Force Publique for Belgian repression.

Soldiers mutinied at Camp Hardy, an army base on the road between Léopoldville and Matadi port. They beat white officers and penned them up with their wives in a corner of the camp. Clear-eyed observers had seen trouble approaching for a while. Army units had exhausted themselves supervising the election. On Independence Day, most of the Force Publique's 24,000 soldiers were confined to barracks while the Congo celebrated. The decision to retain 1,000 Belgian officers, a third of their wages paid by Brussels, had not helped. Their replacement by Congolese would be a long process. By independence only a handful of Africans had been promoted to 'master sergeant' rank and twenty officer cadets sent to a Brussels military academy.

'Everybody knows that we, the army rank and file, are treated like slaves,' a soldier had written to *Emancipation* newspaper back in April 1960. 'We are punished arbitrarily because we are macaques. We may read no newspapers published by black civilians. There is no human contact between our officers and ourselves, but rather a relationship of domination that turns us into racially inferior slaves.'[12]

After the elections, disenchantment spread to include the new government. Lumumba told his soldiers they would not get promotions until they were properly trained.

'Prime Minister Lumumba has said that in spite of independence, no second-class soldier will become a general,' wrote another soldier to *Emancipation*. 'How hurtful it is to tell the people such things. Mr Lumumba considers us unable to do the jobs of our own officers, but with what rank, may we ask, did any general in the Force Publique begin his military career?'[13]

Lieutenant General Janssens, head of the Force Publique, seemed unconcerned, even though the Force Publique had mutinied four times in the last sixty-five years, most recently in 1944. Like his soldiers, he had taken no leave for months while policing the handover of power. He was too tired to think straight. He attended a Fourth of July party thrown by Americans in Léopoldville.

'The Force Publique? It is my creation,' he told guests. 'It is absolutely loyal.'[14]


News of the Camp Hardy mutiny pulled nerves tight in Léopoldville. Lorryloads of soldiers raced around the streets. Philippa Schuyler heard rumours of rape by mutineers. Western journalists in Léopoldville were reluctant to investigate, fearing it would play into the hands of the right wing back home.

'The implications were extremely ugly and would not be popular with many of our customers,' thought Reuters correspondent Sandy Gall, a tall Scottish 32-year-old with experience of hotspots like Suez and Hungary.[15]

On 5 July, there were reports of violence from other parts of the Congo. A Belgian woman was raped sixteen times by soldiers at Kisantu. Two women were raped at Banza-Boma. Other reports came in from Madimba and Matadi. Later that day, Lieutenant General Janssens tried to calm the capital's garrison at Camp Léopold II.

'Independence is good for civilians,' he said. 'For the military there is only discipline. Before 30 June you had white officers. After 30 June you will still have white officers.'[16]

Lumumba gave a radio speech to the nation making it clear he would not promote Congolese NCOs to officer positions without proper training.

That evening, soldiers at Camp Léopold II held a meeting to discuss their grievances, particularly a slogan Janssens chalked on a blackboard during his talk: 'Before Independence = After Independence'. They took hostage officers who tried to disperse them. Soldiers from Thysville, near Camp Hardy, refused to intervene. Military police eventually broke up the trouble.

The Force Publique had a radio network that linked bases across the country. Rumours crackled through the air like electricity. Nerves stretched tighter. On 6 July, soldiers in Inkisi attacked local Belgians. Twenty women were raped there over the next two days.

A delegation of soldiers in Léopoldville met Lumumba and demanded pay rises, promotions and the departure of white officers. Lumumba refused. Another group tried to force their way into the parliament building. A newspaper man asked who they were protesting against.

'Belgian officers and some of our rulers,' came the reply.[17]

Kasa-Vubu and Lumumba flew to Camp Hardy, site of the original disturbances, to calm the mutineers. Then trouble broke out in Thysville and nearby towns. Civilians joined in. What was left of the party atmosphere curdled. Drunk Africans beat whites on the street.

On Thursday 7 July, Lumumba gave a press conference in the capital to deny any rape or looting had occurred. The same day the first trainload of Europeans pulled into Léopoldville from Thysville. The passengers were beaten men, crying children, women bleeding down their thighs.

Down south, Katanga remained calm but provincial president Moïse Tshombe surprised many Congolese by asking Belgium and Rhodesia to send peacekeeping troops. Soldiers were uneasy in their barracks and he feared a mutiny. Brussels and Salisbury refused.

On Friday, Lumumba dismissed Janssens as head of the Force Publique. The prime minister appointed his uncle Victor Lundula, a tired-looking medical practitioner and former sergeant major who shared Albert Kalonji's taste for Hitler moustaches. Lundula turned the Force Publique into the Armée Nationale Congolais (Congolese National Army – ANC) and appointed Joseph Désiré Mobutu, skinny and dark, as his chief of staff. Another former sergeant major, Mobutu was rarely seen without sunglasses and a bow tie. A journalist by day, he moonlighted as secretary to Lumumba. His favourite book was Machiavelli's *The Prince*.

Lundula and Mobutu tried to hold the ANC together by promoting all soldiers a rank and removing Belgians from their positions, with the promise that troops could vote on keeping them as advisors.

At the Catholic Institute in Léopoldville, Sandy Gall interviewed a roomful of nuns, all refugees who had arrived by train from Matadi. Rosary beads clicked. A nun told him that many sisters had been assaulted by drunk Force Publique mutineers.

'That's a very serious allegation,' said Gall. 'How can you be sure?'[18]

'Because I saw it', the nun said. 'And I was raped myself.'

'You were actually raped yourself?'

'Yes. I was raped … several times. They even raped a 70-year-old sister, Sister Agatha. She's sitting over there.'

An old woman in a habit, staring blankly at the wall.


The removal of Belgian officers unstitched the ANC's last threads of discipline. Soldiers from Camp Léopold II mutinied in Léopoldville. They attacked Lumumba's house, then Kasa-Vubu's, smashing glass and throwing stones.

'We are fed up with Lumumba,' said one soldier at a roadblock. 'We are going to do him in.'[19]

Frustrations over money, rank and years of bigotry burst onto the streets. Drunk or drugged solders ordered whites to kiss their feet. Those who did were kicked in the head; those who refused were beaten to the pavement with rifle butts.

Newsreels filmed riots, broken glass, a soldier throwing his rifle at a man's back like a spear, other soldiers kicking in the doors of the Hôtel Stanley on the hunt for Flamands. Lumumba flew around the country trying to ride the tiger with speeches that pinned the mutinies on a Brussels conspiracy to retake the Congo. The horrified Belgian public thought he was blaming the victims.

Civilians led by policemen rioted again in Matadi. At least twenty women were raped there. More refugees arrived in Léopoldville by train. Soldiers mutinied in Sanda, lower Congo. Philippa Schuyler ran round Léopoldville on reporter duty, the memory of the man in her apartment still fresh but determined to get a story. She asked one man why he joined in the riots.

'I don't know,' he said. 'Everybody was doing it so I thought I should do it, too. I wouldn't have thought of it myself, but with all the others acting violent, it kind of seemed the thing to do.'[20]

A curfew was announced for seven in the evening. No one was left to enforce it.


Whites began to flee. Some crossed the river to Brazzaville until the ferry was suspended. Others escaped to Angola, Kenya, Uganda. In Katanga, panicking whites fled south to Rhodesia, where a young Mufulira policeman called John Trevelyn found them beds and listened to their stories. Hundreds of civilians stacked battered suitcases in Léopoldville airport's departure lounge, waiting for flights. Lost children's toys went soggy in a thin lake of piss that spread across the terminal floor from overflowing toilets.

Belgian airline Sabena rerouted its fleet to Léopoldville and began airlifting out refugees. Soon only 2,500 Belgians would be left from Léopoldville's 18,000-strong white population; 300 from Stanleyville's 5,000; just 200 from Luluabourg's 6,000.[21]

'I liked the Congolese,' a man from Orientale province told a journalist at the airport. 'I naively thought they liked us as well. My wife was raped more than thirty times. She has been insane for three days. What more is there to say?'[22]

As the passengers disembarked at Brussels they were met by Belgian police. 'Where have you come from? Were you subject to ill treatment?'[23] Ground crews carried out hysterical women strapped to stretchers. Short-trousered children held hands on the rain-soaked runway apron. Inside the terminal, rows of clerks handed out emergency funds. Lovanium university lecturer Jan Vansina did not need money but the clerk told him he could not leave the airport without it. The cash was a loan from the Belgian government and would have to be repaid. Civilian volunteers waited outside the terminal with their cars, offering to drive refugees to hotels or relatives.

Sabena's airlift halted on the evening of 8 July, when ANC troops occupied the airport at Léopoldville. For days, Belgian Prime Minister Eyskens had been urging Lumumba to allow Belgian military intervention. Some of the mutineers thought they could scare off Brussels by keeping whites hostage on the ground. They miscalculated.

The occupation of Ndjili airport sent Belgian public opinion boiling over; they wanted their people rescued. Eyskens's government ordered in paracommandos to back up the 2,500 troops who had remained in the Congo. Two companies set off from Belgium, others from Ruanda-Urundi. Lumumba, flying across the country stamping out mutinies, saw the intervention as colonialism.

'You are here illegally,' he told a Belgian officer, 'and we have no need of your protection.'[24]

The intervention had the thinnest glaze of legality. The day before independence, Brussels and Léopoldville had signed a treaty of friendship that gave Belgium sovereignty over the Kamina and Kitona airbases, and the right to intervene militarily should the new government require assistance in maintaining law and order. The treaty had never been ratified.

'A Belgian and fascist plot against independence,' said Anicet Kashamura, Congolese Minister for Information, on the radio.[25]

The Léopoldville government claimed to have the mutinies under control. On 9 July, Lumumba and Kasa-Vubu persuaded mutineers in Matadi to release a group of white hostages. The next day, Belgian gunboats and marines landed at the port. A firefight killed twenty African soldiers.

'These military interventions by Belgium in the Congo are really and in all honesty only for the purpose of saving lives,' said Eyskens.[26]

Troops at Camp Hardy mutinied again when they heard about the attack. Two girls, 11 and 12 years old, were among those raped. Soldiers mutinied in the Kasaï capital of Luluabourg. Hundreds of Belgians barricaded themselves in the Immokasaï, a concrete block of flats in the centre of town, while mutineers shot out the windows. The trapped whites painted 'SOS' on the roof in red paint. On 10 July, Belgian paracommandos floated down to rescue them, arriving just as the ANC set up mortars.

The next day, Léopoldville mutineers shot at wounded Belgian soldiers returning from the battle. In revenge, the Belgians occupied Ndjili airport. A firefight left the terminal restaurant a mess of broken glass and blood. In the departure lounge, a BBC reporter led his camera crew through a crowd of cowering white civilians, looking for interviewees.

'Anyone here been raped and speaks English?'[27]

Elsewhere, in Léopoldville, Philippa Schuyler talked with women who had fled to the capital by train. A young social worker from Thysville still carried the shredded bra and panties she was wearing when three soldiers raped her.

'As I was a social worker, there to teach the Congolese women sewing, cooking, social adjustment, and so on, I lived alone,' the woman said:

> and it was easy for the soldiers to break in. I tried to hide in the wardrobe, but they pulled me out, spitting on me, and beat me all over. I grabbed a sewing basket and hit one soldier on the head with it, but he wrenched it out of my grasp. I jabbed him with a pair of scissors but it didn't do any good. My legs were bleeding. I fell on the floor, and they kicked me. I tried to get up but the floor was slippery with blood, and I fell in it. I crawled away, and tried to run into the W.C. and bolt the door, but I wasn't fast enough and they came in after me …[28]

Schuyler collected more stories: the woman raped twelve times in front of her children, the pregnant woman raped at gunpoint, the woman force-fed her own pubic hair before a soldier wrapped sandpaper around his finger and shoved it into her vagina. Belgian women thought themselves lucky if they had just been stripped naked in public and forced to eat dirt.

Schuyler estimated that 600 women were raped in the riots. Belgium put the figure at 300. Rape is always an under-reported crime. At least fifty Europeans had been murdered; forty-two people alone died near the Angolan border. Hundreds more were still missing when Schuyler flew out from Léopoldville to Accra, then on to Brussels. The Congo's independence had become a horror story.

At the height of the mutinies, Moïse Tshombe made a radio broadcast from Elisabethville in Katanga. For some, his announcement showed him to be a puppet of the Belgians, bought for a suitcase stuffed with francs. For others, his words resurrected a murderous tyrant, a Katangese emperor who ate the hearts of his enemies and spiked their skulls on wooden poles. Tshombe was about to become the most hated man in the Congo.

# 4

# EMPEROR MSIRI'S GHOST

## Katanga Declares Independence

'This is Radio Katanga,' said the announcer with a cigarette burning between his fingers. 'Good evening, dear listeners. President Tshombe is going to speak to you.'[1]

It was eight o'clock in the evening of 11 July 1960. Moïse Tshombe, 40 years old, short, round-faced, his normally cheerful features crunched into a look of concern, waited for a technician to give him the signal to talk.

Tshombe was a failed businessman who had discovered a better use for his winning charm in Katangese politics. Out in the villages, he played the traditionalist, talking up his membership of the Lunda aristocracy; in the cities, he wore a suit and told *évolués* that Katanga belonged to them. Few could resist his appeal. Even cynical Belgians left his office convinced they had met the future of Africa.

Unusually for a Congolese, he came from a wealthy background. Tshombe's father had made a fortune after the Second World War buying goods cheap in Elisabethville and selling high in the bush. The profits went into village stores, a sawmill, a hotel and a fleet of trucks with 'J. Kapenda Tshombe et Fils' stencilled on the flanks. As a young man, Moïse took over the Elisabethville office, where he got busy delegating work and enjoying himself.

When he was not driving fast cars or chasing women, Tshombe learned some important truths about Katanga's relationship to the rest of the country. Elisabethville may have looked sophisticated, with its café crowds window-shopping Christian Dior dresses in the shade of mauve jacaranda trees, but beneath the surface polish was a mining town whose copper profits provided 50 per cent of the Congo's income. Locals never forgot the source of their wealth. In some houses, you could find a giant lump of raw malachite, like turquoise waves running over rock, standing in for a coffee table.

Moïse listened as white customers complained about their mining profits subsidising Léopoldville. Black Katangese moaned about losing jobs to immigrants from neighbouring Kasaï province. He filed away the information for future use and went back to his womanising. Debauchery was approaching fast when Tshombe *père* swooped in and married Moïse off to the daughter of Mwata Yamvo Ditende, heir to the Lunda chiefdom.

Married life produced eight children and spurred Moïse into proving he could make it on his own as a businessman. The moneymaking genes must have skipped a generation: Moïse went bankrupt three times before 1951. Tshombe *père* could always be relied on to pay off creditors, but then he died and his son inherited the largest African-owned concern in Katanga. It surprised no one when 'J. Kapenda Tshombe et Fils' slid slowly towards insolvency.

Tshombe discovered his true calling in politics. In 1956, he founded the Groupement des Associations Mutuelles de l'Empire Lunda (Lunda Empire Mutual Assocations Group – Gassomel), a tribal debating club. Two years later, Gassomel joined other Katangese groups to form Conakat, an association of seventeen tribes designed to protect 'authentic Katangese' from Kasaï immigration.[2]

Most Congolese parties kept their distance from Europeans but Tshombe had no problem accepting money from the Union pour la Colonisation (Union for Colonisation – Ucol), an all-white settler group around since 1944 under the leadership of handsome silver fox Jean Humblé. Ucol cared more about provincial autonomy than Kasaï immigrants, but Humblé thought a charismatic black leader like Tshombe could be a useful friend. He discreetly arranged funding.

The white cash alienated some supporters. Jason Sendwe and his Baluba followers decided they preferred Kasaï immigrants to Belgian settlers and pulled out to form Balubakat.

'Not really a bad man', said Sendwe of Tshombe, 'but very fond of money'.[3]

Sendwe's departure limited Conakat influence to the south of the province and a few large towns further north. Despite this, Tshombe became an enthusiastic partisan for Humblé's federalist ideas and held occasional meetings with more extreme settlers, known as ultras, who talked about Katangese independence.

By the time the Congo fell apart in July, Tshombe had become the only black politician with a significant white following. It surprised no one that his announcer on Radio Katanga this evening was a Belgian. Roger Jaspar had fought his way through mutinies and shoot-outs to keep the appointment. His path to the radio studio began when he made small talk about his past as a broadcaster with Tshombe at the Elisabethville Independence Day celebrations.

'Come and see me as soon as possible,' said the moon-faced Conakat leader with a face-splitting grin, 'I will need you.'[4]

Few could resist Tshombe's charm. Now Jaspar, a dark-haired forty-something with a face lined by sun and drink, was sitting in Elisabethville's smoky Radio UFAC studio across a desk from Tshombe and an entourage of serious African men in suits.

The Belgian finished his introduction. A technician pointed and Tshombe began to speak into a condenser microphone. He had an important announcement for everyone in Katanga: he was seceding from the rest of the Congo. For the second time in two weeks.

Back in the late nineteenth century, the Congo's southern province had been a remote empire ruled by Mwenda Msiri Ngelengwa Shitambi, a former Bayeke trader from Tanzania. Msiri muscled onto the Katangese scene by supplying a local chief with the firepower to defeat his rivals. What started as business became personal when Msiri murdered the chief's heirs and took control.

In its early years, his rule brought order. By the time Europeans pushed into the province, the emperor was senile and cruel. Enemies were buried up to their necks and left to starve, others eaten alive by dogs. Skulls white as eggs hung from poles outside Msiri's wooden capital of Bunkeya.

'Human hearts, still beating, were thrown into mugs of pombe [native beer],' said a Belgian observer, 'which were then enjoyed by the whole court. Men were tied to trees, and when they groaned in hunger, were given their own ears, nose, and arms to eat and perished after devouring themselves.'[5]

Both Brussels and London wanted Msiri's empire. The emperor refused all foreign treaties; the gifts and insincere declarations of friendship not enough to win his sovereignty. In 1891, an expedition under Captain William Stairs, a Canadian working for Léopold II, gave up on diplomacy and tried to arrest the Katangese ruler. In a confrontation at the village of Munema, a Belgian named Omer Bodson shot Msiri.

'I have killed a tiger!' shouted Bodson. '*Vive le Roi!*'[6]

Msiri's bodyguard shot him in the spine. The rest of the expedition escaped. Stairs sent the emperor's head back to Europe in a petrol tin.

The Katangese Empire collapsed and Brussels installed the Comité Spécial du Katanga (Special Committee of Katanga – CSK) to administer the territory. Within a few years, Belgian mining engineers discovered huge veins of copper pulsing beneath the red earth in the south. By 1960, Belgian company Union Minière du Haut Katanga (Mining Union of Upper Katanga – UMHK) was digging it from the ground for £100 a ton and selling it to the world for £250.[7]

UMHK had more power in Katanga than any Belgian politician. It started as a nineteenth-century joint venture between the CSK and Tanganyika

Concessions Ltd ('Tanks'), a British outfit founded by legendary imperialist Cecil Rhodes. The company soon dwarfed its parents. UMHK subsidiaries diversified into coal and hydroelectric power, vegetable oils and water processing, flower mills and cattle. Its housing arm, Compagnie Foncière du Katanga, erected whole cities for workers, throwing in healthcare and swimming pools for free. The company wrapped its tentacles around the unexploited wilderness of red dirt and green jungle like a giant squid, and sucked it dry.

The mining giant had already dispatched the last traces of Msiri's empire by the time Belgium passed control of the province from CSK to Léopoldville in 1933. Many in Katanga, then and later, thought joining the Congo was a mistake.

'Katanga has always wanted autonomy,' Tshombe told his cronies. 'And it is only under the colonialist boot that the former Belgian Congo, this ethnic and geographic monstrosity, was unified.'[8]

Men in Elisabethville had been looking for ways to dismember that monstrosity for years. They made their first attempt a week before independence.

On 25 June, the Katangese Sûreté (national police) kicked in a hotel room door and arrested François Scheerlinck. A long-time member of the ultra scene and former Sûreté man himself, Scheerlinck had in his possession a Sabena ticket to Brussels, New York and Washington, and a letter naming him special ambassador for the independent state of Katanga.

'Recognition was […] to be sought in the countries bordering the Congo,' Scheerlinck told his interrogators, 'and in England and Portugal. Simultaneously, an appeal would be made to the UN. For the Katanga provincial government, it would be a race against time.'[9]

Tshombe laughed off any involvement but the Sûreté had enough evidence to pin him as a major player in the plan. The Belgian authorities were shocked. They knew he flirted with secession talk but thought the Conakat leader had committed himself to a united Congo after his recent political successes. In May 1960, Conakat had won twenty-five of the sixty seats in Katanga's provincial assembly and eight of sixteen seats available for the national lower chamber. Jason Sendwe's Balubakat got twenty-three in the province and seven in the chamber. Independents and the MNC shared the rest.

Conakat and Balubakat activists had been beating each other to death in the street since the split. A clash was inevitable when the provincial assembly met to elect a Cabinet at the start of June. Balubakat members walked out, paralysing the assembly by reducing attendance below the required two-thirds. Conakat begged Brussels to allow a majority vote. After two weeks of failing to persuade Balubakat to return, Brussels changed the law. Conspiracy theories buzzed around the decision like flies in an abattoir but Eyskens's government believed it was the only way to force Sendwe's men back to the assembly. It did not work. Balubakat stayed away.

The Conakat-dominated assembly elected a provincial government in its own image. Tshombe became president and moved into his official residence, a white mansion in the centre of Elisabethville with neat green lawns and a finned American limousine in the garage. Seven of the remaining posts went to Conakat, two to independents, and one MNC-Kalonji, with whom Tshombe had signed an electoral pact in May despite his earlier stand against Kasaï immigrants. Balubakat got nothing.

Tshombe's victory quickly turned sour. Lumumba punished him by making Sendwe the Commissioner of State for the province and giving Balubakat two posts in the national Cabinet. Conakat only got one. Sûreté men investigating the Scheerlinck affair thought this was the moment Tshombe got angry enough to think seriously about secession. And support for independence was now coming from the biggest player in Katanga: Union Minière.

UMHK's directors feared for the future under Lumumba. The company had recently privatised itself into a patchwork of shareholders: the former colonial government's share in the company (18.14 per cent) had passed to Léopoldville; Tanks retained 14.47 per cent of the capital; the CSK 8.77 per cent; Société Générale de Belge had 4.64 per cent; and private investors, many French and British, owned the rest. UMHK suspected that Lumumba might nationalise the company without the Belgian government to hold him back. It enlisted Conakat and Elisabethville's ultras to prevent that happening.

'We all assumed that Union Minière arranged everything so Katanga would become independent,' said Henriette Cardon-Sips. [10]

It was public knowledge that the mining company had gifted expensive houses on the previously all-white boulevard Elisabeth to Tshombe's friends in the weeks before Scheerlinck's arrest. Godefroid Munongo, Conakat's second-in-command, known around town as 'the only black man with a European brain', got a sprawling villa with a good wine cellar. [11] The Sûreté suspected the the mining company had used Munongo to get at Tshombe. Munongo, grandson of Emperor Msiri, denied everything.


Thirty-six years old in 1960, Godefroid Munongo exuded a charisma as cold and dark as the Atlantic Ocean. Gold-rimmed sunglasses hid heavy-lidded eyes. He looked like a professional torturer.

'You must remember one thing,' he told anyone curious about his relationship with Moïse Tshombe, officially his boss. 'Tshombe was a good chief. But he was subordinate to me.' [12]

A department head in the Pensions Service and aristocrat of the Bayeke tribe, Munongo was Conakat's founder and original president. He created the party after 160,000 Kasaï immigrants strategically outvoted Katangese natives in the 1957 local elections. Even Jason Sendwe's Baluba, linked by blood and family to the new arrivals, joined Conakat in protest.

Msiri's grandson stepped down when his politics caused problems at work. Some observers believed he retained control of the party, hand tight on Tshombe's shoulder. Others thought Tshombe used his strong-willed subordinate as a shield for unpopular decisions. The truth may have been simpler.

'Munongo is a very loyal man,' Tshombe said, 'but if I tell him to do something he doesn't like, he simply refuses.'[13]

Whatever the relationship, the two men trusted each other. Attempts by Conakat's enemies to split them always failed. Tshombe had the charm, the diplomacy and the ability to compromise; Munongo was the ruthless conscience, the incorruptible spirit. Together, the pair, both close to tribal royalty (Munongo's brother was chief of the Bayeke; Tshombe had married the Lunda chief's daughter), made up the yin and yang of Conakat.

Munongo denied any connection with Scheerlinck's secession attempt and refused to implicate Tshombe. Sûreté men took out their frustrations on senior Conakat man Évariste Kimba, a rare Baluba in the ranks. They beat him until he confessed that the party had made plans to join an independent Katanga to the Rhodesian Federation. Alarm bells went off in Brussels. Belgium had been suspicious about Anglo-Saxon intentions in Africa ever since it had raced British explorers into Msiri's territory.

Lieutenant General Janssens paraded the Force Publique along the border while Salisbury gave vaguely convincing excuses for a series of secret meetings held with Conakat men in Rhodesia. Scheerlinck got deported. UMHK was too big to touch. Eyskens considered expelling the noisiest Belgian ultras but did nothing and tried to keep the affair quiet. Independence was too close.

For the first week of July, Katanga managed to avoid the murder and rape that lit up the rest of the country. Elisabethville locals splashed about in the Lido pool, trudged round the golf course and ate imported lobster in the concrete slatted Sabena guest house. The place was so quiet that John Roberts, a young Englishman backpacking through Africa, left town in search of adventure.

But the province remained tense. On Thursday 7 July, Tshombe, in Léopoldville trying to talk to Lumumba as the army mutinied around them, asked Belgian and Rhodesian troops to intervene in Katanga as a pre-emptive attempt to prevent disorder. Both governments refused. The next day, trouble broke out in Elisabethville between Force Publique soldiers and white officers.

One man was killed. On Saturday, Katangese civilians turned back a trainload of Europeans fleeing to Rhodesia. Munongo called Tshombe to discuss the mutiny. He got Lumumba.

'So I asked for instructions from Lumumba because Tshombe was not there,' was how Munongo remembered the conversation. 'Lumumba said, "Let them plunder, rape, kill. Then we will start all over again, without Europeans."'[14]

False rumours buzzed around Elisabethville that the Rhodesian army had crossed the frontier. Union Minière closed down its mine works and evacuated the families of white employees. Panic spread like plague. That evening, Force Publique soldiers in the capital opened fire on a group of Europeans in the city centre. The Italian vice consul and five others died in a storm of bullets.

The shooting broke the nerve of Elisabethville's white population. They drove south in panicky convoys, bribing Rhodesian border guards with cash and jewels. Even Belgian officers fled. British journalist George Gale, a hard-drinking Welshman from the *Daily Express*, found a major behind his desk with head in hands, unable to stop his men running away.

'*Vous êtes un lapin en uniforme,*' Gale told him ('You are a rabbit in a uniform').[15] The major said nothing, just squeezed his skull tighter.

Not everyone in Katanga ran. By Sunday, whites in Jadotville had formed self-defence groups and were fighting mutineers through the town's eucalyptus trees. Authorities in Elisabethville demanded an intervention from Brussels. The Belgian ambassador in Léopoldville warned that Lumumba, already furious at paracommandos elsewhere in the country, would never forgive meddling in his richest province. Brussels politicians argued amongst themselves. On three occasions, Eyskens gave orders for intervention then changed his mind, once recalling aeroplanes that had already taken off from Kamina airbase.

The violence spread. In Jadotville, Belgian agronomist and occasional radio presenter Roger Jaspar watched mutinous soldiers shooting the glass out of hospital windows. Fighting began in Kabolo and Kongolo. Eyskens finally gave the order. Captain Commandant Guy Weber flew two companies into Elisabethville. Other paracommandos landed in northern cities and took control.

Tshombe hurried back to Katanga to find Munongo had already decided the province's future.

'When Moïse returned to Elisabethville, I was dead tired after two days of fighting and nonsense,' said Munongo:

> In the meantime Belgian paracommandos had crushed the mutiny. So I said to Moïse: 'You must do your duty'. […] We talked a long time. And I told Tshombe: 'You do not have two choices, only one. Unless you declare Katanga's independence, I will do it'. I knew that people would support me.[16]

Tshombe was persuaded to make another attempt at secession. Few believed he did not ask UMHK for advice first. Within hours, the news reached Belgian Minister of Foreign Affairs Pierre Wigny, a square-faced aristocrat with a neat centre parting. Wigny warned that Brussels would not recognise an independent Katanga, concerned that Léopoldville would fall into the arms of the Soviet Union without the province's copper profits.

No one in Conakat listened. Early in the morning of 11 July, Tshombe woke the British consul for advice about a radio broadcast. Afterwards he visited American consul William C. Canup to discuss Washington's position.

'In general we wish Tshombe discouraged,' the State Department telegraphed Canup, 'but do not wish to close door completely since detachment Katanga could conceivably be in interest West if rest of Congo continues in present status.'[17]

The same day, in the centre of Elisabethville, all chaos and Belgian soldiers riding jeeps, Roger Jaspar searched for the Conakat leader, remembering the invitation from Independence Day. On the way, he met an old friend who directed him instead to the Radio Elisabethville studios, where a Belgian called Maurice Verbruggen was trying to get a local broadcast service going.

Usually limited to rebroadcasting programmes from Léopoldville, Radio Elisabethville's only competition was a few private short-wave stations like Radio UFAC, operated by a war veterans group across the road, and the Radio College, a heap of modernist concrete and glass on avenue Wangermee. Radio Katanga's first broadcast that afternoon, with Jasper at the microphone, was a brief announcement that Pius Sapwe had been appointed police chief, part of Munongo's Africanisation of the police force. Afterwards a message arrived from the Provincial President's residence: Tshombe would make a special radio announcement at eight o'clock that evening.

The broadcast took place in the better-equipped UFAC studios across the road. Tshombe and his entourage turned up early. He showed no surprise at Jaspar's presence. At eight o'clock, a red bulb lit up and Jaspar introduced Radio Katanga. A technician pointed at Tshombe.

'The Katangese government has decided to declare the independence of Katanga,' said the Conakat leader into the microphone. 'And this independence is total.'[18]

The next day, Lumumba and Kasa-Vubu commandeered a Belgian military aeroplane and headed for Elisabethville. Munongo, new Katangese Minister of the Interior, took over the control tower radio as the plane circled overhead.

'The order has been given to troops at the airport to fire on all aircraft which do not have authorisation,' said Munongo. 'If Lumumba promises not to leave the terminal I will talk with him, and President Tshombe will welcome President Kasa-Vubu.'[19]

He listened to Kasa-Vubu and Lumumba arguing over the open mic. The prime minister refused to accept the conditions. The aeroplane flew off. Munongo gave a rare smile. Back in Léopoldville, a furious Lumumba asked Ralph Bunce of the United Nations for military aid to end the secession. Bunce contacted his bosses in New York.

Katanga had amputated itself from the rest of the Congo. Support from Belgian capitalists, Rhodesian imperialists and ambiguous signals from America had persuaded Tshombe that his province could function as a new nation. In neighbouring Kasaï province, Lumumba's one-time friend Albert Kalonji was already thinking about his own secession. It would all go wrong and men from Elisabethville would find themselves in the front line trying to stop Kalonji's new country from collapsing and taking Katanga with it.

# 5

# *L'AFFAIRE DU SUD-KASAÏ*

## Albert Kalonji and the Diamond State

The Baluba bowmen wanted revenge. They showed John Roberts their vials of poison: liquefied crocodile brain, toxic herbs and juice boiled from putrid meat. An arrowhead dipped in any one would paralyse an enemy and slowly shut down his internal organs. It was a horrible way to die. Other Baluba warriors waved antique Arab muzzle-loading rifles in the air and swung *panga*s, waiting impatiently for Roberts to lead them into battle.

The dark-haired 22-year-old from Somerset tried to look commanding. He was only here because a hippopotamus had bitten his canoe in half somewhere along the River Luapal.

The son of an architect, Roberts had done two years' national service back in Britain as a second lieutenant. He got out in 1957 with the ability to lead men, bayonet sandbags and polish boot leather to a black mirror. It led to a job in the Northern Rhodesian Police. When his contract finished, Roberts set off to backpack across Africa from the Cape of Good Hope upwards.

He began in May 1959. Blisters and bloody feet; riding an ostrich near Coitzdorp; examining bushman cave paintings by torchlight; Basuto girls dancing to jazz 78s on a wind-up gramophone in the bush; catching barracuda off a rich man's yacht headed for Lourenço Marques; hiding up a tree from a buffalo with two Shangaan Zulus; talking with a white Rhodesian woman who thought him a fool not to realise the only solution to racial problems was 'the machine gun'.[1]

Roberts reached the Congo in time for the 1960 elections and hung around Elisabethville until independence. He stayed with Willy and Henrietta Cardon-Sips, friends of his parents. The sound of marching bands had barely died away when Roberts bought a canoe and continued his journey. The hippo attacked before he got far and he took a bus back to Elisabethville, where he found

Katanga independent and the Congo in chaos. Two months later, thanks to a plump Belgian called 'Uncle Jan', he was in charge of a column of the Kasaï Liberation Army liaising with Baluba tribesmen outside the small town of Luputa.

He told a soldier in sweaty camouflage fatigues to ask the bowmen about witchdoctors. The Kasaï Liberation Army needed all the help it could get. Roberts knew the United Nations soldiers spreading through the country like damp would do their best to stop his attack before it began.


Ralph Bunce had passed on Lumumba's request for help to the United Nations Secretary General, a Swedish civil servant with blonde hair and grey-blue eyes calm as a frozen lake. Dag Hammarskjöld turned it down. The UN's job was peace.

The United Nations had been around since the end of the Second World War. Its optimistic goal of world harmony was often compromised by the competing desires of America and the Soviet Union, its strongest members. American pressure sent UN troops to the Korean War in 1950 and Soviet demands made them sit and watch as the Red Army crushed anti-communist rebels in Hungary six years later. Most of Hammarskjöld's energy went into persuading the superpowers occasionally to vote the same way.

The Swede did not want the UN to be used as a private army to take back Katanga. The Congo's biggest problem, in his view, was the threat of a clash between Belgian soldiers and the ANC. He twisted some superpower arms and secured a mandate from the Security Council in New York to replace the 7,400 Belgians in the Congo with UN soldiers. The first peacekeepers, a Tunisian contingent, arrived in Léopoldville on 14 July, followed by units from Ghana, Mali and Morocco. Belgian soldiers reluctantly gave up their positions to blue-helmeted UN men and flew home.

The process was surprisingly smooth, even surviving a kick in the teeth from Lumumba, when he declared it too slow and asked the Soviet Union to intervene independently. Moscow officially declined but saw a chance to sink its claws into Africa. Soviet aeroplanes and lorries and Czechoslovak technicians began to arrive secretly in Stanleyville. Cold warriors in Brussels were horrified.

'The Congo will become communist within two months,' said Harold d'Aspremont-Lynden, a close colleague of the Belgian prime minister.[2]

Soon after, Harold d'Aspremont-Lynden was on his way to Katanga as head of the Mission Technique Belge (Belgian Technical Mission – Mistebel), a high-powered group of experts full of ideas on how to run the new country. Minister of Foreign Affairs Pierre Wigny was not happy. He had been arguing against taking sides in Katanga ever since Tshombe declared independence, but lost any support in the Cabinet after Léopoldville accused Brussels of organising the secession and broke diplomatic relations.

The army never shared Wigny's doubts about intervention. Even before Mistebel flew in, General Charles de Cumont, head of the Belgian Chiefs of Staff, helped crush the last mutineers holding out in Manono and Kongolo. The fighting was short but bloody. More Europeans died in Katanga than any other province. De Cumont encouraged Belgian soldiers and bureaucrats to return from Rhodesia and appointed Major Jean-Marie Crèvecœur, a short SAS veteran with glasses and a fussy moustache, head of the Katangese armed forces.

When Wigny protested, de Cumont argued that he was just following his brief to protect European civilians. Paracommando chief Guy Weber used the same excuse to spend time at Tshombe's side offering advice. Moustached and tall, muscle already padded with a little flab, the 39-year-old Weber had chased the Nazis out of Belgium in 1944. Now his enemy was communism, which he thought meant Lumumba. It had not been hard for Tshombe to win him over.

'He was the kind of African with whom, after five minutes of conversation, skin colour was forgotten,' said Weber.[3]

On avenue Reine Elisabeth, Jean-Marie Crèvecœur, now a colonel, set up HQ for his new army. He demobilised local ANC forces and expelled those unwilling to serve the new state. Within a few days, he had only 350 men. He acted confident for the press.

'A year from now', he said, 'I will have created a well-trained thousand-strong Katangese army.'[4]

Volunteers began running along dusty roads, clambering up wooden climbing frames, ducking through concrete tubes. Numbers for the Katangese Gendarmerie, an army that sounded like a police force, remained low.[5] Brussels seconded eighty-nine Belgian officers and NCOs. A recruitment campaign in the army netted another 326 military and technical volunteers. Aeroplanes from Brussels brought crates of guns and ammunition.

Munongo thickened the stew by encouraging loyal tribal chiefs to form their own militias. His brother Antoine, chief of the Bayeke, offered a private army of warriors. Kasongo Nyembo, a senior Baluba who hated Sendwe, came on board with 90,000 followers, a sixth of the tribe in Katanga.

D'Aspremont-Lynden bustled around Elisabethville, giving advice, making telephone calls and applying pressure. No one was surprised when Union Minière agreed to re-open its mines and divert taxes from Léopoldville, or when the Belgian National Bank set up an account worth 50 million francs for Jean Kibwe, 36-year-old Katangese Vice President and Minister of Finance.[6] Mistebel men wormed their way into Katanga's new ministries as advisors, sometimes finding local ultras had got there first. Tshombe's Cabinet was young by European standards, most being in their thirties. Paul Mohana, Minister of Social Affairs, was 29.

At an open-air ceremony in late July, gendarmes raised the first two Katangese flags, made by a local tailor, over the town. A green bar slashed the flag from lower left corner to upper right, dividing it into red and white sections. Three red croisettes (lumpy diagonal crosses that symbolised ancient Katangese currency) sat in the white.

'Red for the blood shed for Katanga's freedom,' said Tshombe, 'white for purity, green for hope.'[7]

The Katangese hoped the UN peacekeepers would stay out of the new state. But on 2 August, Dag Hammarskjöld called a press conference in the United Nation's New York headquarters along the East River, all airy white concrete and marble walls. The UN, he announced, had made a decision: troops would enter the province in four days.

'They will have to fight their way in,' Tshombe told reporters when he heard, certain that Hammarskjöld's soldiers would act as an advance guard for Léopoldville.[8]

Kibwe, Weber (now a major) and Minister of Defence Joseph Yav flew to New York, where they pleaded Katanga's case among skyscrapers, yellow Checker cabs and Kent cigarette smoke. The trio failed to impress the Security Council. The Soviet Bloc saw Katanga as a western imperialist plot; recently independent African and Asian nations called it neo-colonialism; and Dwight Eisenhower's America had distanced itself to stop the Cold War extending into Africa. Only Britain and France, both with large mining investments in Katanga, appeared sympathetic.

Tshombe's advisors persuaded him to invite Hammarskjöld to Elisabethville, hoping the Katangese president's famous charm could smooth out a compromise. Tshombe waited at the airport with a brochure called *Welcome to Elisabethville* and a parade of gendarmes. When the UN plane touched down, he found that Hammarskjöld had brought along two companies of Swedish UN troops, who dug in around the runway. Tshombe accepted the manoeuvre gracefully and discovered the Swede had a chilly charm of his own. After long discussions and some unexpected pressure from Brussels, which wanted to keep on the UN's good side to avoid awkward questions about Mistebel, Tshombe agreed that peacekeepers could replace Belgian soldiers.

'Who can I trust,' said Tshombe, 'if I cannot trust the United Nations?'[9]

If he could have seen a few weeks into the future, with ANC troops pouring over the border from Kasaï province leaving dead bodies and burning towns behind them, he would not have been so sure.

It was a warm evening at the end of August in an Elisabethville cocktail bar when Uncle Jan asked Roberts if he wanted to help Katanga. Roberts rattled the ice cubes around his glass.

'I think I can safely say that adventure is my hobby,' he said, 'almost, in fact, my career'.[10]

Uncle Jan was a recruiter for South Kasaï, the Congo's newest secession. He sketched out the area's recent history over a fresh round of cocktails. The May 1960 elections in Kasaï had been a straight fight between the province's Balubas and their long-time rivals, the Lulua. The Baluba supported native son Albert Kalonji, an accountant with a mystical side (he was fascinated by Rosicrucian myths of the sixteenth century) and a burning dislike for Lumumba dating from the break-up of the original MNC.

'He makes friends easily,' said a colleague of Kalonji, 'but he is not loyal to them'.[11]

The Lulua sided with Lumumba's MNC faction. Their votes got Lumumba's men seven out of ten seats in the provincial assembly and Kalonji's MNC splitters the remainder. Kalonji thought he could negotiate his way to assembly leader but some shady deals blocked his chances. The political row escalated into ethnic violence.

Lulua chased Kalonji's followers out of villages in the north. Thousands died. An old woman, face ridged with tribal scars, boasted that she had burnt fifty-two Baluba huts with their inhabitants still inside. A Lulua raiding group kidnapped a 2-year-old called Emile and roasted him over a fire. A Portuguese trader tried to rescue him but his car was attacked:

'I get out and start to run for that check point. I forget all about Emile, because he [is] not crying. When I get to the check point, the soldiers go back but Emile [is] gone. What [are they] going to do with that baby?'[12]

Cannibalism was widespread. Both sides would eat the rump and leave the rest. A pair of Baluba men loaded their truck with sixteen Lulua women and children, promising to take them to a festival. They drove to a nearby village where fellow Baluba hacked up the passengers with *panga*s and cooked them. Human flesh tastes like sweet pork.

At least 250,000 Baluba refugees came south to their ancestral heartland of South Kasaï, trudging through the sun to settle near the diamond mining town of Bakwanga. Malnutrition turned children into pot-bellied skeletons, legs like bowed twigs, knee joints bulging. Even the healthiest adults had anaemia. Hospitals ran out of saline solution and glucose, and the refugees kept coming.

By the eve of independence, the Belgians thought the province had stabilised. Police kept quiet about decomposing body parts in the bush. Kasaï authorities discreetly pushed through a law that any meat sold at market must have animal hide attached to prove it was not human.

Violence returned within days of the handover ceremony. Kalonji blamed the new government. On 11 July, he dodged mutinous soldiers in Léopoldville to ask the American consulate for funds to overthrow Lumumba. Larry Devlin, CIA Station Chief in the Congo, turned him down. A few days later, Belgium did the same. Kalonji returned to Kasaï and ditched Congolese nationalism for something more local.

On 8 August, he joined other Baluba leaders in Bakwanga and declared South Kasaï an independent state. Kalonji appointed himself president and Joseph Ngalula the head of government. The new state sliced the province north-west to south-east, scooping up most of Kasaï's industrial diamond deposits. Its main mining company, the Société Internationale Forestière et Minière du Congo (Forminière), created with American help back when Léopold II still owned the country, quietly agreed to divert its future taxes to Bakwanga.

Kalonji raised the South Kasaï flag: a red stripe over green, with a yellow 'V' cutting through both: 'V' for *Victoire*. This second secession so close on the heels of Katanga enraged Lumumba. The UN urged negotiation. Lumumba ignored the peacekeepers and gave orders to retake the territory.

The assault began on 23 August. A thousand ANC soldiers from Stanleyville slotted themselves around Soviet lorries deep in the bellies of transport planes. Former Thysville camp commander Léopold Nzulu was in charge, advised by Lumumba's brother-in-law Jacques Omonombe and the Secretary of State, Jacques Lumbala. The attack force touched down in Luluabourg, the Kasaï capital, and drove south.

Kalonji had 250 policemen and 200 soldiers to stop them. His armed forces paraded around Bakwanga's bungalows with ancient .303 Lee Enfield rifles and old British army helmets that looked like rusty soup dishes. In the evening of 24 August, Kalonji got in a jeep and headed to Katanga, telling his ministers he would ask Tshombe for help. That night, the ANC entered South Kasaï territory and shot any Baluba they saw. Local tribesmen fought back with spears and bows against automatic weapons. Villages burned.

At least 5,000 Baluba were killed, many tortured, women raped. ANC troops shot dead American journalist Henry Noble Taylor along with a lorryload of refugees near the South Kasaï capital. Lumbala and Omonombe organised the arrests of Lumumba's political enemies and looked on as ANC soldiers murdered children. South Kasaï troops fell back into the streets of Bakwanga. As news of the fighting spread, Sandy Gall of Reuters asked Colonel Crèvecœur if it was safe to visit the South Kasaï capital.

'It is in friendly hands,' Crèvecœur told him. [13]

Gall chartered a light aircraft in Northern Rhodesia, splitting the cost with George Gale and Dickie Williams of the BBC. The South Kasaï capital was a dirt strip airport in cattle ranching land, surrounded by a few streets of hibiscus-gardened European bungalows and a sprawl of African huts. The trio found Bakwanga airfield full of Soviet Ilyushin IL-14 and Antonov AN-12 transport planes. A Tunisian UN lieutenant ushered them into a jeep, one hand on his Sterling sub-machine gun.

'*Ça c'est ma Bible*,' he said, tapping the barrel. This is my Bible.[14]

'Are things that difficult?'

'Yes. Very difficult indeed'.

Crèvecœur's information was wrong. The ANC had entered Bakwanga on 27 August, sending Kalonji's soldiers fleeing through the bush towards the Katangese border. Injured Baluba soldiers were dragged out of Bakwanga hospital and shot. On 1 September, at least seventy civilians, including children, were executed. Hundreds more died when the ANC burned down a church. Two hundred Baluba refugees were dying every day of starvation and the UN troops present lacked the manpower to help.

Gall explored the South Kasaï capital. The houses were empty, the diamond mine closed. ANC guards had 200 local whites locked up in the Club Belge, rationed to three glasses of water a day. The whites avoided eye contact with the Congolese soldiers noisily drinking beer at the bar. Back at the airfield, about to board their aeroplane, Gall and friends were arrested by a bearded solder and dragged off to an army base. Soldiers robbed and beat them until military policemen rescued the trio. The UN put the reporters on a DC-3 to Léopoldville. As they took off, more Soviet Ilyushin Il-14s were coming in to land.

Tshombe allowed South Kasaï's leaders to take refuge in Elisabethville. Kalonji set up base in a cottage in the grounds of Tshombe's presidential palace.

'I shall fight on from the outside,' he told journalists. 'Like General de Gaulle'.[15]

Other Conakat men found it hard to forget that Kasaï Baluba had been their immigrant enemies only a few years before. Munongo refused to hand over any weapons and would not even discuss the issue with Tshombe. Albert Kalonji had to beg UMHK to intervene.

'Know that I protect Katanga,' he wrote to Henry Fortemps, the UMHK assistant director general. 'If I cannot resist then you will be swept away.'[16]

He got his guns. Brussels sent money to fund a new army.

The Kasaï recruiting office was a few doors down from the cocktail bar. Roberts signed up. He bought a second-hand Belgian army uniform, razored off the insignia and sewed on a red V, then reported to Kalonji and Ngalula for his orders. Ngalula spoke good French and English, and seemed friendly; Kalonji had a colder personality.

'I felt that I personally could trust him, as I was obviously one of his officers,' said Roberts, 'but I should have hated to come up against him.'[17]

Kalonji introduced Colonel Gillet, a French big game hunter and war veteran from Orientale province, as his aide de camp but the real tactical brain was Colonel Crèvecœur, camped in a cattle farm on the Katangese side of the River Lubilash with a tableful of maps. Taking back South Kasaï was a priority for Elisabethville. ANC patrols from Bakwanga were already probing over the border in what looked like preparation for an invasion of Katanga.

Kalonji's exile army consisted of two companies with 120 men each, recruited mostly from Baluba émigrés working in Katanga. Roberts was put in charge of forming a third company. He chose the biggest men from a line-up of 800 Baluba, passed out Sten guns and loaded them on a train for the front line. Five Belgian paracommandos joined Roberts's company at Kamina, scratching the painted insignia off their helmets, but left when they sensed the resentful anger of Kasaï soldiers at their former colonial masters. A few Europeans were tolerated, like Flemish commandant Georges Vleigh and Lieutenant Jules Kimm.

During the train journey, Roberts discovered a group of his soldiers around a bloody Congolese man with the flesh peeled off his arm. The soldiers had made him eat it. They claimed he was a spy. Roberts handed him over to Kaniama prison and barely returned to the station in time to stop his men lynching a group of Benalula tribesmen, allies of the Lulua.

He had just reached the border when 300 of Lumumba's ANC troops crossed into northern Katanga on 8 September and headed for Kongolo, a riverbank town where locals grew coffee and rice in the dark soil. Crèvecœur rushed Katangese gendarmes to meet them. Roberts's company slipped around the fighting into South Kasaï.

Baluba villagers joined his column carrying poisoned arrows. Roberts asked their witchdoctors to boost morale. Soon his company were wearing twine charms around their shoulders with ends covered in pounded paste hanging over the heart. The witchdoctors taught Roberts some magic. On 14 September, as his men prepared to attack the small town of Luputa in the south of the province, Roberts got a local boy to stick a wooden idol in the ground to represent the enemy, draw a circle round it, then knock it down. He asked one of his men if the ceremony was useful. 'Captain Roberts, it make me feel good,' said the man, 'like I protect my family. It make me feel strong, a real man.'[18]

Roberts's troops marched towards Luputa. In Elisabethville, Kalonji accused Lumumba of genocide as black smoke rose over Bakwanga. He wanted revenge. In Léopoldville, CIA agent Larry Devlin took possession of a vial of poison with instructions to inject it into the prime minister's toothpaste. A lot of people wanted Lumumba dead that autumn.

# 6

# ASSIGNMENT – LÉOPOLDVILLE

### How to Overthrow the Congolese Prime Minister

'What do you call a drunken Congolese soldier, with steel helmet and dark glasses pushing a gun into your stomach?' Journalists in the bar of Léopoldville's Hôtel Stanley drank their whisky and waited for a punchline they all knew. 'Monsieur!'

Roadblocks covered the Congolese capital like a rash. A knot of petrol drums, rubble and ANC soldiers demanding papers as they pushed FN FAL muzzles in your face and breathed whisky fumes. If you stayed calm, gave out cigarettes and grovelled, you might live to file your story.

The only other sign of life on Léopoldville's streets were the women who squatted by the sides of the road frying meat in palm oil. The city stank of smoking fat and fear. Lumumba's government had declared martial law. Opposition newspapers had been shut down. Gabriel Macoso was the first journalist to be arrested for criticising the government. Political demonstrations were banned. Police opened fire on an anti-government march to show they meant business.

Most journalists tried to stay indoors. New CIA Station Head Larry Devlin thought that was smart. Back in July, he had been picked up by ANC soldiers, two days after his arrival. They beat him, put a revolver to his head and played Russian roulette. The hammer came down on an empty chamber. The soldiers laughed and let him go. A few weeks later, Devlin ventured out and found himself in front of a firing squad of drunk soldiers. A passing Congolese politician saved him.

Cheating death with seconds to spare was all part of the job for Devlin, a ruthless American patriot in his late thirties with slicked back hair, a taste for single-breasted suits and a cigarette permanently between his fingers. The San Diego native had seen action in Europe during the Second World War before marrying a French girl and studying for a Masters at Harvard University. In the winter of 1948, a professor invited him into his office for a chat. A few months later, Devlin joined the CIA.

The Congo used to be a safe posting. Agency friends told Devlin to pack his golf clubs. The closest the CIA had got to any action in Léopoldville was back in May 1960, when it persuaded Lumumba to ignore a snappily dressed Trinidadian arms dealer linked to Fidel Castro, who offered to outfit the Congolese Air Force after independence. Devlin set off to Léopoldville expecting rest and relaxation. He arrived in the middle of the Cold War.

Lumumba's appeal to the USSR had shaken America. Things got worse when the prime minister visited Washington in the last weeks of July and requested military aid to end Tshombe's secession. In breaks from the talks, Lumumba told the Capitol's politicians that the US had only become a success because it had imported African slaves to run the country. The Americans found his politics unhinged; Lumumba's request for a nightly whore offended them.

'His words never had anything to do with matters under discussion,' said Douglas Dillon, Deputy Secretary of State. 'You had a feeling he was gripped by this fervour that I can only characterise as messianic. He was just not a rational being.'[2]

Dillon refused to provide military assistance or women, and advised trust in the UN. Lumumba flew to New York for discussions with Soviet diplomats. Devlin, who had accompanied him to Washington, stayed behind to brief CIA Director Allen Dulles on the dangers facing the Congo.

'While I never believed Lumumba was a communist', said Devlin, 'I did believe he was politically naïve and inherently unstable.'[3]

A lipless, moustached pipe smoker, Dulles listened as the Congo station chief talked about Lumumba's contacts with Moscow, the materials arriving daily in Stanleyville, the Soviet spies buzzing around Léopoldville. Lumumba was pasting himself into the scrapbook of America's enemies, on the same page as Cuba's Fidel Castro and Rafael Trujillo of the Dominican Republic.

Devlin returned to the Congo authorised to spend up to $100,000 on any operation to remove Lumumba from power. 'In high quarters here', cabled Dulles:

> it is the clear decision that if Lumumba continues to hold high office, the inevitable result will at best be chaos and at worst pave the way to a Communist takeover of the Congo with disastrous consequences for the prestige of the UN and for the interests of the free world generally.[4]

Devlin tucked an automatic in his waistband and toured his Léopoldville contacts. The news was good: Kasa-Vubu had distanced himself from Lumumba after the South Kasaï invasion, fearing civil war; Baluba politicians hated the prime minister for the massacres in Bakwanga, with the exception of Jason

Sendwe, who had his own problems in Katanga; Mobutu's loyalty snapped after he was told to ignore Soviet propaganda leaflets circulating in the army; only General Lundula, head of the ANC, remained true in the MNC stronghold of Stanleyville. Even the United Nations had turned, with Hammarskjöld briefing journalists that the South Kasaï campaign had been genocidal.

'Lumumba gets worse and worse,' the UN's Ralph Bunce wrote to his wife in August as he packed his bags for America. 'He is the lowest man I have ever encountered. I despise Gizenga, but I hate Lumumba.'[5]

Devlin was pushing at an open door.

Other secret services came to the same conclusion: Lumumba had to go. Britain's MI6 put Daphne Park on the job. High in intelligence, low on glamour, the 39-year-old consul to Léopoldville had grown up in a Tanganyika mud hut listening to lions roar in the distance. Her father was a gold prospector. In London during the war, she trained resistance fighters for missions into occupied territory, and drifted inevitably into the spy world. An attempt to grab Nazi scientists in post-war Berlin impressed no one when Park's inadequate German mixed up a missile scientist with an expert on bumble bees, but a posting to Moscow allowed her to shine as a spy. Of espionage she said:

> It's about knowing human beings and being able to relate to a very wide range of people. People talk to you if they want someone to know what's happening and you're the person they trust. But you have to retain your own values, you have to believe in your own country.[6]

Park worked a parallel path to Devlin. Secret meetings, money changing hands, promises kept and unkept. When Lumumba's private secretary wanted to defect, she smuggled him out of the Congo in a Citroën 2CV.

'Nobody ever takes 2CVs seriously. But that's not why I had it; if they'd let me loose in anything bigger, I'd have been lethal. My director once told me the bravest thing he'd ever done in his life was to be driven around by me.'[7]

The Belgians had more direct plans. At the end of July, Captain Guy Dedeken found himself in Brussels being interviewed by Major Jules Loos, advisor to the Ministry of African Affairs. Loos wanted details on his military skills and moral flexibility. Dedeken, former leader of a Force Publique commando unit, had been held hostage in the ANC camp at Luluabourg with his wife and five children. He had no love left for the Congo.

Loos introduced him to General Baron de Cumont, recently returned from Elisabethville. De Cumont gave Dedeken a mission: kidnap Lumumba and take him to Brazzaville in the neighbouring Republic of the Congo.

In early August, Dedeken visited the former French colony. Brazzaville contacts got him an audience with Abbé Fulbert Youlou, a blank-eyed defrocked priest and the country's president. Youlou disliked Lumumba and sympathised with Tshombe. He agreed to host the operation. Dedeken recruited Baluba warriors from South Kasaï for his team and had Lumumba shadowed around Léopoldville.

Someone talked. Europeans in Brazzaville casually asked Dedeken if he was planning to assassinate the prime minister. He denied everything but no one believed him. Dedeken's moral flexibility went no further than kidnapping but others with less restraint were thinking murder. An anonymous former member of the Belgian-Congolese security services circulated the 'Plan L' memo, suggesting Brussels assassinate Lumumba by poisoning his medicines.

Baron Robert Rothschild, now the head of Mistebel after D'Aspremont-Lynden returned to Brussels as Minister for African Affairs, shut down Dedeken's kidnapping mission. The captain headed off to join Kalonji's army in South Kasaï.

Another path for subversion soon opened up. Louis Marlière, Mobutu's military advisor and closest white friend, informed Brussels that the ANC colonel had his own plan to get rid of Lumumba. The Belgian government passed Mobutu 20 million francs. Devlin also handed over thick bundles of francs courtesy of the CIA. The colonel reread *The Prince* and counted his money.


On 5 September, domestic resentment boiled over, helped along by foreign bribes. Kasa-Vubu gave a national radio broadcast claiming Lumumba had destabilised the country by sending troops into South Kasaï. He sacked Lumumba as prime minister, along with six ministers, and asked Joseph Ileo, President of the Senate and a member of Kalonji's MNC faction, to form a new government.

Lumumba made his own broadcast, sacking Kasa-Vubu, and urged the people to rise up in support. The UN saw civil war in its crystal ball and closed all airports in the Congo that night. The next morning, it shut down Léopoldville's radio station; George Ivan Smith, a 45-year-old Australian UN official with a well-used face, pulled vital parts from the transmitter station. Soviet technicians, their shirts sweat-stained rags in the humidity, failed to fix the sabotage.

Tshombe, whose gendarmes were still fighting ANC troops in Kongolo, made an enthusiastic broadcast from Elisabethville supporting Kasa-Vubu's move: 'Lumumba, the usurper should be put before a high court to answer for his crimes.'[8]

For the next nine days, Léopoldville was in chaos. Kasa-Vubu and Lumumba each claimed to be rightful leader of the Congo. Their supporters clashed on the streets. Devlin scurried around with wads of francs for his contacts, and the United Nations tried to keep the peace without taking sides but tainted itself in the eyes of Lumumba by accepting a million dollars from the US to prevent ANC soldiers mutinying after their wages failed to arrive. Mobutu took credit for the money.

The president and prime minister threatened to arrest each other; the Congolese Chamber of Representatives and the Senate voted through contradictory resolutions; Foreign Minister Justin Bomboko, an oversexed Kasa-Vubu loyalist who had loudly criticised Lumumba, narrowly escaped arrest by ANC troops at the rundown Hôtel Regina, his favourite spot for chasing women. Mobutu confided that they had orders to execute him.

On 14 September, Kasa-Vubu declared parliament suspended but parliament refused to accept the order. Lumumba demanded UN troops arrest his enemies, but the peacekeepers ignored him. Mobutu made his dramatic entrance into politics that evening. At a press conference in the Hôtel Regina, he declared military rule until 31 December 1960, with all political decisions to be made by the Collège des Universitaires, a panel of university graduates. Bomboko came out of hiding to head the Collège. The army shut communist embassies and expelled their representatives. Lumumba was out of power. Mobutu had intended to get rid of Kasa-Vubu as well, but Devlin changed his mind.

'You've got a legitimacy problem,' Devlin told him. 'Only Kasa-Vubu can solve that.'[9]

Mobutu reluctantly allowed Kasa-Vubu to remain president. The real power remained with the colonel and his friends, known as the Binza group after their upscale Léopoldville neighbourhood. Key members were Bomboko, Victor Nendaka, head of the Sûreté, and Cyrille Adoula, a former trade union leader. All knew Devlin well.

'We must have confidence in the effort of Colonel Mobutu,' said Tshombe in Elisabethville, 'to restore order out of chaos.'[10]

Lumumba refused to give up. On the morning of 15 September, he urged the ANC in Camp Léopold to rise against the new regime. His audience included Baluba soldiers who had refused to join the South Kasaï invasion back in August. Halfway through his speech they attacked him with bottles and knives. Lumumba took refuge in the officer's mess until UN troops escorted him home and ringed the house with guards. Kasa-Vubu asked the UN to arrest his prime minister. The UN claimed strict neutrality. The next day Lumumba asked the UN to fly in troops from Stanleyville, where General Lundula remained loyal among the mango trees and mosquitos. The UN again claimed neutrality.

On 18 September, the day the ANC invasion of Katanga was finally stopped and pushed back over the Kasaï border, a soldier tried to assassinate Mobutu at

Camp Léopold. Pierre Mulele, former Minister of Education, had organised the attack on Lumumba's orders. Two further attempts by Mulele, assisted by Maurice Mpolo, Minister of Youth and Sports, and Lumumba's choice for new ANC head, also failed.

'Lumumba wants my hide?' Mobutu said. 'I want his!'[11]

Lumumba stayed at home, guarded by UN troops. He drank heavily and chain-smoked weed, rarely changing out of his pyjamas as he gave speeches to a sleepy entourage.

On 19 September, Devlin received a top-secret cable instructing him to await the visit of a senior agent. A week later, Sidney Gottlieb, club-footed CIA chemist and LSD expert with a passion for folk dancing, met Devlin at the Café de la Presse with instructions from Dulles. President Eisenhower had decided to assassinate Lumumba. Gottlieb passed over a box containing rubber gloves, a mask, a syringe and a glass vial of poison that would give the impression of death by natural causes when injected into the target's toothpaste. Dulles claimed Eisenhower had suggested the assassination in a private meeting. Others thought Dulles had taken an off-hand comment from the president and gone rogue.

'At no time and in no way', said General Andrew Goodpaster, Eisenhower's personal military staff officer at the White House, 'did I ever know of or hear about any proposal, any mention of such an activity. It is my belief that had such a thing been raised with the President other than in my presence, I would have known about it.'[12]

Devlin would later claim he could not understand why it was necessary to kill a politician already kicked out of power, but his cables to Washington in the autumn of 1960 were gung-ho about the assassination. Attempts to get past the UN guard on Lumumba's house failed and the poison expired. In early October, Devlin dropped the murder kit into the dark waters of the River Congo.

UN relations with Mobutu, already shaky after the coup, deteriorated when the colonel sent his troops into Léopoldville to arrest Lumumba supporters. The undisciplined troops robbed and raped. On 10 October, ANC officers appeared at UN headquarters with a warrant for Lumumba himself. When the UN refused to co-operate, Mobutu threatened to beat them into the sea. The colonel took great pleasure in listening to the pleas of Virenda Dayal, a hamster-cheeked Indian civil servant who had replaced Bunce as Hammarskjöld's Special Representative.

'Until a few days ago', said Mobutu, 'the UN treated me like a child. Now I've shown them what I am. General Rikhye [Hammarskjöld's military advisor] took me to the Indian military hospital, and he invited me to lunch. In three months I got nothing. In two days, everything'.[13]

Dayal managed to negotiate the tension down a notch; Lumumba remained in his house guarded by the UN. But the peacekeepers felt besieged. Lumumba supporters blamed them for his overthrow, Mobutu's men made it clear they were not wanted and Mobutu's Belgian advisors blocked their political efforts. Léopoldville newspapers loyal to the new regime let everyone know Dayal had an official helicopter on standby to take his wife shopping in Brazzaville. The UN man took out his anger on Devlin. He had a nice line in chilly condescension.

'I so admire America and Americans,' he told Devlin. 'You make the very best air conditioners, the best refrigerators, so many fine machines. If you would only concentrate on making your machines and let us ponder for you.'[14]

Devlin smiled blandly.

Despite the threats and arrest warrants, Lumumba refused to remain prisoner in his home. He gave press conferences in the Hôtel Regina. On another occasion, *Time-Life* correspondent Edward Behr and an Indian journalist joined a convoy ferrying Lumumba, his friends, bodyguards and a gang of large women in colourful dresses around Léopoldville's dance halls. The women poured shots of Grand Marnier into everyone's beer. Lumumba drank, danced with the ladies and made speeches to puzzled patrons.

'The imperialists will be defeated,' said Lumumba. 'The imperialists who are responsible for the crushing of the revolution, whether in Africa or Asia. Take India …'[15]

The Indian journalist showed interest.

'Take India. The white men crushed the revolution in India. The white men killed Gandhi.'

'You bloody fool,' said the Indian journalist. 'We killed Gandhiji.'

Lumumba's bodyguard pulled a pistol. Lumumba paid no attention:

I am going out tonight to die like Gandhi. If I die it will be because the whites have paid a black man to kill me … Fetch Kasa-Vubu, fetch Mobutu. Tell them Lumumba challenges them to a duel. Tomorrow I will die with the people. I will be the people's hostage.

He walked unsteadily to the car. His entourage followed.

United Nations guards waited back at his house. Elsewhere in the Congo, UN patrols in helmets blue as a robin's egg trudged through jungles, along dirt roads, past shaggy-thatched mud huts. Ethiopian, Indian, Irish and Moroccan troops flew into Katanga province to join the Swedes. Some would have fun, drinking beer in the sun with friendly Belgian settlers, splashing around Elisabethville's Lido pool. Others would find themselves fighting for their lives down remote bush tracks against the people they had come to protect. Jason Sendwe's Baluba of northern Katanga had begun to kill.

# 7

# WE ARE THE UNITED NATIONS

## Swedish and Irish Peacekeepers in Katanga

The wall behind the wardrobe was covered in dried blood.

Private Tom Kenny of the Irish UN arrived in Niemba with the rest of his unit at the end of October. Looters had stripped the one-street town in the north-east of Katanga and smashed what they could not carry. Doors hung off their hinges. Clothes and broken furniture lay on the ground. The few inhabitants who remained blamed local Baluba; the accused denied any involvement and pointed the finger at outsiders from Jason Sendwe's Balubakat.

Kenny, tall and blonde, had signed up with the Irish army a few years back and was thinking about turning it into a career. He found a billet in a house whose Belgian owners had disappeared during the riot. He rearranged the bedroom furniture to make more space and found dark red blotches covering the wall, floor to ceiling. The Belgian owners.

Katanga took a lot of getting used to for Irish farm boys who joined the army to escape a life digging potatoes. From the moment the plane touched down at Kamina airbase, the Irish felt like explorers on an alien planet. Pale as a priest's collar, they burned fierce red in the sun. Every morning, they ran their fingers over mosquito bitten scalps bumpier than a toad's back.

'Like all the other lads who went, I knew little or nothing about the Congo,' said Irish UN soldier Tommy Gavin, 'only that it was in Africa, and in those innocent times the Irish always associated Africa with only one thing – collecting money for "the black babies."'[1]

The Irish arrived as the 32nd and 33rd Battalions. They spread into northern Katanga from bases in Goma and the eastern port of Albertville, finding poor communications, blazing heat, bad roads, suspicious Belgian settlers and cultural clashes with other UN troops.

'The Moroccan and Tunisian troops were out and out dirty bastards,' said Dubliner Tony Norris. 'We went to take over a billet and there was a line of lockers down the centre of the room, which they had used as toilets. We had an unbelievable job cleaning out the place.'[2]

The UN Security Council held Tshombe's secession responsible for recent violence in the north. Up in Niemba, Tom Kenny realised the situation was more complex than that when local Baluba ripped up half a mile of track and derailed a steam train carrying 100 people. The Irish arrived with blankets and baskets of fruit. Only five passengers had survived: all women, one a nun. They had been gang-raped.

'The women's faces were covered in blood,' said Kenny, 'and the nun's clothes were all torn.'[3]

Niemba town remained quiet, even after an Irish soldier shot and wounded a local Baluba chief's son, mistaking him for an intruder. Everyone believed the accident had been forgiven. On 8 November, Kenny joined an eleven-man patrol to check a local bridge after reports of sabotage. That morning, a Baluba cook in the Irish kitchen requested the day off and never came back. The patrol's leader, Lieutenant Kevin Gleeson, thought the Baluba easy-going people who were suffering because they had remained loyal to Léopoldville. He blamed the train derailments and looting on incitement by Tshombe's gendarmes. Stig von Bayer, a Swahili-speaking Swedish interpreter attached to the Irish, caught Gleeson before the patrol left and warned him to be careful.

'No problem', said Gleeson. 'They know we are the UN and are here to help the Balubas.'[4]

Von Bayer told him that at least ten tribal chiefs sympathetic to Elisabethville had been executed by Baluba courts. Sendwe's teenage supporters in the Jeunesse Balubakat (Balubakat Youth) burned Chief Vincent Yangala alive and carried his penis through the streets of Manono on a spear.

Gleeson shrugged.


Jason Sendwe had never accepted Tshombe's secession. He declared northern Katanga the 'Province of Lualaba' and refused to recognise Elisabethville's authority. Tshombe offered Sendwe the vice presidency and four ministerial posts but got no response.

In early August, Tshombe bypassed Balubakat and appealed directly to Katanga's tribal chiefs at a meeting in Elisabethville, hoping the bright searchlight of his charm would overcome doubts about independence. The Jeunesse Balubakat ordered their tribal leaders to stay at home. A chief who disobeyed was swarmed by Jeunesse with sharpened bicycle chains and lashed to death.

Drums beat louder through the jungle, carrying orders for Sendwe's men and hate for Conakat. On 13 September, Jeunesse under 20-year-old Laurent-Désiré Kabila occupied the northern town of Manono for five days, attacking

Europeans and gendarmes. Further south, another Jeunesse gang, who wore witchdoctor fetishes made from human body parts to make them bulletproof, murdered officials in Bukama.

The next day, Katangese gendarmes hunted Baluba around the Luena coalmine, shooting fleeing civilians in the streets. At least sixty died. Later that month, Sendwe's men killed twenty-two people, including children, at Mukulakulu. Jeunesse leaders stitched severed hands to their hats as decoration. Older Baluba pulled up train tracks and attacked wreck survivors, raping the women. Katangese gendarmes in the north fired on Balubakat protests, led prisoners into the bush and returned alone. Baluba overran Kongolo, in the far north of the province, before Katangese gendarmes under a Belgian captain called Balthus retook it on 5 October. The following day, Kabalo Jeunesse captured a ten-man Katangese patrol led by Grégoire Kulu. They rammed sticks into the amputated stumps of Kulu's legs, doused him in petrol and made him walk. After a few steps of haemorrhaging torture, they threw a match.

Hammarskjöld proposed neutral zones to separate Conakat south from Balubakat north, policed by Swedish troops. Tshombe's trust in the United Nations had faded after it did nothing to stop the ANC invasion from Kasaï, but on 17 October he accepted the plan. His gendarmes were understrength, Katanga's attempts to establish legitimacy had been unsuccessful and thousands had died on both sides. He needed to disengage from the Baluba until the rainy season came in at the end of the year.

Baluba violence continued in the north as chiefs used the secession to settle scores. Kabongo Boniface, an important tribal leader, died when the Jeunesse forced a tube down his throat, poured in petrol and set him alight. Gendarme garrisons in outposts of northern Conakat support like Albertville and Kongolo lived in fear.

As clouds gathered for the rain, ready to turn roads into rivers, the province of Lualaba squatted in the north, glowering at Tshombe's southern heartland over a fence of UN soldiers.


On the drive up the bush track, Kenny noticed a leopard skin hat nailed to a tree. He wondered what it signified.

Gleeson and several soldiers were examining the fallen bridge when Private Joseph Fitzpatrick, a young Dubliner, called them back. Hundreds of Baluba were coming out of the forest carrying rifles and bows. Others rolled a tree trunk across the track to block the Irish vehicles' retreat.

'Jambo,' said Gleeson. 'We greet you in peace.'[5]

A shot came from somewhere, then the air clattered with wooden arrows. Gleeson fired bursts from his Gustaf sub-machine gun and the Irish ran up the track towards the bridge. As bullets and arrows sliced around them, they waded through the river and into the bush beyond. Poisoned arrows knocked some into the tall grass. Kenny had an arrow tangled in his collar and two more in his buttocks. His face swelled up blue and yellow. The Irish took cover by a large anthill. Arrows hit Gleeson in the knee and arm.

'Take cover lads,' he said, 'we'll all be killed.'[6]

Then he curled up to die. Kenny fell as the Baluba surged forward. A mob of leopard skin, ragged clothes and screaming faces bludgeoned him into a bloody mess and left him for dead. The other Irish scattered, Fitzpatrick running further into the bush, shooting down Baluba with a rifle he had to reload after every shot. He hid in a thicket, trembling with diarrhoea and sweat, until the tribesmen left.

Two days later, a joint Irish and Ethiopian patrol found Kenny wandering dazed down the track. Fitzpatrick emerged onto a path near some Ethiopian soldiers shortly after. The other Irishmen were dead. Twenty-year-old trooper Anthony Browne had reached a nearby Baluba village, where he begged a group of women to help him. They took his money and their men beat him to death.

The Baluba claimed they had been fired on first. The UN speculated that the Irishmen had been misidentified as Belgian soldiers. A Baluba prisoner told interrogators that a witchdoctor had ordered the tribe to kill anyone coming down the track. The interrogators asked why the tribe had not attacked a more heavily armed Irish patrol the previous day.

'They looked too tough,' said the prisoner.[7]

The ambush was still news when Tommy Nilsson, blonde and square-jawed, arrived in Elisabethville at the end of November 1960 with Sweden's 10th Battalion. The 19-year-old jazz lover from Malmö had been doing national service in the military police when his commander waved him over one day in late November. Nilsson had plans to be a detective when he got out and hoped it was news about the police academy.

'Pack your bags', said his commander. 'You're going to Africa.'[8]

Sweden had not done much fighting since it crushed Norwegian independence during the Napoleonic Wars. The Katanga peacekeeping mission should have been big news for a country lucky enough to avoid the trenches of the First World War and fascist invasion in the second. But no one in Malmö took it seriously.

'It will be a piece of cake,' a friend told Nilsson. 'You'll be fighting against natives armed with knives and arrows.'[9]

A piece of cake. Nilsson thought about Niemba as he lined up with rifle and kit bag alongside other conscripts on the airbase tarmac. In Katanga, his unit moved out to Kasenga, near the border with Northern Rhodesia. They made base at the Hôtel Luapula, a place of cool white stone, brick bungalows and palm trees. Life was easy. They played football with the local children; drank with the Belgians, all dark hair and short-sleeved shirts and bad teeth, but generous with their beer; assembled and disassembled light machine guns. White UN troops and settlers got on well now. Both hated the Baluba.

Nilsson and his comrades patrolled local villages, mud-brick huts with thatched straw roofs. The inhabitants walked barefoot, wearing a patchwork of European and African clothes: women with shaved skulls and brightly patterned dresses, the older women with scarves wrapped around their heads, the men wearing shirts and shorts donated by mission stations, perhaps an old greatcoat from the war, the children pot-bellied and naked. Swedish armoured cars nudged past farmers herding bony crepe-skinned cows.

In breaks from patrols, the UN men went sightseeing at Johnson Falls on the River Luapula. Nilsson posed for a photograph next to a white van in the African sun, a sticker in the windscreen: 'Pour le Président Tshombe, pour La Victoire et la Liberté'. He posed for another by a dust-brown termite mound tall as a tree; it looked like a mouldy Egyptian obelisk. News came that the Irish had arrested some of the Baluba responsible for Niemba. The Belgians handed out Simba beer to celebrate.

Towards the end of the year, the Swedes transferred to Elisabethville. There were patrols through the African districts in southern Elisabethville: brown brick bungalows in the UMHK workers' suburb and traditional round huts with conical thatched roofs for those who worked elsewhere. The Swedes walked Indian file along Elisabethville's wide roads, the grass borders yellowing in the sun. Off-duty, they splashed around in the Lido, an art deco swimming pool complex built in the western outskirts of the capital. Nilsson floated in the pool and watched the bush stretching away into the distance. Trips to the zoo and exotic animals behind wire fences. A Sweden-Ireland UN volleyball match. Walking through Post Office Square one day, Nilsson noticed a fresh ingredient added to the Katanga stew: white men in uniform, pale as Europe.

Local UN initially confused the new arrivals with the 231 Belgian soldiers, half of them officers, who had remained behind as volunteers in the Katangese army when Brussels ordered its soldiers home. They were known as Minaf soldiers, after the Ministère Belge des Affaires Africaines (Belgian Ministry of African Affairs) that paid part of their wages. Another fifty-eight had joined the police force; over 1,000 Belgian civil servants worked for the Katangese government.

Belgium's official advisors also remained, jockeying for power. Lieutenant Colonel André Grandjean had been appointed advisor to Minister of Defence Joseph Yav. This created tension with Crèvecœur, who saw Grandjean's shadow fall across his gendarmes. Both men fell out with Tshombe's advisor Major Weber. And specialists flown in by Mistebel and its successor organisation, the Bureau-Conseil du Katanga under the University of Liège's Professor René Clemens, found themselves competing with Elisabethville ultras to influence ministers.

Brussels sent Colonel Frédéric Vandewalle, a craggy 48-year-old intelligence veteran with ears like an elephant, to take charge of the mess. He set up base in the Belgian consulate and brought the factions into line.

'This Belgian Colonel, who had been Sûreté chief in Leo, Deuxième Bureau expert, with a demonic but sometimes outrageously Machiavellian intelligence, strongly impressed Tshombe,' said Guy Weber, half-admiring, half-worried for his own job.[10]

But the newcomers Nilsson saw were mercenaries, not professionals from Brussels. One soldier of fortune, in the country longer than the rest, had recently got a lot of press in Katanga and abroad. John Roberts's story was all over the newspapers.

The cell was dark and damp. It smelt of piss and human waste. Liberian United Nations soldiers watched John Roberts through the barred window as he sat on a slab of dirty cardboard that doubled as a bed. He felt like an animal in a zoo.

The attack on Luputa had been a disaster. Roberts lost half his forty-strong attack group to an ANC ambush, a confusion of flashing FN automatic fire and screams. Lumumba's men bayoneted Kimm the Belgian to death. Another nine Kasaïans died in a scrambling retreat through the bush. The ANC wiped out Vleigh's group as it counter-attacked. Regrouping in Gandagika, north of Luputa, Roberts found himself in charge of a demoralised column.

The Kasaï Army of Liberation's other columns had done better, pushing invading ANC troops out of Katanga and back into South Kasaï with the support of Crèvecœur's gendarmes. The UN arranged a ceasefire on 12 September. ANC troops withdrew north to loot Luluabourg and rape eight Belgians. One woman broke her spine jumping from a second-floor window. Kasa-Vubu asked the UN for a neutral zone across the central south of Kasaï to separate the two sides.

Albert Kalonji returned to Bakwanga to give speeches about the rebirth of the sixteenth-century Baluba Empire and hand out political posts to chiefs who had remained loyal. Non-Baluba from the Bemba, Lenze and Basalampasu tribes pledged allegiance to the resurrected South Kasaï, hoping for jobs and money. Kalonji made plans to expand his borders and ordered Roberts to retake Luputa.

Gandagika's chiefs summoned warriors by war drum, the beat sounding out over the bush to be taken up by the next village in relay. Roberts's force of uniformed exiles and leopard-skinned locals entered Luputa to find it deserted and stinking of death. Bodies lay in burned-out houses, blobs of human waste floated in pools of piss, survivors were starving. The Kanioka, a local tribe sympathetic to Léopoldville, waged guerrilla war from the bush.

Liberian UN troops in the area seemed more interested in pimping local women into makeshift brothels than peacekeeping. They were not alone in their interests in the sex trade. Down in Katanga, a recently arrived Irish private had turned an entire warehouse into a whorehouse.

'He made a whole lot of little cubicles,' said Irish journalist Alan Bestic, working for British newspaper *The People*. 'He then went down and recruited a whole lot of young girls on the reasonable assumption that they were young enough to be free of disease.'[11]

The Liberians refused to provide any medical supplies and did nothing to help as the Kanioka tribe circled Roberts's 600 men. The whirlpool chaos of the Congo had overwhelmed the Liberian officers.

'Why can't I understand these natives?' said their commander, Colonel Johnson. 'Why can't I, a black man, understand other black men?'[12]


Roberts organised a ceasefire with the Kanioka. He looted medicines from a missionary station and shot elephants for food. As the situation stabilised, Ghanaian UN troops arrived, even less helpful than the Liberians. Roberts enlisted local witchdoctors to drive them out. UN soldiers left their barracks each morning to find bloody chicken heads staked in the dirt. Constant drumming kept them awake.

The Kanioka-Baluba ceasefire broke down within a few weeks. On 25 October, Liberian troops killed fifty Kanioka tribesmen raiding a Baluba village. More died when UN troops locked prisoners in an unventilated railway carriage. Roberts led his soldiers to the village of Malunda, heart of the Kanioka uprising, and torched its thatched huts.

In the last days of October, he visited Colonel Johnson in Kalende to discuss the situation. Liberian troops stopped him leaving.

'You are under arrest.'

'What the hell for?'

'You'll get the reason later.'

'But you can't arrest people like that.'

'Yes we can. We are the United Nations.'[13]

The Liberians locked Roberts up with a teenage Swiss and two white merchants, one of them Brazilian, accused of being his assistants. He had never seen them before. He escaped twice, the second time in UN uniform, but never got far. The UN deported him and he touched down at Langar airport,

Nottingham on 28 November to find television news crews waiting. He posed with a Baluba bow and arrow.

'If I could have this part of my life over again, I should still join the Kasaï forces,' he said. 'Everything that has happened since in the Congo has convinced me that it was the right decision and that the cause of both Kasaï and Katanga was worth fighting for.'[14] But, he said, the Congo should eventually unite. It was one of the few opinions Roberts and the United Nations had in common.

Down in Elisabethville, the new mercenaries got on better with the UN. They mixed in the streets and drank in the same bars.

'Mercenaries? We met lots of them,' said Tommy Nilsson, 'but it was under friendly forms at this time. Most of them came from South Africa and Belgium but there were also a lot of former French Legionnaires. I also met one from Poland.'[15]

UN soldiers would not be on friendly terms with mercenaries for much longer. The new breed of hired gun stepping off Sabena aeroplanes had plans for Katanga. Some were here to get rich or die trying; some wanted to relive the camaraderie of their war years; some wanted to keep the white boot on Africa's neck. The most dangerous of them, a gang of right-wing Belgian bar flies, thought the secession could be the starting point for a *coup d'état* in Europe to bring fascism back from the dead.

# 8

# LES AFFREUX

## Fascists, Monarchists and Mercenaries in Belgium

Brussels. Rattling trams, spiky gothic churches the colour of stale champagne, black statues of forgotten men, hawkers selling caged pigeons in the market, the bronze Manneken Pis urinating for tourists, the weather chilly after the dry heat of Katanga. It was early September when Hendrick Bas, 40-year-old controller of Elisabethville airport and diehard secessionist, flew to the Belgian capital to talk mercenaries with the head of the Opterion chain of opticians.

The Opterion connection began when a letter arrived in Elisabethville from a group calling itself the Comité d'Action et de Défense des Belges d'Afrique (Action Committee for the Defence of Belgians in Africa – Cadba). Based in the Etterbeck district of Brussels, Cadba claimed to have recruited a volunteer 'Brigade Tshombe' to fight for Katanga. The name at the bottom of the letter was Jean Thiriart, owner of Opterion. Tshombe sent Bas to investigate.

Katanga had been interested in foreign volunteers since a false start in August when a 29-year-old Belgian journalist arrived in Elisabethville with a plan for a mercenary army tucked in his suit jacket. Pierre Joly's goatee, slicked back hair and paunch gave the impression that he had teleported in from a smoky Brussels jazz club. His politics were anything but beatnik. Joly lived deep in the European far right, bouncing between Algiers, Paris, Madrid and his native Liège at the side of colonialist terrorists, veteran fascists, counter-revolutionaries and reactionary Catholics. He mixed extremist politics with a reputation as a louche man about town, more likely to be found in a café than out chasing a story.

'A Walloon specialist in drunkenness', said a disgruntled French contact.[1]

Smarter minds on the far right suspected Joly of being a stooge for the French secret services: Service de Documentation Extérieure et de Contre-Espionage (External Documentation and Counter-Espionage Service – SDECE). They accused him of passing back information, sabotaging plans and worse. In 1959 Joly had acted as front man for some German arms dealers when they supplied weapons for a botched coup in Guinea that failed to reverse the country's independence from France. Many thought the SDECE was behind it all. The journalist denied everything.

Joly's brother-in-law worked for UMHK and arranged an interview at Tshombe's presidential palace. Joly proposed a Katangese army led by French veterans of the Algerian war. He threw around names, including Colonel Roger Trinquier, well known in military circles for his theories of counter-revolution. Tshombe liked the idea of independence from Belgian aid but the plan stumbled when Joly demanded 100 million francs a year for the new army, twice what the Katangese leader could afford. Negotiations broke down, helped along by Guy Weber, who suspected the journalist of pushing a French plot to control Katanga. Sûreté men escorted Joly to the border.

But the mercenary idea took root with Belgian settlers, whose idea of independence did not involve taking orders from men in Brussels. When the Cadba letter came in, ultra advisors in the presidential palace convinced Tshombe to investigate. Bas took a Sabena jet to the Belgian capital for an appointment on Wednesday 7 September with Jean Thiriart.

At the Opterion offices, Thiriart turned out to be an athletic and intense 38-year-old, in good shape for a businessman. Tall and muscular with cropped hair, Thiriart exercised regularly, canoed most weekends and skydived when he got time away from running his company and chairing the National Union of Opticians. He lived in solid bourgeois comfort with his wife and children in an upscale part of Brussels. Only twenty cats prowling the house hinted at any bohemian colour. Thiriart seemed an unlikely contact for mercenaries but close friends knew his radical side. As a teenager, the owner of Opterion had belonged to far-left groups like the Jeune Garde Socialiste Unifiée (Unified Young Socialist Guard) and the Union Antifasciste. His German Jewish stepfather taught him Marx and Yiddish. Rumours circulated of strange adventures during the war.

The meeting at Opterion was brisk, businesslike and frustrating. Thiriart claimed to have 3,000 volunteers. French volunteers. Bas asked to see them. Thiriart explained that they were in France and went into another room to call Paris. He returned without new information. The meeting ended inconclusively but they arranged another in a local café, where Thiriart promised to reveal more about the Brigade Tshombe. The airport controller left, suspicious.


Cadba was born in Etterbeck's Café Tanganyika, a popular hangout for Africa veterans. In early July 1960, a group of regulars stayed late at the Tanganyika listening to the radio news as independence fell apart in the Congo. Cigarettes and coffee, beer glasses down to the late night dregs, shots of genever. The radio announcer talked about fleeing Belgian civilians, rape and murder. The more the men listened, the angrier they got.

The Café Tanganyika crowd took action. On 9 July, they worked late into the night preparing a leaflet setting out the aims of their new organisation. Cadba wanted further military intervention in the Congo, help for refugees, support for the royal family and the arrest of politicians responsible for the Congo disaster. The drinkers at the Tanganyika, led by Paul Teichmann and Charles Demoulin, were royalists, still bitter at Léopold III's 1951 abdication.

'This is nothing less than a revolt against the government's criminal improvidence,' said Teichmann.[2]

A successful Cadba rally around a local statue of Léopold II inspired the group to think bigger. Like many Belgian rightists, Cadba obsessed about the Algerian situation, where France was fighting urban guerrillas to keep its North African colony. In 1958, a putsch by army units in Algiers had brought General Charles de Gaulle back to power in France after ten years in the wilderness. Cadba organised a public meeting in Brussels on 17 July, hoping for their own de Gaulle moment. Leaflets called on soldiers and policemen to disobey parliamentary authority: 'Algiers and Léopoldville, two fronts, one war'.[3]

No one listened. Fewer than 300 people attended a final rally at the end of the month. Cadba had run out of fuel. The motor only started again when a Cadba organiser who used the names Tisch, Themistocle and Thucydide, but was really Jean Thiriart, received a letter from a Brussels monarchist living in a Buvrinnes chateau.

'The time for waiting has passed: ACT!' said the letter writer.[4]


Count Arnold de Looz-Coswarem was the 65-year-old leader of an illegal paramilitary group called the Corps Franc Roi Baudouin (King Baudouin Free Corps). Despite a grand name, the Corps Franc seemed to consist only of the count; his friend Jean Cassart, a reserve colonel in his fifties with round glasses and a comb-over, famous for escaping a Nazi prison during the war; and Léon Jacobs, a former Congo hand, journalist and policeman.

De Looz-Coswarem despised democracy. He worshipped King Léopold III. During Léopold's post-war exile in Switzerland, the count dreamed up schemes to smuggle him back into Belgium, unable to decide between an armed assault on the Brussels parliament to clear the way or just stuffing the king into the boot of his car. The plans came to nothing and the count went to prison when he threw a tear-gas grenade into parliament in the name of absolutist monarchy. He got out in plenty of time to see Katanga secede.

The count's letter to Cadba announced the formation of a volunteer unit to fight in Katanga called the Brigade Tshombe. Thiriart liked what he read. He pushed the recruiting drive in the Cadba magazine *Belgique-Afrique*.

'Legions of volunteers will be able to recruit ten times more regiments,' he wrote, 'by responding to the appeal from thousands of young Europeans, Germans, Belgians, Hungarians, Italians, who are sick of seeing Europe scorned and humiliated from the outside, swindled, cheated, and abused from the inside'.[5]

It was an unusual way of recruiting men to fight in Africa, but Cadba had some unusual plans for the Brigade.

Bas turned up at a café in the Place du Marché to find Thiriart drinking coffee with Colonel Cassart. The Opterion head repeated his claim to have 3,000 Frenchmen ready to fight. He refused to give more details until he got a guarantee that the Brigade Tshombe would remain under Cadba control. Bas demanded more information.

Over a fresh round of café au lait, Cassart admitted they had exaggerated their manpower figures. Thiriart's articles in *Belgique-Afrique* had got little response, so in August the Corps Franc Roi Baudouin gang turned to Le Cosmos, a rough Liège bar in the rue du Plan Incliné full of ex-military men who liked to drink. Owner Jacques Haquet was a former paracommando who had left the army in 1952 and moved into the bar business.

Léon Jacobs asked Haquet for recruits. The bar owner had recently distributed his own pamphlet about Katanga and his hate for democracy ('the half measures and the measures for nothing, the hollow and twisted phrases'), and agreed to look around. Soon ex-paracommandos, Korean war veterans and right-wing bar flies were parading through Jacob's office.[6] He took their details, promised 15,000–25,000 francs a month on a six-month contract and sent them for a medical. In a month, he had thirty men. A similar effort in Brabant's Café l'Edelweiss by owner Charles Lambert recruited another twenty.

Fifty Belgian drunks, said Bas, were very different to 3,000 Frenchmen. Thiriart sensed he was losing his audience and spilled the reason he wanted to retain control of the Brigade Tshombe: Cadba and the Corps Franc Roi Baudouin needed it for a *coup d'état* in Belgium. The idea had sprouted during long discussions at de Looz-Coswarem's chateau. The count and his cronies envisioned a battle-hardened gang of mercenaries bringing about direct rule by the king. The Cadba leadership, all hard-line monarchists, approved. The Brigade Tshombe would fight in Katanga then return to clean out Brussels's political cesspool.

Thiriart, the only senior Cadba figure who was not a monarchist, had his own reasons for supporting a right-wing coup. As a 17-year-old he had rebelled against his Jewish stepfather by joining the Légion Nationale, a Belgian fascist group. He mixed far-right ideology with remnants of his far-left past.

'The most beautiful, the most exciting part of my life, I admit, was the German-Soviet pact,' he said. 'National Socialism was not an enemy of Communism, but a competitor.'[7]

When the Germans invaded Belgium in May 1940, most Légion Nationale militants went underground into the resistance. Thiriart moved into the collaborationist milieu as a member of AGRA (Amis du Grand Reich Allemand – Friends of the Greater German Reich), a Belgian group bankrolled by Heinrich Himmler's SS with a circular swastika as its emblem. Later in the war, Thiriart trained with SS-Obersturmbannführer Otto Skorzeny's commando teams and hunted resistance fighters in occupied France. He did three years in prison after the liberation and remained politically quiet for the next decade, building up Opterion, marrying, and polishing his middle-class respectability. Congolese independence re-awoke the political animal in Thiriart. He saw the crisis inspiring a coalition of royalists, conservatives and the extreme right to take power in Belgium, with the Brigade Tshombe as its military wing.

'Plastic explosive will be the mouthpiece of anti-communism in the second half of the twentieth century,' Thiriart said to his confidants.[8]

Cassart and Thiriart asked Bas for his opinion. He told them they were fools. He had no intention of involving Tshombe in a *coup d'état*. The meeting ended with both sides swearing at each other as waiters ushered them out of the café.

An unhappy Hendrick Bas called on Pierre Joly to see if the original French mercenary plan could be resurrected. The paunchy journalist cared only about the news from Algeria: General Raoul Salan, a veteran officer who fought for France in both world wars and Indochina, had exiled himself to Madrid and was calling for the overthrow of the French government in protest at President de Gaulle's negotiations with Algerian nationalists. Joly barely registered Bas's presence.

The airport controller had a last card to play. Cassart had overconfidently named the cafés where the Brigade Tshombe recruited. Bas visited Le Cosmos and L'Edelweiss. He found owners and potential mercenaries unenthusiastic about a coup. Belgium still had the death penalty for treason. They agreed to cut out Cadba and deal directly with Bas.

He booked seats on a Sabena flight to Elisabethville for the most promising mercenaries but somebody leaked the news to the Associated Press. The UN complained. Prime Minister Gaston Eyskens intervened to cancel the flights but was privately intrigued by the idea of subcontracting military aid. He asked the Ministry of African Affairs to look into it.

Bas's expedition had come at the right time. Eyskens believed the fall of Lumumba had removed the need for an independent Katanga. He put gentle pressure on Elisabethville to rejoin the Congo, with the promise of high office for Tshombe and his Conakat friends if they obeyed. When the Katangese showed no enthusiasm, Eyskens looked into ways of reducing overt Belgian support. Mercenaries seemed a good solution.

By the end of September, reporters had forgotten about Bas's recruits. The airport controller put fifty of them on a flight to Elisabethville. Commandant Armand Verdickt, head of intelligence for the Katangese gendarmes, ran background checks on the new arrivals. He discovered that the men from Le Cosmos and L'Edelweiss had done more time than a clock. Army deserters, burglars, car thieves and a rapist. The few without criminal records were alcoholics or drug users, behind on alimony payments, in trouble for driving unroadworthy taxis. Marcel Poelman wrestled, unsuccessfully, under the name 'the Black Angel'.

'These are not soldiers,' said Verdickt. '*Ils sont les affreux!*' (They are horrors!).[9]

The mercenaries joined Groupes Mobiles: fifteen white soldiers and fifteen Katangese gendarmes packed into a few jeeps, supported by another thirty Katangese gendarmes in a lorry, led by a regular Belgian officer who had stayed on as a volunteer. The regulars always seemed to be bulky men with cropped hair, beer bellies and dainty moustaches, wearing crisp combat fatigues and bush hats with the brim turned up at the left. Les Affreux looked different. They had neck scarves, stubble, cigarettes tucked into the corner of their mouths, rolled up sleeves, revolvers on hips, shorts and socks.

'Reputed to be bad boys', wrote a journalist for the *Libre Belgique* newspaper, 'with the air of pirates (long hair, droopy moustaches) and frightening in combat'.[10]

Their reputation outstripped their performance. In November, some Affreux in Groupe Mobile D set up residency in Kabongo, near the border with Kasaï, to protect the town's airstrip. The group quickly fell apart when Poelman the wrestler convinced the other mercenaries to desert with him. Only Charles Masy, blonde-haired and goggle-eyed with a wife back home and ambitions to own a bar, refused to quit. Masy had been 14 when German tanks rolled into Belgium. After three years of occupation, he joined the resistance, playing the innocent well enough to fool the Gestapo when they arrested him. At the liberation, he joined the Belgian SAS but things went wrong and he ended up in Katanga to escape a charge for beating up a Brussels policeman. He was not the kind to run away from a fight.

Other Affreux haunted Elisabethville's bars and brothels, telling tall stories to journalists and showing little enthusiasm for the bush. Locals avoided them.

'They were swaggering around all over the place, pissed out of their heads, with large whores on their arms,' said Irish journalist Alan Bestic. 'If you angered them they would shoot you in a minute. It was an ugly scene.'[11]

The first amateur wave of mercenary recruitment had finished. De Looz-Corswarem retreated to his chateau. Colonel Cassart used contacts in Elisabethville to become an arms dealer. Jean Thiriart and Paul Teichmann abandoned Cadba to create the Mouvement d'Action Civique (Civic Action Movement – MAC), a far-right party more interested in Algerian politics, European unity and karate lessons.

Professionals took over. Major Jules Loos, last seen arranging Lumumba's kidnapping, contacted 65-year-old Colonel Adelin Marissal, a retired veteran of both world wars. Marissal hated communism as much as he loved Belgium. He had been loudly talking up the Congo as the front line in a war against the Soviets. Loos steered the colonel into a meeting in a government building with an aristocratic 46-year-old former resistance fighter, all thick grey hair and semi-circle of a moustache. Harold d'Aspremont-Lynden, the Minister of African Affairs. The minister asked Marissal to recruit mercenaries for Katanga, warning that Brussels would deny all knowledge if the plan was uncovered. Ministry assistance would be limited to vetting volunteers to prevent any more Affreux slipping through.

Marissal agreed and began hiring through his parachute club, targeting ex-military men and offering 25,000 francs a month with a million franc life insurance policy. He called his mission the Clan des Amis du Congo (Friends of the Congo Clan).

Unknown to Marissal, another recruiter was on a similar road. In late July, former settler Jean Gérard had begun advertising in *La Libre Belgique* for skilled personnel to work in Katanga. The responses were mostly ex-military. Gérard soon had a list of potential mercenaries. He contacted Jacques Masangu, head of a Katangese delegation in Brussels funded by UMHK. Masangu liked the mercenary plan but wanted more men. Gérard organised a recruiting station in a Namur café, north-east Belgium, aiming for volunteers from the parachutist camp at Marche-Les-Dames. An assistant called Beaumont recruited at nearby Seilles, a village coated grey by local limestone quarries. Beaumont gilded the truth by telling volunteers that Baudouin I, known to be sympathetic towards Katanga, had approved their enlistment.

Marissal only became aware of Gérard's work on 7 October, when the Katangese delegation requested the Ministry of African Affairs run background checks on 228 potential mercenaries. Both projects wanted to digest the other but D'Aspremont-Lynden let them run in parallel. The more Belgian mercenaries in Katanga, the better.

By winter 1960, around seventy of Le Cosmos's criminals and a handful of Gérard's volunteers had joined Tshombe's 7,000 gendarmes in Katanga. They headed into the bush to battle the Baluba. One mercenary already in the country, Welshman John Trevelyn, had a different enemy. He was out on Lake Mweru fighting for his life against an opponent with sharp teeth and scales.

# 9

# THE RHODESIAN CONNECTION

## Copper Country and Katangese Nationalism

When the crocodile came to life in the bottom of the boat, 23-year-old John Trevelyn was sitting in the stern holding a Mannlicher rifle. Five minutes earlier, the dugout canoe had been drifting along Lake Mweru's shore line in the darkness as the South African in the bow guided a torch over the reeds. A wire connected the torch to a portable battery. Two young Katangese men sat in the centre of the dugout with paddles raised.

The long cone of light passed over a pair of glowing red points. The South African moved the beam back to illuminate the eyes of a sleeping crocodile. He rested the torch on the dugout ledge and picked up his Mannlicher. No sound except the rippling of water. He aimed the rifle. The shot echoed around the lake. Between the eyes. The Katangese hauled in the corpse, heaving the scaly body onto their pile of dead crocodiles. They paddled off in search of another. Crocodile belly skin fetched a good price for shoes and handbags.

The South African had just turned to say something to Trevelyn when the dead crocodile erupted, thrashing in the bottom of the boat. The light went out as the four men scrabbled away from the snapping jaws, the dugout rocking, crocodile claws scraping the sides.

Trevelyn's rifle went overboard. He grabbed a machete. A hunter once told him you could last two minutes, three minutes maximum, in crocodile waters. Then they got you.

'*Pangas* swung blindly,' said Trevelyn. 'The live croc hidden amongst the dead ones snapped its jaws seemingly everywhere in total darkness: the boat rocked dangerously. Finally …'[1]

The four men hacked the crocodile into bloody chunks in the bottom of the boat. Panting with effort, they paddled to shore by moonlight. Trevelyn never went crocodile hunting again.

John Trevelyn grew up on a North Wales farm. His earliest memory was watching a burning German bomber crash into nearby fields. The farm had an outside toilet and no gas or electricity. He milked cows by lamplight. At 17, he joined the Parachute Regiment and spent three years in the Middle East and Cyprus. He remembered how Greek women used to throw shaken bottles of Coca-Cola at the wall to make a noise like a hand grenade. Back in Britain, he saw an advert from the British Crown Agents looking for ex-soldiers to work in Northern Rhodesia. He joined up and spent his twenty-first birthday at Lilayi Police College.

Trevelyn was on duty as shift commander in the police station at Mufulira, a copper mining town 10 miles from the Congolese border, when the first white refugees came over the border at independence, some of the women on the verge of a breakdown.

'As an ex Brit Para I thought I'd seen most things by then but …'[2]

Mufulira got it easy. Most Katanga refugees ended up in Ndola, a bigger town to the south with its own airport. Mattresses packed Ndola synagogue wall to wall for the new arrivals. Private houses opened their doors.

'My family accommodated six to seven families in our home at any time for about two weeks before the refugees went on elsewhere,' said Mervyn Bloomberg, young son of the owner of a car rental firm. 'Many of the men stayed on as they wanted to go back once the fighting subsided to see if they could get their possessions. I can remember the members of the Jewish community cooking hundreds of meals to support the refugees.'[3]

Up in Mufulira, Trevelyn met a Belgian officer called Pierre who was heading back into Katanga province. He told Trevelyn to look him up if he ever came to Elisabethville. In December 1960, Trevelyn and a friend decided to take up the offer. They joined a trickle of Rhodesians already heading across the border, like Jimmy Mandy, a 40-year-old war veteran of North Africa and Malaya, red-faced and alcoholic. In 1953, drunk, he had fallen three floors down a lift shaft and broken his neck. He soon bounced back.

'Man, I have a party or two, something goes wrong,' he said. 'No money and then my feet begin to itch again.'[4]

Trevelyn did not need money. He had six months' wages in his pocket as an end-of-contract bonus. The Welshman wanted an outlet for the frustration he felt at the activities of Kenneth Kaunda, a rising star of domestic politics pushing for an independent black Northern Rhodesia.

'The atrocity stories coming in and the shit we had put up with regarding UNIP – the NR Independence Party – and Kenneth Kaunda, the President in waiting, had got under our skin,' said Trevelyn. 'Political expediency of those days let him get away with murder – literally. This was a sort of payback time – in advance.'[5]

The Central African Federation (CAF) was established in 1953 to bring together Southern Rhodesia, a partly self-governing British colony, with the British protectorates of Northern Rhodesia and Nyasaland. The white minority lived in a world of old-fashioned Britishness, with starched nannies wheeling baby carriages through red dirt streets and everyone wearing Sunday best to the church. Pubs served up local brews like Lion lager but kept British licensing hours. The Federation had some fine talk about racial tolerance but only existed so Rhodesia's whites could keep control of the copper business in the black-dominated north.

Prime Minister Raphael 'Roy' Welensky ran the Federation. Son of a Lithuanian Jew, Welensky was a former boxer and railway engineer with a face like an Easter Island statue.

'Half-Jewish, half-Afrikaner, 100 per cent British,' he said of himself.[6]

By the late 1950s, Welensky was smart enough to see trouble heading for white-ruled Africa and did everything he could to strengthen the Federation. He floated the idea of an African version of NATO (ATO – the African Treaty Organisation) uniting white-controlled colonies, hoping to gain American support by posing as an ally in the Cold War. London and Washington squashed the idea. A plan to jam Soviet radio broadcasts coming out of Egypt got brief support from Portugal before collapsing.

After these failures, Welensky welcomed contacts with Belgian ultras like Jean Humblé in Katanga. Soon Rhodesian representatives were holding secret meetings with top Conakat men in Salisbury hotel rooms. In March 1960, Welensky suggested an independent Katanga join the CAF, hoping to use it as a buffer against African nations further north. The failed June secession delayed the plan and Belgian intervention after independence crushed it completely. Few observers even thought it feasible. Thanks to the activities of men like Kenneth Kaunda, the Federation was already falling apart. Lord Alport, the British High Commissioner in Salisbury, thought Welensky was using Katanga to distract himself from the possibility of black majority rule in Northern Rhodesia, like a man planning an extension to a house already on fire.

'The excitement and flurry', thought Alport, was just a way for Welensky to dodge 'the less interesting but perhaps more difficult problems of the constitutional future'.[7]

The CAF continued to support Katanga after the secession. White Rhodesians welcomed an anti-communist neighbour that favoured capitalism and white expertise. Some even fell for Tshombe's charm, a surprise to journalist Sandy Gall, who knew first-hand how much they hated black politicians of any persuasion.

'They're not fit to run a *shamba* [farm], let alone a country, man.'

'Yes, but that's a matter of training. In a few year's time …'

'But, Jesus, man, you don't know the African. You just don't understand his mentality. These fellows were swinging from the trees when I first came here and now you want to dress them up in dinner jackets and make them run the country.'

'I'm not saying there should be independence overnight. What I am saying is that the democratic process was started by the British, has been developed by successive governments and must inevitably lead to one man, one vote.'

'When they can't read or write? They don't know what an election is, let alone a free election. You must be a bloody communist, that's what you are.'[8]


John Trevelyn and his friend drove over the border into a red dirt wilderness of giant baobab trees, trunks thick as a house, topped with sparse green leaves. Like many Northern Rhodesians, Trevelyn had spent time in Elisabethville before independence, pub crawling and chasing girls in bars open twenty-four hours a day. Now hyenas chewed at bodies lying by the roads.

'No roadside vendors either, no children happily selling drinks, food, souvenirs, hands out, palms upturned shouting cheerfully, running alongside the car. Things had changed.'[9]

After 50 miles, the road crossed the River Lubumbashi and the Union Minière chimney stack appeared in the distance above the vegetation. Elisabethville. The city's wide boulevards paved with hexagons of volcanic rock; roundabouts decorated with Katangese crosses made from flowers; blacks and whites mingling on the streets; the Volkswagen Beetles and Peugeot 403s parked at the side of the road in diagonals like teeth on a saw; African women in brightly coloured wrapped skirts carrying straw shopping baskets on their heads; revving cars, chattering people, cha-cha on the radio; the Katangese gendarmes with red bands around their white helmets; the huge Christmas tree in Post Office Square behind wooden barricades, wilting in the heat.

Trevelyn and his friend found Pierre, who took them to the police barracks. They signed up after a brief interview in English and Swahili. The pair were attached to a ten-man unit operating out of Pweto at the northern tip of Lake Mweru, one of the chain of great lakes along Katanga's eastern border. A leathery German veteran of the Légion Étrangère (Foreign Legion), known as 'the Kraut', gave the orders. Trevelyn respected him but had little time for the Belgian soldiers:

They were thinkers rather than doers. The Belgians were mainly admin soldier types whose main purpose was to administer the country. Mostly they had no idea how to lead their soldiers who were black locals whose fighting capability depended a lot on tribe, training, leadership. African soldiers like showmanship and one good white officer could do wonders by example, jokes, and a general mixture of firm discipline and humour. Africans can laugh at themselves and at others. Then they will kill you just as easily as you would swat a fly.[10]

The group holed up in Pweto over Christmas for the rainy season. The rain pecked at a roof made from flattened petrol drums then fell so hard it seemed the sky was trying to kill the ground. Dirt paths bubbled over. After the rain, the group roamed west and south of the lake, patrolling Kilwa, Minga and Kiniama by jeep.

They spent their down time drinking and hunting crocodiles on Mweru. Communications were erratic. Without a radio, the group lived in their own time warp, only catching up on events when they surfaced in Pweto or on rare visits across the border into Northern Rhodesia to pick up mail. Trevelyn's mission was to protect settlers out in the bush from local Baluba and the ANC troops starting to slip south through the UN neutral zones. Lumumba's men were on the march again.

Stanleyville was a town of pastel inter-war buildings more suited to the French Riviera than Africa. It was there, after Lumumba's arrest, that Antoine Gizenga declared himself Prime Minister of the Congo, dismissing Kasa-Vubu and Mobutu as traitors. The Congo now had two rival governments to go with its two secessionist states. Gizenga, a depressed-looking 35-year-old with a mouth like a trout, appealed to the Soviet Union for help.

'If the imperialists think that we will surrender', he said, 'or if they think they will kill off the Congolese people's liberation movement, they are wrong'.[11]

Soviet premier Nikita Khruschev authorised a $500,000 payment to Pierre Mulele, the Stanleyville representative in Cairo. Spies suggested that Mulele skimmed some cash for himself. The Soviets looked the other way. Gizenga needed money to keep his 6,000-strong version of the ANC loyal.

'It is clear that if the army does not receive wages it will refuse to fight,' reported Czech newsman Dushan Provarnik from Stanleyville:

> The Gizenga government has to pay its soldiers at least the same money that Mobutu gives his own soldiers, i.e. 2,000–6,000 Congolese francs depending on grade. Under the existing circumstances, when the government has no revenues, as taxes have not been raised, these expenses are a heavy financial burden.[12]

Attempts to supply Gizenga with arms and advisors were less successful. A Czech air bridge from Prague through Egypt failed when Nasser refused access to his airspace. Lumumba's former confidant Kwame Nkrumah seemed happy to help but somehow Soviet weapons sent via Ghana never reached the Congo. The Ghanaian leader did not reveal he was talking trade treaties with the Americans.

On 26 December, Gizenga's Stanleyville ANC troops took Bukavu, capital of Kivu province, from men loyal to Léopoldville. Anicet Kashamura, Lumumba's former information minister, became provincial governor. His troops roped opponents to the back of their jeeps and dragged them around town, leaving slick trails of blood and flesh.

The Stanleyville ANC moved south along Lake Tanganyika and marched like army ants into northern Katanga to join Jason Sendwe's Balubakat guerrillas. On 8 January, Gizenga's men fought their way into Manono, a town loyal to Tshombe in the central north and part of the UN neutral zone. The Jeunesse under Laurent-Désiré Kabila tortured and executed Katangese gendarmes.

The UN announced it would take no action against Gizenga's men but urged Tshombe to keep the ceasefire. To Elisabethville's surprise, the Belgian government agreed with the peacekeepers and took the opportunity to pressure Tshombe more firmly on rejoining the Congo. The Katangese began to wonder if they could find better friends elsewhere.


In early 1961, Trevelyn got talking to a man in a Pweto bar. The man asked him what it was like being on patrol. You drove along bush tracks, Trevelyn told him, dirt roads that went in no time from open landscape to a humid jungle, perfect for ambush work. It was lousy to get into and lousy to get out of. You were stuck, so you went slowly round bends and watched the sky to see what the vultures were doing. The open spaces were the worst. A bend, a dip shrouded by a low copse of scrub, a dried up riverbed. You fired off a burst or two at any sites that felt bad and watched what happened. If chimps fell out of the trees or birds took off, then that was OK. If not, then you kept firing. You kept your FN FAL rifle on semi-automatic. On full automatic the barrel climbed into the sky so fast you could only hit clouds.

The man bought Trevelyn a beer and told him the latest rumour: a prominent Congolese politician had disappeared in Katanga. Something bad had happened to him. Lumumba, Patrice. Trevelyn shrugged and drank his Simba. The name did not mean much.

'We were soldiers, not politicians or news media looking for a story,' he said. 'Soldiers thought about fighting, staying alive, eating, drinking, and women.'[13]

How could the disappearance of one politician affect Katanga?

# 10

# PISSING BLOOD IN KATANGA

## The End of Patrice Lumumba

The arm stuck up through the ground, black and bloated, crusted in flies. Gérard Soete and his crew of Katangese policemen scraped away at the dry soil around it with shovels. Three corpses were entangled in a shallow grave. Soete's men dragged the bodies onto canvas sheets. They filled in the grave and lifted the corpse-heavy bundles onto the back of a truck.

They drove for 150 miles, bumping over dirt tracks and rough road. Night was falling when Soete indicated a place to stop. The policemen pulled the dead men off the truck bed and began to dig again. This time they dug 6ft down. Soete ordered his crew to roll in the bodies and fill the grave.

Arrogant and good-looking, Soete had served in the Belgian Air Auxiliary Police Service in 1945, helping to police a defeated Germany. The next year he joined the Elisabethville Sûreté. When Tshombe declared independence, Soete rallied to the new Katangese state as advisor to the Chief Commissioner of Police. Hiding these bodies was the ultimate test of his loyalty.

Despite the fresh graves, the deaths would not remain secret. News of them spread like a pool of blood from under a locked door.

On 25 November, the United Nations recognised Kasa-Vubu as official head of the Congolese delegation. Two days later, Patrice Lumumba dodged his UN bodyguards during a thunderstorm and fled Léopoldville. Trapped in his house, lost in a cloud of dagga smoke, mourning the recent death of his young daughter, Lumumba had impulsively decided to head for Stanleyville. He intended to enlist Gizenga's army to take back the country.

His entourage begged him to stay and wait for the investiture of incoming American president John F. Kennedy, a boyish Boston Democrat addicted to painkillers and women. Kennedy was known to be opposed to Katanga and unsympathetic to colonialism.

Thomas Kanza, a Lumumba supporter, said:

> After Kennedy takes over the White House a UN Security Council meeting will take place and the Congolese parliament will be reconvened. Lumumba will walk from his house to the parliament, which was less than 100 meters from his house, and if the parliament renews its confidence in Lumumba's government, he comes back as prime minister.
>
> If the parliament refuses confidence, he becomes the leader of the opposition. But Lumumba, God knows why, decided to leave the residence, to travel all the way from Léopoldville to Stanleyville.[1]

The former prime minister could have outrun Mobutu's men if he had not stopped to give speeches. At one town, he spent five hours denouncing Mobutu, Kasa-Vubu, the West and the Catholic Church. Gilbert Pongo, a captain in the Léopoldville ANC with a taste for zebra-stripe polo shirts, caught up with him in Kasaï province. The United Nations refused to allow Ghanaian troops on the scene to intervene. New York did not want to get involved.

Lumumba arrived back in the capital by aeroplane on the afternoon of 2 December, bloody and bruised. Camera crews filmed Mobutu's men beating him again in a flatbed truck at the airport. The next day, they moved him to Camp Hardy at Thysville. He walked with difficulty.

The former prime minister's charisma still shone bright. On 13 January, he persuaded the camp guards to mutiny. Senior figures from the Léopoldville government flew down and a forceful speech from Mobutu restored order. The Collège des Universitaires decided to move Lumumba somewhere no one would listen to him. Kasa-Vubu asked South Kasaï to put Lumumba on trial for the Bakwanga massacres. Albert Kalonji considered it, discovered he still had a few drops of sympathy for his old MNC colleague, and refused. Léopoldville cabled Tshombe.

On 16 January, Tshombe's gendarmes rounded up hundreds of Africans in Elisabethville, along with a few Europeans, like the Katangese National Bank director who objected to his staff being taken away. Tshombe claimed they had conspired against him.

'Some three hundred Africans had been arrested,' wrote British journalist Richard Cox, who had been in the bank director's office when gendarmes came through the door, 'ostensibly because of a plot against Tshombe, more probably to clear the city of possible Lumumba supporters'.[2]

On Tuesday 17 January, a gang of Mobutu's men arrived at Camp Hardy. They told Lumumba that he was being taken to Léopoldville, where he would be reinstated as prime minister. Lumumba believed them. They took a light aircraft to Moanda. There, Lumumba, with fellow prisoners Maurice Mpolo, the projected ANC head, and Joseph Okito, a senator from Lumumba's home town, climbed into a waiting DC-4. Already on board were soldiers chosen from Kasaï Baluba serving in the ANC. Mobutu may have thought them the only troops loyal enough to be trusted. Or he may have hoped they had not forgotten the massacres at Bakwanga.

The flight lasted several hours. The three prisoners were tied to their seats and beaten for the entire journey. Lumumba's goatee was torn out. The crew locked themselves in the cockpit. Defence Commissioner Ferdinand Kazadi watched the violence and did nothing.

'It's true, but you know the ANC soldiers', he said. 'They are brutes and we couldn't stop them beating the prisoners! We had no authority over them.'[3]

At 4 p.m., the DC-4 requested permission to land from Elisabethville control tower. The Belgians in the tower asked for the flight plan. The pilot refused. After fifteen minutes of argument, he admitted he had Lumumba on board. The men in the control tower reached for the telephone. They contacted Gendarme Chief of Staff Major Paul Perrad and tried but failed to reach Tshombe at the presidential palace.

Perrad rang Munongo, who gave permission for the aeroplane to land. Captain André Protin, a Belgian officer in the gendarmes, saw Munongo preparing to meet the flight, nervous for once in his life, with Jean Kibwe and Minister of Public Works Gabriel Kitenge. At 16.50 the DC-4 touched down. Two platoons of military police surrounded it under the command of Captain Julien Gat, a bearded Belgian in battledress.

Also on the scene were Major Guy Weber, who had been in earshot when Perrad learned about the flight; Police Chief Pius Sapwe; and Crèvecœur, Vandewalle and Carlos Huyghé, a Belgian settler in the gendarmes, who were at the airport by coincidence, having just touched down from an inspection tour of Tshombe strongholds in the north.

At 17.00 Lumumba, Mpolo and Joseph Okito left the aeroplane. The Katangese military police beat the three men with their rifles and pushed them into a lorry, then drove off in a convoy through a hole already cut in the airport fence. Watching Swedish UN troops were told by their HQ not to intervene. Twenty minutes later, the convoy arrived at the Maison Brouwez, a low white villa requisitioned earlier that day.

Munongo, Kibwe and Kitenge stayed at the house for forty minutes. Lumumba and his two companions were beaten again. By this time, advisors had found Tshombe at Elisabethville's Cinéma Palace attending a film screening organised by Moral Rearmament, the American Christian peace movement. The Katangese president headed home and ordered his ministers to join him. Jean Kibwe would later claim that he, Tshombe and Munongo pushed through the decision to kill Lumumba.

'Lumumba is a great criminal,' said Kibwe. 'He started this chaos. He is responsible for thousands and thousands of deaths, and unparalleled destruction. He was a relentless enemy of Katanga. He wants our skins.'[4]

The meeting lasted into the evening. At eight o'clock, cars left Tshombe's house filled with Katangese government ministers. Minister of Defence Joseph Yav refused to attend, having been Lumumba's Minister of Economic Affairs, the sole Conakat man in the first Congolese Cabinet. Tshombe, Kibwe and Minister of Foreign Affairs Évariste Kimba were drunk on whisky. When they arrived at the Maison Brouwez, they found Police Commissioner Frans Verscheure waiting outside for orders.

At 20.30, the prisoners, the ministers, Katangese gendarmes and policemen, Verscheure and Captain Gat drove in convoy into the bush outside Elisabethville. The journey took forty-five minutes. A grave was dug in the beam of car headlights. Gat assembled a firing squad from the Katangese soldiers. The prisoners were shot, Lumumba last. He had a look of angry contempt on his face when the bullets hit. As the Congo's first prime minister lay in a pool of blood, Gat finished him with a shot to the head. Gendarmes rolled the bodies into the grave. Lumumba's arm remained above the ground, pointing at the sky. The convoy headed back to Elisabethville.

Later that evening, a group of Belgian advisers, including Vandewalle, Weber and Jacques Brassinne met at Professor René Clemens's apartment in the Immokat residential block to piece together what had happened.

'They say Lumumba is dead!' Weber wrote in his diary. 'In any event, he was beaten last night by a group of ministers.'[5]

The next day, Verscheure, sleepless, red-eyed and guilty, confessed everything to fellow Flamand Gérard Soete. They forced him to do it, he said. Soete sympathised. He thought the murders pointless while the UN held Katanga in the palm of its hand. Soete asked around and discovered that local Katangese miners had heard the shootings. Soon the bush outside Elisabethville was buzzing with rumours of firing squads and dead men in the ground.

Munongo ordered Soete to move the bodies. The Belgian assembled a team of Katangese assistants and reburied the dead men near the Rhodesian border. A week later, Munongo ordered Soete to destroy the corpses completely.

On Wednesday 25 January, Soete took two jars of sulphuric acid, empty barrels and some Katangese policemen to the burial site. His brother Michel accompanied him. They spent the first day failing to find the grave and returned on Thursday. When they finally found the site, they dug up the bodies and drove to another location. By torchlight, scarves wrapped around their faces to block the smell, they hacked the three corpses into pieces. They dropped each piece – a foot, a forearm – into a barrel. They drank heavily as they dismembered.

Soete chopped off Lumumba's head. He spat into its face then sat down in the guts and flesh. Drunk and emotional, he started crying.

'I'm doing this instead of you, you white cowards,' he said.[6]

He used a pair of pliers to pull two of Lumumba's teeth. He put them in his pocket. Soete poured acid into the barrels and stinking white smoke rose up. One of the Katangese assistants spilled some and burnt his foot. Soete and Michel mashed up the remaining bones and burnt what was left. They buried the sludge and went back to Elisabethville.

Destroying the bodies had taken five days. Soete and his brother took a two-week holiday in South Africa to recover.


When John F. Kennedy took power in January, he wanted to know why Lumumba had disappeared. Larry Devlin claimed to know nothing and organised an investigation. David Doyle, the CIA's man in Elisabethville, tried to infiltrate Tshombe's office by hiring a local European gigolo to seduce the president's loyal secretary. She was not beautiful. Doyle met his contact a week later.

'I wasn't able to go through with it,' the gigolo said.

'Why not? What happened?'

'Oh, she came out with me every night. We dined and then went to her place for a nightcap.'

'Well?'

'David,' he said. 'I did my best for you. But have you ever tried to stuff a marshmallow into a piggy bank?'[7]

Despite the gigolo's failure to perform, details of the murder soon spread around town. No one involved could keep his mouth shut. Soete grumbled about it to fellow policemen; Minister of Information Lucas Samalenge told drinking buddies; Verscheure informed close friends about his role in the executions.

Elisabethville gossip split between blaming the Belgians for Lumumba's death in a conspiratorial web that involved the CIA and MI6, or viewing the assassination as a blood pact between Léopoldville and Elisabethville, the murder being Mobutu's price for accepting an independent Katanga.

At the end of the month, in the dining room of the Hôtel Léopold II, Katangese vice president Jean Kibwe repeated the whole story to a Frenchman called Colonel Roger Trinquier. The colonel had promised to teach Katanga the lessons of war learned in North Africa if Tshombe would make him commander of the gendarmes. Every Belgian loyal to Brussels hated him.

# 11

# THE COUNTER-REVOLUTIONARIES

## Katanga Asks France for Help

A portable field battery in an anonymous Algiers villa, wired with metal clamps to the nipples or testicles; a roomful of French paratroopers and cigarette smoke; constant questions in a flat, bored voice. Tell us what you know and the pain will stop. Tell us what you know and the pain will stop. Then the electricity, the white light behind the eyes and the spasms. Algerian independence fighters who survived the torture called it *la gégène*. The French army called it counter-revolution.

France had been in Algeria since 1830, another tile in a mosaic of foreign invaders that included Phoenicians, Romans and Ottomans. Men from Paris built roads and villas, dug out farming grids and changed the country's demographics with a salad of white immigrants from France, Italy and Spain, known as *pieds noirs*. The settlers worked side by side with native Algerians but never believed in equality. By 1954, Algerians of the Front de Libération Nationale (National Liberation Front – FLN) had begun their fight for independence. The first battles took place in the monotonous sunlight of the steppes. Within two years, the FLN were in Algiers's narrow streets. Men calling themselves urban guerrillas planted plastic explosive in cafés and knifed any policemen brave enough to chase them into the Casbah.

Paris unleashed the army. Among the men in green was a trim 48-year-old with greying hair, jaded eyes and ideas for a new kind of warfare. Colonel Roger Trinquier had joined the infantry at 20 to escape peasant life in the Hautes-Alpes. He fought river pirates in 1930s Indochina and confronted the Japanese in wartime Shanghai. In the post-war years, he led native groups behind Viet Minh lines. By the time he arrived in Algiers as head of a paratroop regiment, Trinquier had ditched the tactics taught in officer training school and become a convert to Colonel Lionel-Max Chassin's radical new ideas of counter-revolutionary warfare. Chassin knew that it took more than a gunfight to defeat an insurgency. The French had to judo flip the guerrillas' own tactics against them. Senior officers were slow to accept Chassin, so his partisans enlisted Belgian journalist Pierre Joly to spread the word. Joly published a selection of their writings in the underground book *Contre-révolution*.

Trinquier put the ideas to practical use in Algiers. He introduced small mobile combat units for street fighting, relocated sympathetic civilian populations, initiated social reform to cut away the FLN's support and gathered intelligence by any means necessary. Crackling field generators, drowning torture, rubber hose beatings. Prisoners always talked.

In May 1958, Trinquier joined the putsch that brought General Charles de Gaulle back to power. The army had convinced itself that de Gaulle would keep Algeria French, but within two years the general authorised free elections in the colony, the start of an inevitable slide to independence. The French public cheered, sick of war and torture; the army felt betrayed. General Raoul Salan, a senior figure in the putsch, moved to Madrid and founded the Organisation de L'Armée Secrète (Secret Army Organisation – OAS) terror group to fight de Gaulle. Trinquier drove part of the way to the Spanish border with Salan but turned back, too loyal a soldier to take up arms against Paris.

Troubled by his allegiances, stuck in an administrative post in Nice, Trinquier received a letter from Africa on 5 January 1961. Georges Thyssens had a job for him as head of the Katangese armed forces.

Trinquier's name had come up during a meeting between Katangese Minister of Defence Joseph Yav, a 31-year-old butterball of colourful American shirts under a black Homburg, and his new advisor Jacques Duchemin.

French journalist Duchemin had got the job after impressing Yav during an interview in Brussels. He quit the newspaper business and arrived in Elisabethville on 2 December 1960 aboard a Sabena DC-7 packed with Belgian civilians returning to Katanga. The numbers of whites in the Congo had been slowly climbing since the independence exodus: Katanga had 20,000, Léopoldville 9,000 and Kasaï 2,000.[1]

One of Duchemin's first suggestions caught Yav's attention: recruit a Frenchman to run the Katangese armed forces. Paris already sold the secession weapons through Abbé Fulbert Youlou's Republic of the Congo, a former French colony, and de Gaulle had approved the delivery of three Fouga training jets (a pre-independence order that took its time) to Katanga by a Lebanese businessman. France would not object, according to Duchemin, if Katanga sheltered under its wing. Yav passed the suggestion to Moïse Tshombe.

The Katangese president was enthusiastic. He had no problems cutting ties with Belgium after the recent pressure to reunite the Congo. Duchemin's plan could free Katanga from the whims of Brussels and open up a new future in French Africa, a network of former colonies that still took orders from Paris.

Duchemin suggested three senior French soldiers: de Massu, de Bigeard and Trinquier. The third name sounded familiar to Tshombe. When Pierre Joly of *Contre-révolution* fame had turned up in August with his plan for a French-led mercenary army, he had mentioned Trinquier as possible commander. Tshombe authorised Thyssens to write to the colonel in Nice.

The move angered Brussels and its advisors in Elisabethville. Major Guy Weber tried to sabotage Duchemin's plan by spreading rumours that Thyssens intended to use French mercenaries to install a dictatorship under Munongo.

If the rumours contained any truth then Thyssens had picked the wrong partner. Munongo would never side with a white man against Tshombe. Recently, drinking in a bar, a European had said something that annoyed the Minister of the Interior. Munongo slapped the man's face so hard his teeth rattled.

'Don't think I've forgotten you Belgians killed my great-grandfather,' he said.[2]

Trinquier cleared the offer with French Foreign Minister Pierre Messmer, a pouchy-faced war veteran and de Gaulle loyalist. Messmer gave the green light.

'The Belgians are already aware,' said Messmer at his office in Paris's leafy place du Maréchal-de-Lattre-de-Tassigny, 'and look on this project with the greatest displeasure'.

'Should I go or not?'

'You should go. It will be a little more difficult, that's all.'[3]

Messmer confided that de Gaulle's ambition was to reunite Katanga with the rest of the Congo and run the country from Elisabethville. He recommended keeping that secret from Tshombe as long as possible. Trinquier asked how official his visit would be. Messmer thought it over.

'I think it would be a good idea,' said Messmer, 'to detach you from the army for your mission and reinstate you afterwards'.[4]

At ten in the morning on 26 January 1961, a newly civilian Trinquier touched down at Elisabethville airport in a Sabena jet accompanied by his bodyguard Michel Rey. The Frenchman looked conspicuous as any ex-soldier, grim-faced in a boxy sports coat and sunglasses. Joseph Yav met Trinquier at the airport and briefed him on the situation as they drove into Elisabethville. The pressure from all sides to end the secession, the UN neutral zones, Balubakat and the Stanleyville ANC occupying parts of the north, questions being asked over Lumumba's disappearance.

'You see, we need a solid army to cope with this situation,' Yav told him. 'We are counting on you and the officers you recruit to save us.'[5]

Trinquier booked a room at the Hôtel Léopold II, an off-white block at the intersection of avenue de l'Etoile and avenue Fulbert Youlou. The hotel was infested by newspaper men, mercenaries and ultras. In the bar, smiling Katangese servers kept the whisky flowing as foreign correspondents hammered at portable Olivettis, a copy of Joseph Conrad's Congo novella *Heart of Darkness* nearby for inspiration. Belgian settlers conspired in the lobby under spinning ceiling fans. Monsieur Blatter, the sour-faced Swiss manager, patrolled the dark panelled corridors scowling at his guests.

Professor René Clemens visited Trinquier at the hotel that afternoon and warned him that the Minaf Belgians objected to his presence. If he took the job, they would leave. The colonel protested that he was there to help. Clemens told him to keep his help. The Belgians were big enough to go it alone.

Guy Weber was less polite. He cornered Trinquier the next morning before a meeting with Tshombe at the presidential palace. Weber did not want outsiders interfering in Katanga; he had personally shot down offers of help from other foreigners, including Jean Thiriart's former Nazi commanding officer Otto Skorzeny.

'I want to say to you, before the meeting,' said Weber, 'that we are still the masters in Katanga and nothing happens without our agreement.'[6]

The meeting did not last long. Weber and Crèvecœur loudly objected to giving a Frenchman command of the gendarmes. They protested their loyalty. Tshombe listened serenely, then pointed out that Brussels paid a third of their wages. They served two masters. That evening, Tshombe telephoned Trinquier to offer him the job. The Katangese president wanted to replace all Belgians in his service with French volunteers.

Trinquier investigated the situation in Elisabethville: the UN posts near the airport, Groupe Mobile units training under Belgian officers, journalists gossiping in bars, the red dust landscape outside the town criss-crossed by aeroplanes and jeeps. He retreated to his room at the Léopold II to write a report.

In Trinquier's opinion, the Baluba in the north could not defeat Tshombe's gendarmes in open battle. They would inevitably turn to urban warfare, like the FLN in Algiers. Before long, the blue flash of plastic explosive would be destroying Elisabethville cafés and bars. To fight Baluba terrorists, Trinquier planned to recruit French mercenary officers for the gendarmes, train Katangese officers in Chassin's techniques and introduce *la gégène* to sub-Saharan Africa. In five years, Tshombe's army would be run by Katangese counter-revolutionaries.

The biggest problem Trinquier could see was opposition from senior Belgian officers. But that could be stamped out with the help of Elisabethville's ultras.

His bodyguard Michel Rey had asked around. Local whites saw the colonel as a new dawn for Katanga.

'Young officers were waiting with impatience for me to take command,' said Trinquier. 'They hoped I could change the atmosphere and at last they could do some serious work. The civilians as well. What struck us was the kind of hate they felt towards Belgium. They rejected it; all of them were prepared to take Katangese nationality and follow President Tshombe.'[7]

He met some ultras in the hotel. They talked about racial tensions in the gendarmes. This did not surprise Trinquier. He had seen Crèvecœur and fellow advisors ignore Katangese Cabinet ministers in the same room. Trinquier may have been a ruthless enthusiast for torture but he thought racism fatal to counter-revolution.

Later, Trinquier met vice president Jean Kibwe for dinner at the hotel. Kibwe needed advice.

'We have killed Lumumba and his two companions,' Kibwe said. 'The press, especially the left-wing press, are asking us daily what happened to them. We are going to be obliged to announce their disappearance. What can we do to make this news of as little consequence as possible?'[8]

'Lumumba is dead,' said Trinquier. 'You cannot bring him back to life. Sooner or later the world will find out about his disappearance. It is better to clear the ground and announce it straight away, then wait for the storm to pass.'

If Kibwe did not want the Katangese government to take the blame, Trinquier suggested, then just tell the press that the prisoners had been shot while trying to escape. Kibwe thanked him. He was unapologetic about Lumumba's murder.

'Even if his death has, for us, serious consequences,' Kibwe said, 'we will not regret it.'[9]


Colonel Frédéric Vandewalle did his best to stop Trinquier. He cabled Brussels with nightmare scenarios, warning that the Frenchman's appointment would cause the Belgian mission to fall apart. The response was chilly. After the initial shock of betrayal, Foreign Minister Pierre Wigny had accepted France's ambitions in Katanga, privately relieved to give up responsibility and escape the international condemnation that had been raining down. He had no objections as long as UMHK could continue to mine copper. Vandewalle counter-argued about creeping French influence and loss of morale. Wigny ignored him.

Guy Weber joined the battle, writing notes to Tshombe:

The decision of the Katangese government to give command of its armed forces to a FRENCH officer is SERIOUS and has given the officer corps a psychological shock. The Belgian cadre has always served with loyalty and there is no question of any bad feeling. But it is my duty not to conceal the consequences of this action.[10]

Three pages of closely typed frustration and conspiracy theories about Thyssens followed. Tshombe waved away the charges and told Weber to smooth the way for a French takeover.

On 31 January, Trinquier had a final meeting with Weber. Earlier that day, Tshombe had ordered Marissal and the delegation in Brussels to stop accepting Belgian volunteers. Weber finally got the message; through clenched teeth he assured Trinquier of a clean handover. The next day, the colonel flew back to Paris with a signed contract in his pocket that made him the most powerful white man in Katanga.

Trinquier reported to Messmer, but did not tell him about Lumumba's death. Messmer gave the green light for a recruiting office in the rue Cambon, near the Ritz. The colonel began discreetly looking for army veterans and adventurers with the right politics.

'Our young men instinctively realised that the battles that were being fought in Katanga were the same that we are fighting in Algeria, Laos or Angola,' Trinquier said. 'It is our freedom and our civilisation that we are defending.'[11]

The first volunteers, including fellow Algeria veteran Roger Faulques, signed up. Trinquier had limits. He turned away a man called Robert Denard who had done time in a Moroccan jail.

The Belgian advisors in Elisabethville had not given up. In early February, Vandewalle persuaded Tshombe to allow military action in the north, ostensibly an attempt to free the Lubudi–Luena railway from Baluba ambushes. Vandewalle's real aim with Operation Banquise was to show Tshombe he did not need the French to retake northern Katanga. Crèvecœur got out his maps. No one saw any reason to tell Brussels about the plan. Trucks and jeeps rolled into Baluba territory.

On 15 February, a day that saw a total solar eclipse over Europe, Munongo announced Lumumba's death at a press conference in Elisabethville. He claimed that the former prime minister had escaped from custody in Katanga and been murdered by villagers. No one believed him. A journalist asked if Munongo had killed Lumumba.

'Prove it!' said Munongo.[12]

Tshombe remained calm.

'The fuss over this evil man will soon die down,' he said. 'The people have no memories here. *C'est fini.*'[13]

Stanleyville troops in Bukavu broke into a convent, stubbed their cigarettes out on a nun's breast and decapitated a Belgian priest. Seven Kasa-Vubu supporters were stabbed to death in Léopoldville; Gizenga executed fifteen political opponents in Stanleyville, including Gilbert Pongo, who had arrested Lumumba in Kasaï and been captured a few weeks later trying to retake Bukavu. Gizenga's men kept Pongo in a barrel of salt with his legs slashed open before the execution.

In South Kasaï, the authorities killed six Lumumba supporters sent to them by Mobutu. Kalonji's followers sliced off the prisoners' skin in strips, roasted it and fed it to them.

'The tribunal of chiefs and our people have done nothing else than follow the example of the Allies,' said André Kabeya, South Kasaï Minister for Justice, 'who in Japan and Germany have sentenced and executed political and military leaders guilty of war crimes.'[14]

Left-wing students protested Lumumba's death across Western Europe, claiming him as a symbol of anti-imperialist struggle. African-Americans jeered United Nations delegates from the public gallery of the New York headquarters. The Soviets claimed Hammarskjöld had masterminded the murder and demanded the withdrawal of UN troops from the Congo. Soviet Bloc secret police organised demonstrations. Riots took place outside Belgian embassies in Moscow, Belgrade and Cairo.

The United Nations wanted Lumumba's death investigated. Tshombe stalled by talking about double standards.

'To the best of our knowledge, the USSR and communist Hungary have never granted the commission of investigation established by the United Nations the right to conduct an investigation in Hungary,' Tshombe wrote to the UN, 'and Mr. Hammarskjöld was not even allowed to visit Budapest. Katanga does not see why there should be one law for the rich and another for the poor.'[15]

Only Vandewalle got any joy from the political hurricane. Lumumba's death made Katanga toxic in Paris. Pierre Racine, director of Prime Minister Michel Debré's Cabinet, summoned Trinquier to Debré's official residence at Hôtel Matignon and cancelled the mission. Trinquier, warlord dreams dancing behind his eyes, refused to accept the decision. The discussion escalated into an argument. Paris police appeared at Le Bourget airport to prevent Trinquier leaving the country. Detectives parked outside his house, revving their engines in the bitter cold.

Vandewalle hoped a successful assault on the Baluba and their Stanleyville allies in northern Katanga would be enough to put the final stake through the Frenchman's heart. But his operation would spark an international incident when the Compagnie Internationale, Katanga's first unit of English-speaking mercenaries, found themselves in a stand-off with UN soldiers at a grassy airfield, both sides wondering who would shoot first.

# 12

# SOLD UP THE RIVER

## The Rise and Fall of the Compagnie Internationale

The third finger on Richard Browne's right hand was worth 100,000 francs. The small print in the rest of his contract promised a million francs if he went blind or insane. His wife got the million if he died. Smaller print detailed compensation for losing other body parts.

The recruiter in room 801 of Johannesburg's Pritchard House Hotel had put together a nice package of incentives. High wages, insurance, combat zone allowance. Browne finished reading the contract and reached for a pen.

Thirty-five-year-old William Richard Browne grew up the second son of a well-off farming family in Blandford, a Dorset market town on the River Stour. Older brother Percy was Tory MP for Totnes. Browne preferred fighting to begging for votes. He joined the army and took on communist rebels in post-war British Malaysia, stalking them through sweating jungle with a Sten gun in his hands. Demobbed and back in Britain, he quickly lost all tolerance for drizzling rain and bowler-hatted respectability. Browne immigrated to South Africa.

He set up home with his wife in Halfway House on the Johannesburg–Pretoria road. He liked the sun, he liked to drink and he had no problems with Apartheid. In early March 1961, he saw an advert in the *Rand Daily Mail* looking for 'ex-servicemen in search of adventure' placed by Scottish émigré Roderick Ian Russell-Cargill, a recruiter for Katanga.¹ Elisabethville needed men for police duties in the aftermath of its northern operations, where 500 gendarmes had taken town after town, leaving burned out houses and dead bodies behind them.

A UN report stated:

It is thus clear that the offensive launched by Mr. Tshombe on 11 February is aimed, not merely at opening up the Lubudi–Luena railway, as he had declared, but the subjugation of the entire region populated by the Baluba tribe, by the use of overwhelming force, including the burning of villages and the elimination of all opposition and resistance and the terrorization of the population.[2]

The UN passed two resolutions in response: one to remove all unofficial foreign personnel in Katanga and the other authorising force to prevent civil war. Orders went out to arrest any mercenaries if a firefight could be avoided.

Brussels, never happy with Operation Banquise and anxious to avoid confrontation with the UN, told Crèvecœur to shut down his reconquest of the north. It was a small victory for the UN at a dark time. At the start of February, Mobutu had dismantled his Collège des Universitaires and appointed Joseph Ileo, a veteran politician missing a few teeth and fond of bow ties, as prime minister. Ileo's new government was friendly towards Katanga and South Kasaï, and antagonistic towards the United Nations.

On 28 February, Tshombe, Ileo and Albert Kalonji met in Léopoldville. They agreed to pool their armies to resist UN forces and arranged a 5 March summit in Tananarive, Madagascar to discuss the Congo's constitutional future. Only Gizenga declined to attend.

Richard Browne did not care much about the finer points of Congolese politics. Down in the Pritchard House Hotel, he scribbled his signature on the contract. He was now commander of a South African mercenary company headed for Katanga.

Johannesburg was Ian Russell-Cargill's second attempt at recruitment. The first, in Rhodesia, got shut down by the authorities and some bad timing. Back in January, Stuart Finley-Basset, a 58-year-old Ndola businessman and proud owner of a smoking chimpanzee, had offered mercenaries to Elisabethville at £200 a head. His boasts about the deal attracted unwelcome attention from the United Nations. Salisbury had a word and Finley-Basset moved his operation to Frankfurt, Germany, where it soon ran down.

Newspapers were still talking about the affair when Russell-Cargill opened his own office in Salisbury. Local police advised him to pack up and try elsewhere. With help from Major Carlos Huyghé, a good-looking Belgian ultra who advised Joseph Yav, Russell-Cargill relocated to South Africa and placed discreet adverts in *The Star* and *Rand Daily Mail*.

The South African government had trouble balancing its Apartheid policy of racial segregation with support for an anti-communist black nation like Katanga. Too many generals and secret policemen choked at the thought of being on the same side as an African. But Pretoria managed to look the other way when Russell-Cargill booked a room at the Pritchard House Hotel and got to work.

The first man through the door was tall, bulky and moustached with a British accent. Richard Browne. He got £180 a month and the rank of captain. The other forty men who answered the advert were a mixed bag of local and foreign: a lot of tanned South Africans with hair the colour of butter, a few transplanted Britons, Italians, expatriate Belgians, a Greek from Istiaia and Israeli Harry Sher. All had previous military experience, except for two former motorcycle policemen. The youngest was 19, the oldest 49. 'The reasons for joining up were various,' said a young volunteer:

> I don't think anyone came just for the money. It was mainly adventure, boredom, to stop the communists moving south. Katanga was a very nice peaceful country until the Congolese and the UN attacked it. Tshombe was a good and very popular President and happy to employ a white person if a black one could not do the job. Hence the need for us.

In early March, the mercenaries flew to Katanga, where they got two weeks' training in route marches and rifle practice at the mining town of Shinkolobwe. A good marksman with an FN FAL 7.62 rifle could put a round through the bullseye at 300m. At 50m, it made a human head look like a melon dropped on concrete.

On 26 March, a second group of mercenaries, twelve South African and seven Italian, arrived. A third group of nineteen South Africans arrived on 30 March under Jeremiah ('Jerry') Cornelius Puren, a lanky, bald former RAF navigator with a broken marriage behind him and dreams of political power ahead. Puren quickly fell out with Browne and ditched training whenever he could to schmooze politicians in Elisabethville. Other Compagnie men spent their off-duty hours in Le Relais nightclub drinking with UN soldiers, who ignored Hammarskjöld's orders about arrests and instead offered good money for Baluba souvenirs to impress folks back home.

The mercenaries soon discovered that, despite Russell-Cargill's promises, they were not in Katanga for police duty. They would be expected to fight. Crèvecœur formed them into the Compagnie Internationale and assigned an English-speaking translator. One mercenary deserted when he heard the news. Russell-Cargill turned up on an inspection trip shortly after and had to do his own disappearing act when angry mercenaries threatened him with a kicking.

In late March, Crèvecœur ordered Browne to select a battle group of fifty men. The Compagnie bustled around the vehicle park in Shinkolobwe, loading kit onto lorries and converted Volkswagen Kombi minibuses. Browne supervised, swagger stick in his hand, shouting orders, tough but paternal. Puren did his best to undermine him by telling anyone who would listen that Browne was drunk.

A Belgian officer lectured the Compagnie's officers in a prefab hut. He proposed tactics so ruthless that Browne objected.

'You were supposed to shoot at them all,' said one Compagnie Internationale man:

> that was the instructions you got, shoot at the lot, destroy them, burn the village, kill the chickens and goats, chop the trees down so if they go into the jungle and come back they won't find anything there ... But our captain was what you might call a humanitarian type and he believed in mercy, if you know what I mean.[3]

The officer waved away Browne's objections. Crèvecœur intended to capture Jason Sendwe's capital of Manono, a tin mining town full of fruit trees, and retake the north. Operation Banquise had been shut down two months earlier. Now it was reborn as Operation Conga. The Minaf Belgians were the bosses again. Vandewalle and his friends had blocked Colonel Roger Trinquier from ever taking command in Katanga. No one could stop them from crushing Sendwe's Baluba.

Trinquier's loyalty to France had limits. The money in Katanga was too good to forget about. He complained to Messmer that the policemen outside his house kept the neighbours awake all night with revving car engines. Trinquier gave his word of honour to remain in France if they left. Messmer agreed. On 25 February, Trinquier slipped away and headed for Katanga via Salisbury. Commandant Roger Faulques, Captain Yves de la Bourdonnaye, Captain Égé and Georges Thyssens, helping with recruitment in Paris, went with him.

They found a changed situation. Weber's conspiracy talk and Crèvecœur's success in the north had chopped at the roots of Tshombe's faith in Trinquier. The axe cut deeper when the French government, angry at being tricked, pressured Elisabethville to stop the colonel entering Katanga. Tshombe cared more about having a hotline to de Gaulle than giving a job to Trinquier. He agreed to tear up the contract.

Trinquier was in a Salisbury hotel when he got the news. Thyssens tried to honey the rejection with a promise to change minds in Elisabethville, but the Belgian had his own problems. Weber had found out that Thyssens employed some dubious characters to help with recruitment in Paris, notably Jacques Sidos, senior member of the neo-fascist Jeune Nation group. Sidos had done time after the war for collaboration with the Germans. Weber took it as further proof of his conspiracy theory about a coup.

'Those who are working for their personal interest by using unfair or fraudulent practices are to be eliminated in the name of public morality,' he said.[4]

On 4 March, the Rhodesian authorities, under pressure from Katanga and France, threatened to deport Trinquier. Three days later, the colonel illegally crossed the Katangese border and holed up in an Elisabethville house owned by a sympathetic Belgian ultra. Faulques and the others joined him. An African servant in an *askari* served drinks. They sat around smoking and talking, looking like wrestling coaches headed to an official function in their plaid sports jackets and slacks. Trinquier never took off his sunglasses. Ultras made phone calls around town to find someone who could help.

The Katangese president was at the Tananarive conference. Kibwe and Munongo received Trinquier and apologised for the cancellation of his contract. But the decision could not be reversed. Guy Weber took pleasure in discussing the situation with Trinquier.

'He explained to me that I was being used by a "gang" to overthrow President Tshombe to benefit some adventurers who had taken advantage of my good faith,' said Trinquier. 'Then he reproached me for having obtained more favourable material conditions for my officers than those enjoyed by the Belgian officers; this difference in material treatment seemed to affect him deeply.'[5]

Weber told Trinquier that the other Frenchmen could enlist in the Katangese forces if they agreed to serve under Belgians. But the colonel would have to leave the country.

'In the Congo', said Weber, 'it is the Belgians who run things.'[6]

Faulques, de la Bourdonnaye and Égé talked it over and took the offer. On 11 March, Trinquier left Elisabethville on a Sabena passenger jet. The remaining French officers he had recruited back in Paris had to make their own way to Elisabethville, an amputated stump of a promised army.

The victorious Belgians in Katanga decided to restart their operations in the north: Operation Conga. Brussels reluctantly agreed.

Ian Gordon was a missionary's son and former policeman who washed out of the Bechuanaland force with damaged eyes after a murder suspect resisted arrest too enthusiastically. On 25 March, Gordon was Compagnie Internationale second-in-command as it moved from Mitwaba to Mpiana, building bridges and pushing lorries through swamps on the way. Like a lot of ex-cops, Gordon had a jaundiced view of humanity. He was not impressed by the Katangese gendarmes sent in support. The majority had little training and less discipline.

Barbaric tribal warriors, he thought, who would kill anyone and burn anything. The Belgians warned Gordon that the Katangese would not leave their trucks if caught in an ambush. It was best to toss in an unprimed hand grenade to get them moving.

Things improved when the Compagnie Internationale linked up with a column of 200 better-trained gendarmes and thirteen Belgian officers, led by Captain Protin, for the advance on Manono. Lorries rumbled along dusty roads, pushing past women balancing bright cloth bundles on their heads and Katangese farmers herding skinny cattle. Then the roads were empty on the approach to Manono and the ambushes began. Baluba guerrillas attacked eighteen times in 15 miles.

The Baluba hid in slit trenches, three men to one rifle. When the rifleman caught a bullet the next man grabbed the gun from his hands and carried on shooting. Arrows flew out of the trees. Stanleyville ANC units backed up the ambush with machine guns and 81mm mortars. No one took prisoners.

Ben Louw, a Belgian in the Compagnie, was hit by a blunderbuss as he charged a Baluba trench. A comrade bandaged his head wound. Louw ripped his shirt open.

'Stuff my ear,' he said, 'look at this.'[7]

Two jagged chunks of metal had gone into his shoulder blade and right lung.

At 14.30 on 30 March, the Compagnie headed into Manono. Nigerian UN troops near the city showed no interest in stopping them but insisted that the Belgians drop leaflets by aeroplane to announce the attack. Browne's men went in as the spearhead against an enemy dug in among lemon and papaya trees.

'The Baluba were useless soldiers,' said a young mercenary:

> They were totally controlled by their witchdoctors and were always high on drugs whenever there was a battle. To a certain extent so were the Katangan troops as they were told if they wore white man clothes they would be shot but if naked the bullets would turn to water! So after the first shot, they all stripped off![8]

After a two-and-a-half-hour fight, thousands of Baluba and ANC fled into the bush. The Compagnie Internationale headed for the airfield in commandeered jeeps while Katangese gendarmes put their clothes back on and mopped up the town. Nigerian UN troops shared bottles of beer with the exhausted victors. Close to the runway, the Compagnie found a warehouse full of elephant tusks and malnourished prisoners with tales of Jeunesse cruelty.

The gendarmes had lost five men in the attack; the Compagnie five wounded but no dead. Neither Browne nor Gordon bothered to count the fallen enemy.

'The Gizengists, riff-raff of the old Force Publique, are an undisciplined rabble,' said Browne. 'The Balubas are just Congo savages, usually crazed by dagga and Native liquor.'[9]

James Stewart, commander of the reserve platoon, had been shot in the arm and was evacuated by helicopter to Elisabethville. Jerry Puren was promoted captain to take his place. His unit split off into Operation X-Ray, run by a Commandant Liègeois, and tramped through the humid jungle to take Niemba and then Nyunzu, a strategically vital town that turned out to be a sandy street, a railway line and some boarded up shops.

Reinforcements for the Compagnie had arrived back in Elisabethville. Lieutenants Mike Hoare, an accountant and safari organiser, and Alistair Wicks, a smooth old Harrovian with polished manners and a pipe, turned up leading two new platoons of South Africans. They headed to Shinkolobwe for training. Browne managed to speak with them by telephone and got the impression that Hoare wanted his job. He decided to deal with that problem when the fighting was over.

On 7 April, Browne's battle group moved toward Kabalo, an inland port where river steamers connected with the railway from Albertville. A senior UN officer on the scene claimed the Ethiopians had already divided the town into Compagnie Internationale and Baluba zones. No fighting would be necessary.

Crèvecœur took no chances. Browne and thirty of his men would land at Kabalo airstrip in a Katangese DC-4, with gendarmes in two aeroplanes behind them. More Katangese troops, Belgian officers, and several Compagnie Internationale men would approach by the river on the *Constant de Burlet* ferry under the command of Belgian Captain Waulthier. A priest called Forgeur would accompany them. Another Katangese group with Compagnie officers would arrive by armoured train.

Browne remained confident. Operation Conga seemed unstoppable.

At 10.30 a.m. on 7 April, the oval door near the tail of the DC-4 opened and a white man in combat green rappelled to the grass of Kabalo landing strip. More followed until there were thirty of them running for the edge of the airfield. The DC-4 took off. An Ethiopian general in a blue UN helmet watched them from the end of the runway.

'Where is our side of the town?' Browne called to him.

'You do not have a side of the town,' said the general. 'You are all under arrest.'[10]

Browne's men raised their weapons. The general waved his hand and hundreds of Ethiopian soldiers stood up from the long grass around the airfield. The Compagnie Internationale waited in the humid air, fingers sweaty on the triggers. After a long silence, broken only by the humming of insects and distant aeroplanes, Browne told his men to drop their guns.

The UN locked the mercenaries in Kabalo railway station. Balubas on the opposite bank of the river fired on the *Constant de Burlet* as it docked and sent it back round the bend of the river. The armoured train had been ambushed en route and never arrived.

The ferry returned the following morning. Balubas opened fire; the Katangese returned fire; the Ethiopians joined in. A UN mortar shell dropped down the ferry funnel and blew the *Constant de Burlet* apart. Katangese gendarmes fell into the river as the ferry sank. Crocodiles slithered among the bodies in the bloody water, grabbing swimmers and rolling them under the surface. Balubas and Ethiopians kept firing into the bloody, oily water.

A Katangese boat picked up survivors down river. A Compagnie Internationale man among them claimed to have seen Forgeur die. The priest had swum to the bank and pleaded for a ceasefire, he said. A UN soldier shot him in the face.

A few days later, an Ethiopian lieutenant dragged Browne, Gordon and another mercenary out of the railway station and put them in front of a firing squad. Katangese patrols had been probing Ethiopian positions. Two UN soldiers died in a firefight at a bridge 8 miles outside the town. The Ethiopians wanted revenge.

'They kept the guns pointed at my chest for half an hour,' Browne said.[11]

The Ethiopian colonel arrived, hit the lieutenant with his swagger stick and sent the mercenaries back to the railway station. On 10 April, the UN transferred the Compagnie to Kamina airbase. Three men shared a 7ft by 12ft room; the daily meal was a pilchard on a bed of rice. One mercenary contracted tuberculosis.

In his interrogation, Browne insisted that he signed on for police duty and claimed the Compagnie had been 'sold up the river' by the Belgians.[12] Other mercenaries talked about fighting communism. Dr Mekki Abbas of the UN wrote up a report and sent it to New York, where it was read by Conor Cruise O'Brien, a 43-year-old Irishman ready for Katanga. O'Brien was cynical about any claims of mercenary idealism.

'My own recollection, from reading the interrogatories in New York,' he said, 'is that, in about twenty-five of the thirty cases, the motives given ranged from financial reasons to financial reasons.'[13]

The Compagnie was moved to Léopoldville, then deported to Brazzaville across the river. Browne, Gordon and a few of their men were having lunch in a restaurant when Norwegian UN colonel Bjørn Egge pulled up a chair. He asked if they would serve as military advisers in Laos, where the American-backed government was fighting North Vietnamese guerrillas.

'At that time we didn't trust the UN, and still don't, and so we declined,' said one mercenary, 'especially as we heard the life expectancy was three months!'[14]

Egge accepted the rejection and told them what had happened to Mike Hoare and Alistair Wicks. With Browne's men under arrest, only the reserve company and the newly arrived South Africans training in Shinkolobwe remained. They had not lasted long.

They found Oakford lying in a foetal position, eyes wide and terrified. He had a wooden arrow in his stomach. The tip was poisoned with a paralytic. A young mercenary who had signed up back in South Africa, Oakford had stepped into the trees to avoid using the primitive camp toilets and a Baluba tribesman stalking the perimeter had picked him off with a single bow strike. Mike Hoare's men riddled the trees with bullets but the bowman had vanished. Oakford died within hours.

Hoare's and Wick's platoons of South African mercenaries had touched down at Elisabethville in late March. They were still in training when the rest of Browne's Compagnie Internationale drove north, got captured and was officially disbanded to soothe the UN. Crèvecœur turned his Anglo-Saxon trainees into the fourth commando of a Belgian motorised unit and sent them on a supply run to Captain Liègeois in Nyunzu.

Hoare took command. The 42-year-old son of empire, born in Calcutta to Irish parents but carrying a British passport, changed his unit's title to the more impressive 4 Commando and stamped his own discipline on the men: no beards, pointed shoes, rolled-down socks or anything beatnik. Hoare did not want his men confused for Affreux.

The 4 Commando leader had served in North Africa during the war but saw less action than he liked to claim. His command did not impress everyone. John Trevelyn, the Welshman who joined Tshombe's forces the previous Christmas, met the new arrivals when they moved through Pweto.

'Mike H and I didn't get along,' said Trevelyn:

> He was old school Brit Army and I was a young ex-Brit Para – chalk and cheese. When he arrived he was groping: I was by then an old hand. He wanted me under his wing and I said no. Besides which his 'men' were best left alone – at that time they hadn't a clue and I was too young to train them … Personally I didn't like him nor his men. We were a mix of black and white soldiers who knew both the area and what we were doing. His crowd were a bunch of mostly deadbeats run by a bunch of leftovers.[15]

Hoare lost one man on the mission when an unhinged Scotsman ran into the jungle and got left behind. Then Oakford went down. Morale dropped further as the rain fell and lorries sank into the mud. Katangese drivers stole supplies and got drunk. Hoare, usually cool as spreading fern, began to wonder why he had come to Katanga.

His convoy reached Nyunzu on 6 May. They found a Malaysian UN unit standing over the remains of Jerry Puren's reserve unit. Puren himself was in Elisabethville sorting out problems with pay, happy to swap the jungle for a soft bed in the Hôtel Léopold II. Hoare's men unloaded their trucks and set up camp. Three days later, they fled into the jungle when the Malaysians tried to arrest them.

'The campaign to free Katanga from mercenaries has begun,' said a UN spokesman the next day.[16]

'Those you call mercenaries', said Munongo, 'we call Katangese soldiers who are defending the interests of our country.'[17]

It took four days of hacking through the bush with an oil bath compass before 4 Commando emerged at Katangese-controlled Niemba. Then a long journey back to Shinkolobwe to be debriefed by Roger Faulques, recently installed as chief paracommando instructor. Faulques congratulated Hoare on his escape and sympathised that 4 Commando lost two men to the jungle on the way. He explained that operations in the north were ending. Belgium had a new government. At the end of April 1961, the country had voted in a leftist coalition of Socialist Party and Christian Democrats. Paul-Henri Spaak, once a top tennis player (Davis Cup, 1922) but now a Winston Churchill lookalike fond of pastries, got the post of foreign minister.

'For me, the Katangese situation was most difficult,' Spaak said. 'I was fundamentally and profoundly opposed to secession.'[18]

The foreign minister had another reason to be suspicious of Katanga: he was affiliated with financial interests that resented the success of Société Générale de Belgique, a banking behemoth whose shareholdings in UMHK made many suspect that it pulled at least some of the strings in Elisabethville. Spaak's first move was to order the Minaf men to avoid confrontation with the UN. Conga and X-Ray soon ground to a halt, although Crèvecœur had the consolation of occupying most of the east and large parts of the north.

Faulques offered Hoare a whisky. He had more bad news. Belgian officers were complaining about 4 Commando's lost supplies and abandoned lorries. In June, the unit would be split into small groups to reinforce Katangese garrisons in the south as part of a major reorganisation of the gendarmes. Hoare's command was over.

As he drove his jeep through Shinkolobwe, Hoare saw posters of Tshombe's face pasted everywhere. '*Il souffre pour nous.*' He suffers for us.[19]

Hoare did not know that, far away in Brazzaville, Colonel Egge had made another offer to Richard Browne and his men. Would Browne rescue an important man from a Congolese prison? The mercenary leader turned down the offer. Too dangerous. Moïse Tshombe had gone to Coquilhatville convinced he had achieved his political dreams. He ended up behind bars.

# 13

# COCKTAILS WITH CRÈVECŒUR

The United Nations Sends in Conor Cruise O'Brien

'Have you come to bring order or disorder? asked Jean Kibwe, the Katangese vice president.

'Is it to sow the good wheat or the chaff?' asked Joseph Kiwele, Minister of Education.

'Are you a communist?' asked Godefroid Munongo.[1]

Conor Cruise O'Brien tried not to sneer. He had little tolerance for minds less razor-sharp than his own. Big-headed, with a side parting in his thick black hair that started a few inches above the ear, the Irish civil servant and academic had recently quit his day job to become the United Nations' special representative in Katanga. Hammarskjöld handpicked him for the post, assuming anyone who wrote literary criticism that well must be a good diplomat.

The Irishman spent the spring of 1961 prepping for his mission at the UN's New York offices, deflecting advice fired at him by Hammarskjöld and a gang of Ivy League Americans doing their best to keep Soviet hands off the levers of power. O'Brien, a man of the left, did not need advice from cold warriors.

'I am a Machiavelli of peace,' he said to friends.[2]

He agreed with the boys in New York about one thing: Katanga had to go. Hammarskjöld's circle believed the continued existence of Tshombe's country would lead to civil war and open the door to communism. O'Brien saw the secession as a Belgian capitalist conspiracy to defraud the Congolese people. Before he left New York in June, O'Brien asked advice from senior UN figure Gustavo Durán, once a communist lieutenant colonel in the Spanish Civil War, now a peacekeeper who bought his clothes in upscale Martha's Vineyard.

'The Congolese?' said Durán. 'You will hate them all – all without exception. Mobutu, Gizenga, Munongo, left, right, blacks, whites – all horrible.'[3]

Durán's words came back to O'Brien as he sat in an Elisabethville govern-ment office facing Munongo, Kiwele and Kibwe. Tension had been growing between the Katangese and the UN since early April with the arrest of the Compagnie Internationale. Gendarmes blocked Elisabethville airport runway for three nights, protesting the arrival of fresh peacekeepers. Swedish troops cleared the runway and arrested twenty-eight Katangese.

Tshombe led a 10,000-strong protest to the airport. Windows were smashed, UN vehicles overturned. Businesses in Elisabethville refused to serve peace-keepers. The next month, Munongo distributed machetes to his followers for an anti-UN march. Scraping sounds echoed around the capital as marchers sharpened their blades on the pavement.

'You'd be surprised what a little violence can accomplish sometimes,' said Munongo.[4]

The antagonism was still crackling in the air at O'Brien's first meeting. He ducked the trio's questions and assured them that the UN's only goal was to bring peace to the region. They did not believe him. The Irishman did not care. Privately, he regarded the ministers as naive puppets of the Belgians. Hammarskjöld had sent him to cut the strings.

One puppet was already down. Moïse Tshombe had been in a Léopoldville jail for the last month.

In early March 1961, Tshombe and every important Congolese political leader except Gizenga had come together at Tananarive in Madagascar to discuss the future of their country. Tshombe wanted a confederation of autonomous Congo states, the crushing of Gizenga's government in Stanleyville and the withdrawal of the United Nations.

'We must act in concert to take over the destiny of our country once more,' Tshombe said. 'There must be a common front against interference from the Security Council, the Afro-Asian states, and the UN forces, if these are to be prevented from imposing a sort of mandate on the Congo.'[5]

Kasa-Vubu supported the plan. This made little sense to UN officials, whose troops were propping up his government. They decided the confederation was a pay-off to Tshombe for murdering Lumumba. New York sent Robert Gardiner, a senior Ghanaian civil servant, and Nigeria's Francis Nwokedi to lean on the Congolese president. Behind closed doors, the pair gave up control of Matadi and Port Francqui; promised not to remove Mobutu's foreign advi-sors; offered UN military support for Léopoldville's actions; and planted doubts that Tshombe would hand over a fair share of his copper taxes. CIA man Larry Devlin applied pressure elsewhere in Léopoldville.

Kasa-Vubu and Mobutu resisted briefly, then agreed to abort Tshombe's confederate dream. On 24 April, Kasa-Vubu announced a new conference in the Équateur province capital Coquilhatville to debate the decisions made at Tananarive.

'We have resolved our problems ourselves,' said a suspicious Tshombe, 'and now we want both West and East to leave us alone.'[6]

But against the advice of his advisors he flew in, taking Évariste Kimba with him.


A painted line ran through the streets of Coquilhatville marking the equator. Belgians enjoyed being photographed straddling it. Few other foreigners saw anything to like in the city.

'Coq's a pisshole,' said an American official.[7]

In an air-conditioned conference hall Kasa-Vubu asked delegates to tear up the Tananarive agreement and replace it with a federalist system that brought Katanga and South Kasaï back under his control. He promised funding from the United Nations to make it all work. Tshombe sneered at the idea that the UN could help the Congo when the organisation had its own financial troubles. He knelt on the conference hall floor to illustrate Léopoldville's subservient attitude to foreigners.

'You are abandoning the sovereignty of your country to the United Nations,' he said. 'I denounce this agreement with the United Nations as lacking all validity.'[8]

Tshombe and Kimba tried to leave Coquilhatville on 26 April. ANC troops locked them in an airport building. A parade of Congolese politicians came to visit, asking them to reconsider. Tshombe refused.

'I don't care to discuss politics with men who for the past fifteen months have done nothing else than driven flashy cars, maintained fifteen mistresses, and lived off the best, while the country is in chaos and I am the only one who really works,' he said.[9]

The other delegates ratified the new agreement without him. On 9 May, Tshombe was charged with rebellion, repression and use of illegal currency. Three weeks later, he and Kimba were transferred to Léopoldville. The pair ended up in Binza Camp, like Lumumba before them. Munongo, Kibwe and Kiwele formed a triumvirate to run Katanga in Tshombe's absence.

Katangese representatives visited Abbé Youlou in Brazzaville with a suitcase of cash to fund a rescue attempt. The abbé discussed it with Paris and declined. Some senior UN officers thought the Congo was closer to civil war than ever with Tshombe in prison and considered springing him using Richard Browne's captured mercenaries. The plan failed to go anywhere. Tshombe remained behind bars.

Colonel Crèvecœur invited Conor Cruise O'Brien for Sunday cocktails at his villa. As O'Brien mingled with Belgian officers and their wives, glass in hand, Crèvecœur did his best to make a good impression. He dripped poison about Frenchman Roger Faulques and the mercenaries now clustering around him. All extremists, said Crèvecœur and sipped his drink.

Crèvecœur and Major Mattys, a veteran of Operation Conga, passed around arrows and a blunderbuss captured from Baluba rebels. Guests talked about savagery and cannibalism. O'Brien, who thought himself a rebel, did not sympathise.

'Here in this room, they seemed to murmur, was our common civilisation,' O'Brien thought, 'which included, yes indeed, also white UN people – and out there were the forces of darkness.'[10]

The group discussed attacks on UN soldiers in the rest of the Congo. On 3 March, Sudanese troops had got into a firefight with Léopoldville ANC soldiers, leaving one Congolese dead. Two days later, more fighting killed several Sudanese at Matadi seaport. In April, Léopoldville ANC troops had murdered forty-seven Ghanaian soldiers at Port Francqui, Kasaï after taking them prisoner. O'Brien nodded politely but refused to take the bait. Crèvecœur's wife glared at him over her glass.

After the party, O'Brien pressured Crèvecœur into providing a list of foreign soldiers and advisors active in the province. It arrived the next month. As of 14 July, Katanga employed 306 mercenaries, 230 of them Belgian. Numbers had been dropping for the last few months. Fifty mercenaries had deserted by the end of April. Another eighty-five, most of them Mike Hoare's men unhappy with their new duties, left the country two months later, when Elisabethville allowed them to break their contracts.

Hoare joined the exodus, having spent several weeks unsuccessfully searching for the two men who went missing during 4 Commando's May escape.

'I am sorry,' Crèvecœur told him:

You must face the facts. They will both be dead. In a year or so some missionary in the bush will report their death. News filters through to them via the tribesmen in their area. Eventually they hear everything this way. There is nothing you can do about it and nothing we can do.[11]

Hoare went home to his air stewardess girlfriend in Durban, seething at the UN and the Belgians.

Conor Cruise O'Brien was certain that Brussels pulled the strings in Katanga. Journalists prowling Elisabethville's government buildings were less sure. A Belgian advisor promised newsman Richard Cox an interview with Kibwe.

Cox waited outside the office as the advisor strolled in confidently. Muted conversation got suddenly louder.

'I said NO!' roared Kibwe and slammed his fist on the desk.[12] The Belgian ran from the room.

When Cox did get his interview, Kibwe talked about plans to break Brussels's monopoly on Katangese business.[13] The vice president had already invited a German firm to make paper in the province, an Italian firm to build roads and a British/Rhodesian/South African firm to start mining operations near Elisabethville. American mining companies were also interested. Kibwe boasted that UMHK, the spider at the centre of the Katangese web, had been ordered to shift its headquarters from Brussels to Elisabethville. The mining giant's protests, he said, meant nothing.

In another office, Godefroid Munongo was equally adamant about the position of Europeans in Katanga. 'It's ridiculous to say we take orders from the Belgians,' he said, while Minaf advisers sat silently. 'They take orders from us. Why shouldn't we hire them as long as they are under our control? They understand our language and people, and it's convenient for us. When we don't need them any more, we'll send them away.'[14]

He was contemptuous of those who suggested the secession had been engineered by Brussels.

'I did not need the Belgian government to declare independence for Katanga,' he said. 'Never'.[15]

O'Brien had no time for that kind of talk. Within three days of his arrival, he began to cut strings. Colonel Guy Weber, Tshombe's chief advisor, flew back to Brussels on 17 June to avoid arrest. Three hundred Elisabethville residents cheered him off at the airport. UN troops deported Professor René Clemens soon after, decapitating the Bureau-Conseil du Katanga. Then, on 22 June, O'Brien heard some news on Congolese radio that made him smile. After two months of imprisonment, Tshombe had called a press conference in Léopoldville and announced the secession was over. He was flying back home to make it official.

'I owe my life to God and the Virgin Mary,' said Tshombe when he arrived at Elisabethville airport.[16]

O'Brien thought he owed more to the 100 million Congolese francs Munongo paid into the Swiss bank accounts of Léopoldville's leaders. Thousands turned out to greet Tshombe's aeroplane, chanting and dancing across the tarmac. Standing behind Tshombe in the passenger jet doorway was Colonel Ndjoku, Crèvecœur's replacement as head of the gendarmes. O'Brien allowed himself a little hope. Perhaps the secession really had ended.

That hope soon evaporated. Ndjoku left a few weeks later, when no one would obey his orders. Then the Katangese parliament announced that it would not uphold any agreement made with Léopoldville. Tshombe expressed regret. No one believed him. He was grateful to have been released, but not grateful enough to keep his word.

O'Brien stepped up the expulsion of white advisors. He was helped by a tidal wave of backstabbing that washed through Elisabethville after the arrival of Belgian civil servant Charles Muller, on a mission from Spaak to change Katangese minds about reintegration. Local ultras decided he must be a communist when they saw their own names on a deportation list he provided O'Brien. In revenge, ultras passed over lists of Minaf advisors they wanted gone. Katangese soldiers joined in with the names of white officers whose jobs they desired. Then Tshombe's ministers pointed the finger at anyone who tried to stop them taking bribes.

'We must clean all the Belgians out of the government,' said Conakat spokesman André Kapwasa.[17]

O'Brien happily arranged deportations. Belgians flew out of Elisabethville faster than pigeons after a gunshot. Colonel Crèvecœur went to Brussels on leave with his wife and did not return. Vandewalle was one of the few who remained, strolling round town in civilian clothes as the Belgian *chargé d'affaires*.

The Katangese did not want to see all Belgians leave. Tshombe's men became furious when Swedish UN troops arrested George Thyssens, who had overcome doubts about his loyalty to become an important advisor. Gendarmes snatched Muller in revenge and he vanished into a local jail. When the UN tried to spring him, Charles Mutaka-wa-Dilomba, 28-year-old speaker of the Katangese assembly, threatened O'Brien with a Fouga jet attack. The Katangese Air Force had only a single operational Fouga (one snagged a power cable, the other had engine problems) but Mutaka-wa-Dilomba did not share that information. O'Brien calmly retaliated by offering to swamp Elisabethville with Gurkha soldiers.

'Is that the language you usually employ around here?' asked Tunisia's Mahmoud Khiari, UN Chief of Civilian Operations in the Congo, listening in on the call. 'In Léopoldville we are used to a quieter kind of democracy.'[18]

'It is quite remarkable that they can say we're wrong and they're right, when we represent the whole world community,' said O'Brien. 'Unless they change their attitude, we shall have to crush them.'[19]

Ultras loyal to Munongo decided that Brussels was behind Thyssen's problems and broke into the Belgian consulate. Fifteen-year-old Victor Rosez and his teenage friends smashed windows and burned an effigy of Spaak. Munongo arrested the consulate staff. Jacques Saquet, a young radio operator who had volunteered to stay in Katanga when the rest of his unit went home, remembered being marched by gendarmes to a large roundabout near the Hôtel Belle-Vue and released. UN troops using the hotel as a hospital watched in confusion, re-evaluating their views on Belgian power in Katanga. The incident made the newspapers but Thyssens's deportation went ahead. The gendarmes reluctantly released Muller.

Katanga held its first Independence Day celebration on 11 July. Home-made flags fluttered in the wind.

After Tshombe's return, Conor Cruise O'Brien had regular meetings with him at the presidential palace. A crowd of Lunda tribesmen were always dancing and drumming by the main gate. Tshombe was generous with the ice-cold beer but O'Brien remained immune to the Katangese leader's charm. Others did not.

'People simply can't resist you,' said an admiring UN official.

'I know,' said Tshombe.[20]

The meetings achieved little. O'Brien asked Tshombe to attend a summit of Congolese leaders in Léopoldville; Tshombe agreed if the meeting was changed to neutral territory; O'Brien refused; Tshombe refused to go. The pattern repeated elsewhere. Spaak leaned on Elisabethville to end the secession; Munongo gave a press conference asking for the Soviet Union's assistance as it seemed that Belgium had abandoned Katanga; Spaak backed down; Munongo confirmed his support for secession.

O'Brien used any weapon he could find to damage Katanga. One day, André Cremer, a 36-year-old Belgian mercenary and car thief recently kicked out of the gendarmes, walked into a UN office with stories of an assassination squad. Cremer claimed Munongo had created the squad to target peacekeepers. He knew one name: Hugh Chalmers, a 28-year-old Scot in Groupe Mobile E, based near Niemba. The drunk Chalmers made an unlikely professional assassin.

'Nothing but a two-bit bullshitter,' said a soldier who knew him.[21]

O'Brien never really believed the story but that did not stop him spreading Cremer's accusations around the press pool and demanding that Tshombe hand over Munongo for questioning. The Katangese president refused. A French mercenary called Toupé-Thomé aimed threats at O'Brien.

'The UN? No problem!' he said to journalists. 'Twenty kilos of plastic explosive and I'm in charge.'[22]

A better weapon came along for the Irishman when Léopoldville and Stanleyville agreed a truce and created the Government of National Unity on 27 July. Cyril Adoula, a friendly-looking 39-year-old political veteran, replaced Ileo as Congolese prime minister. The Americans liked Adoula so much that even the appointment of Gizenga as deputy prime minister failed to annoy them. In the excitement over a united Congolese government, no one worried too much over Gizenga's refusal to visit Léopoldville or stand down the Stanleyville ANC.

On 24 August, the new government passed Ordinance 70, decreeing all non-Congolese soldiers not employed by central government to be illegal aliens. Kasa-Vubu requested UN assistance in expelling them. O'Brien seized the moment and asked Khiari for authorisation to use force against white mercenaries. Khiari consulted Hammarskjöld.

The Swede gave O'Brien's plan the green light.


In his house on South Coast Road in Durban, Mike Hoare brooded over recent events in Katanga.

'Over the weekend', he wrote on 28 August to another veteran, 'I was getting very worked up over a scheme to offer Munongo a small unit of hand-picked men to give the UN a go.'[23]

But the day Hoare went to telegram the offer, he discovered that Gurkha troops had occupied the post office in Elisabethville and were intercepting all communications. A bad business. He did not send the telegram.

'I am afraid UN have won the day there,' he wrote. 'I bet Munongo wishes he had held on to us in June.'[24]

The Gurkhas in the post office were part of Operation Rumpunch, O'Brien's plan to cleanse Katanga of its mercenaries. The Irishman thought he could pull the secession's sharpest teeth and force Tshombe to obey the United Nations. It would lead to O'Brien being sent home in disgrace, Hammarskjöld's aeroplane falling out of the sky over northern Rhodesia and war in the streets of Elisabethville. Katanga was going down in flames.

# DUSK

# 14

# RUMPUNCH

## The UN Expels Tshombe's White Mercenaries

He was 5ft 9in of peasant muscle from the Medoc vineyards, topped with thick brown hair and chilly blue eyes. He had piloted patrol boats down the Mekong Delta, been a policeman in Morocco, driven coup plotters around Paris and done jail time for the Pierre Mendès France affair. All it got him was an estranged wife, a son he rarely saw and a bad reputation.

On 10 September 1961, 32-year-old Robert 'Bob' Denard was in the arrivals lounge of Bruxelles-National airport wearing a dirty gendarme uniform. Denard showed his French passport and cleared customs, ignoring the journalists thick as flies around any mercenary getting off a Sabena jet from Katanga. They wanted quotes for the evening edition.

'It's obviously an adventure,' said a suntanned Belgian, 'and more often butcher work than real war. But we are well paid …'[1]

'We're Les Affreux because we like to risk our lives,' said another. 'Especially because risking your life can pay big when it's tough.'[2]

'I thought it was a great life, mine,' said a man with a British accent. 'There were no regular hours, you were free as a bird, you didn't clock-in or clock-out, it was nice weather, you know, you got everything provided, all you could eat, cigarettes and stuff like that. And all the time your money was piling up in the bank.'[3]

Denard pushed past them and headed off into Brussels to track down some of Marissal's clan, who had promised help. The Frenchman's mercenary life had begun eight months earlier, when he read an article in the conservative *L'Aurore* newspaper about Tshombe's foreign volunteers. The piece had a photograph of the only Frenchman serving with the Katangese gendarmes.

'His name was Antoine de Saint-Paul,' said Denard, 'and I envied him.'[4]

Young, steady-eyed, born in the French colony of Tunisia, de Saint-Paul had fought the FLN as a sous-lieutenant in Algeria. He hated communism and saw it in Algerian rebels, student protesters and the United Nations. In January 1961, he flew to Katanga on his own initiative and joined the gendarmes. His example inspired Denard to approach Roger Trinquier, then recruiting at the rue Cambon office. The colonel turned him down. He did not like Denard's past.

Denard ditched the idea of working for Moïse Tshombe. In March, he flew to Brazzaville in a Union Aéro-maritime de Transports (UAT) Boeing and told Abbé Fulbert Youlou's head of security his plan to become a policeman in South Kasaï.

'It is a good thing you want to help these people, Monsieur Denard,' said the security chief, 'they are in real need.'[5]

Access to South Kasaï was harder than it looked. The chief advised him to go via Elisabethville. Denard stayed at the Hôtel Léopold II, where Belgian soldiers spied on him, thinking he was a friend of Trinquier. No one offered help to cross the border. Godefroid Munongo agreed to a meeting, failed to tell Denard how much he disliked Kalonji, and suggested a position in the Katangese gendarmes instead.

On 6 March, the Frenchman became a sous-lieutenant with a six-month contract at 13,000 Belgian francs a month and a higher rank than he had ever achieved in the marines. He spent the days before deployment swimming in the Lido, his nights with African girls. One day, driving his jeep around Elisabethville, he offered Roger Faulques a lift. The Foreign Legion hero knew all about Denard's past.

'Thank you', said Faulques, 'but I prefer to walk.'[6]

Denard got posted to Groupe Mobile C as second-in-command to Lieutenant Cuvelier, a short Belgian in sunglasses with a pistol on each hip. Cuvelier's 100 Katangese gendarmes and twenty Belgians patrolled the area around Kongolo, trying to scare local Baluba by decorating their jeeps with the emblem of a witch on a broomstick. Sendwe's men did not scare easily. Poison arrows flew out of the bush. Elephant traps swallowed vehicles on remote roads. The weeks turned to months.

Uninterested in racial barriers, Denard preferred to spend his time with Katangese soldiers rather than whites. His adjutant Augustine Kabuita had fought in the Force Publique against the Italians in Abyssinia during the war. He educated Denard about tribal factions, pointing out how graffiti on ruined walls indicated whether Lumumbaist or Tshombe factions had torched the village.

Denard encountered Roger Faulques again during a training course at the Paracommando School down south in Shinkolobwe. This time Faulques was more impressed. He selected Denard's group for a parade celebrating Tshombe's release. Denard mixed his white and black troops together for the march down an Elisabethville boulevard. The Katangese crowds applauded. Belgians looked shocked. At a reception afterwards, Tshombe congratulated Denard on his enlightened leadership and gave him command of a unit in Albertville.

Denard's men patrolled the shores of Lake Tanganyika, keeping a wary distance from nearby UN troops. On 28 August Ghanaian troops surrounded the Frenchman's camp and demanded his surrender. Conor Cruise O'Brien's plan to cleanse Katanga of its mercenaries had begun.

At 4 that morning, Indian troops had occupied the Radio Katanga studios. Gurkhas took the post office. Roadblocks went up around the city. Swedish soldiers surrounded Munongo's home. Irish troops arrested mercenaries and Belgian advisors as they stumbled sleepy-eyed out of bed. No one fought back.

'We have these soldiers scared witless,' said an Indian UN officer.[7]

At 5 a.m., O'Brien sent Tshombe a letter explaining Operation Rumpunch's aims. After six hours of negotiations, Tshombe agreed to co-operate. He broadcast a radio announcement officially dismissing all foreigners from Katangese service, then went to bed with what his doctor claimed was a mild heart attack. Confident, O'Brien ordered Munongo released. The Minister of the Interior seemed amused by the UN's bold move.

'You fooled me,' he said and shook O'Brien's hand.[8]

At lunchtime, the Belgian consul contacted O'Brien in a panic, talking about national humiliation and the dangers of firefights in Elisabethville's boulevards. He offered to take responsibility for the repatriation of all foreign soldiers if the UN stopped arresting them. UN troops were already stretched thin by Rumpunch; O'Brien accepted. When the arrests ceased at 3 that afternoon, 338 foreigners had already been taken into custody.[9] Others remained on the loose. Some mercenaries had made a run for their national embassies; others were hiding with locals. A few, like John Trevelyn and his crew, patrolled inaccessible parts of the province.

Trevelyn was unaware of Operation Rumpunch until long after it had ended. In the news-less bush, his unit would surface like a U-boat to pick up supplies and gossip before resubmerging into silence.

'Time came and went without thought,' he said. 'You were a sort of prisoner in your own time warp.'[10]

A few village chiefs had radios but most communicated by drum. One night, en route to a remote mission station, Trevelyn lay awake listening to the drums pounding over the bush, not knowing if they telegraphed tribal news or orders for an attack. The next day, he saw smoke rising above the trees in the distance. The Baluba had reached the mission station first.

Casualties for his group were light: a white mercenary killed within days of joining the group, several Katangese soldiers hit by poisoned arrows and one by a *panga* thrown at close range. On route to the mission station Trevelyn nearly joined the casualty list.

He found a box of what appeared to be long candles wrapped in greased paper abandoned in a hut. He held one up to show his team.

'What's this?' he asked.[11]

His team vanished like cockroaches when a light flicks on. Trevelyn was holding a stick of unstable, weeping gelignite. After a long minute, Trevelyn softly returned the stick to its box and crawled away.

The Belgian consul in Elisabethville had not cleared his plan with Brussels. On 29 August, Spaak, pressured by public outrage at Rumpunch, announced that the Belgian government had no authority over civilian mercenaries and would not help deport them. O'Brien won a small victory when Brussels agreed to withdraw its remaining Minaf soldiers and technical staff. Extremist local ultras quickly wriggled into vacant advisor posts. But the 260 mercenaries still in Katanga, the majority Belgian, were safe as long as they could avoid the UN.[12]

Union Minière provided jobs for mercenaries in its factories and plants. Paul Ropagnol, a crop-haired and moustached Frenchman expelled from the army for anti-de Gaulle activities in Algeria, changed from battle dress into a snappy anthracite grey single-breasted suit and became a UMHK office drone. Indian UN troops discovered another mercenary painting a fence at their base for a local subcontractor.

Katanga could have done without some of the foreigners who remained. Gummarus Sluydts, a 28-year-old from Borgerhout, a Flemish town near Antwerp, tried to convince Munongo that mercenaries could escape detection by disguising themselves as game wardens.[13] Iranian game wardens. The Minister of the Interior did not bother to reply.

Conor Cruise O'Brien had the consolation of knowing he had broken the spine of the Katangese army by deporting its best officers. Tshombe appointed General Norbert Muke new head of the armed forces. A granite-chinned soldier, only recently a captain, and before that a cook, Muke's French was rudimentary and English non-existent. Many thought him illiterate. He sat mute at a press conference announcing his appointment as British journalists joked about giving him bananas. Even the Belgians mockingly called him 'Napoleon Muke'.[14] The UN did not take Muke seriously either; O'Brien believed the ultras had pushed him into power to show how much Katanga needed qualified white men. Others thought it a mistake to dismiss the army's new strongman.

'He was not a bad guy,' said Victor Rosez, friends with the general's teenage son, a polio victim with one leg shorter than the other. 'He was from Kasaï, a

Baluba, but grew up in Katanga. So he knew the languages Swahili, Lingala, and Tshiluba and was familiar to both cultures, so the soldiers trusted him.'[15]

Frenchman Roger Faulques had also escaped the round-up. Tshombe secretly appointed him Muke's chief of staff. Faulques, a tough as blood veteran of Indochina and Algeria, began rebuilding the armed forces around a core of paracommandos he had trained in Shinkolobwe. He integrated remaining mercenaries and promoted Katangese soldiers into officer positions.

The Katangese Air Force had been dismantled by Rumpunch but one of its top pilots, Pierre Magain, had escaped with his Fouga jet. Other mercenaries were already coming back. They flew in from Brazzaville or Ndola, slipping over the border into the secession. Faulques took every man he could get, even extremists with bad histories like Bob Denard. He was prepared to overlook the fact that the former marine had tried to assassinate the French prime minister in 1954.

Bob Denard's teenage years coincided with the German occupation of France. A boy from his village joined the collaborationist Légion des Volontaires Français and sent Denard postcards from Romania, Lithuania, Ukraine … then the postcards stopped. Denard's father joined the communist resistance and disappeared for longer and longer periods. In 1944, Denard and a friend planned to set fire to a German arms dump in a nearby forest. When they got there, they found the dump was a canvas mock-up to fool RAF bombers. They burnt it anyway but the resulting Gestapo crackdown scared the pair too much to repeat the adventure.

Later that year, the Allies advanced into the Médoc and Denard had to shelter from the friendly fire of an American bombardment. Afterwards he guided Free French troops through the countryside in pursuit of retreating Germans. He wanted action and medals like papa. In 1945, he enlisted in the navy as a 16-year-old trainee mechanic. He liked wine, women and fighting; he disliked military discipline.

In Indochina, he piloted a patrol boat down the steamy tributaries of the Mekong Delta. Thousands of miles of black water and overhanging fronds, riverbanks hidden behind a solid wall of foliage that concealed villages, trading posts and enemy snipers. He got badly wounded in a firefight and spent three months in a French hospital. Infection set in but Denard was tough and fought off the doctors who thought amputation was the only solution. He returned to Indochina.

The war was brutal. Denard thought he spotted a missing crew on a riverbank, standing to attention in rows. As his patrol boat drew up he saw the men were dead, castrated and impaled on spikes. After that his crew hesitated less at their machine guns when unsure if a passing boat was friendly or Viet Minh.

Emotions boiled over in the summer of 1948, when Denard and his men, drunk and furious at the Vietnamese, the war, everything, smashed up a restaurant while on leave. He got sixty days in jail. A promised Croix de Guerre was snatched away. Denard felt betrayed. He had risked his life for the French navy, once nearly been killed by a Viet Minh guerrilla who pushed a sub-machine gun into his face only to have it jam. Denard decided to quit when his contract ended.

Before that there was an exchange mission to America. Chewing gum, Chrysler cars, skyscrapers. And a genuinely democratic army where anyone, even a peasant like Denard, could rise to the top. He was impressed.

In the early fifties, a civilian again, he joined a construction company that built army bases in French Morocco. It was a world of white sand beaches, art deco buildings, servants and sitting outside cafés watching cars cruise the wide boulevards. Nearby, Moroccan nationalists primed bombs as part of a campaign to take back the country. Extremists in the French community urged Denard to help even the score.

The ex-marine had distractions enough chasing Gisèle, a teenage girl from a well-off Jewish family. They married and had a son. His employer finished its work in Morocco but Denard stayed on with his new family and joined the police force. Moroccan nationalist attacks ramped up. Denard now had reason to fight back. It was a shallow slope from anti-terrorist actions with the police to counter-terrorist actions with off-duty police, to revenge attacks with the extremists he had earlier ignored. He had an affair with a married woman deeply involved with the ultras, which drew him in further and dripped acid on his marriage.

The ultras could not hold back the tide. In 1954, the French allowed Moroccan king Mohammed V back into the country, the first domino that tumbled the others. Independence was set for two years' time. Denard's new friends wanted revenge on the French government they held responsible for the loss of their colonial dream. He became mixed up in a plot to assassinate the French Prime Minister, Pierre Mendès France, during a visit to Casablanca. Denard's role was minor but committed. The assassination attempt was poorly planned and badly executed. A bodyguard was injured in a sub-machine gun attack during a walkabout. Mendès France escaped unhurt.

The group, including Denard, was rounded up by the transitional authorities. By the time of the trial, the French had already packed their bags and left. The new Moroccan government had no interest in settling scores with the ultras.

The gang received short sentences. Denard, having already spent fourteen months behind bars, was somehow found not guilty. He returned to France and tried to fix his marriage in the Médoc but found their differences were too great. He moved to Paris on his own, officially still a policeman. No one would work with him. Eventually he found employment as a gopher to an assortment of right-wing politicians. Denard had a minor role in the de Gaulle putsch of 1958, ferrying senior figures around Paris. His interest in politics remained minimal and he ignored approaches from the French right in Algeria. His options were running out when he picked up a copy of *L'Aurore* newspaper with its photograph of de Saint-Paul.

When the Ghanaians approached during Operation Rumpunch, Denard's men wanted to fight. The Frenchman radioed Elisabethville and was told to lay down his weapons and surrender. Denard and the other Europeans spent a few weeks in a camp guarded by Irish UN troops, then were expelled to Brussels by Sabena jet. Denard got information on how to return from the Katangese delegation and travel expenses from Marissal's Clan to see his son in France. Then he took a UTA flight to Salisbury in Rhodesia and headed north.

On 6 and 7 September, locals rioted in the centre of Elisabethville. They stoned UN armoured cars and burned civilian vehicles. A mob of young Katangese men invaded the Hôtel Léopold II looking for UN soldiers. Canadian Captain Mario Cole fought them off with a chair and his revolver.

'Fortunately these chaps are not very courageous,' he said to reporters.[16]

O'Brien moved his HQ out of Le Clair Manoir restaurant in the city centre and into the airport. Gurkhas left the post office. On 8 September, Kasa-Vubu officially asked the UN to finish off the secession. The time was right. Katanga had been stripped of its white advisors and its military skeletonised.

O'Brien approached Hammarskjöld, then in Léopoldville, with a fresh plan. UN troops would occupy Elisabethville and force Tshombe to surrender his independence. Hammarskjöld, still committed to peace, wavered, but America supported the idea, having woken to the possibility that Soviet-friendly Gizenga could whip up enough popular support to replace Adoula if the secession continued. Even the British government, previously behind Tshombe, was pushing for a united Congo.

'Chances of United Govt. if Tshombe can be squared over Katanga,' said the Cabinet meeting minutes recording Harold Macmillan's view. 'If Katanga separated off, we shdn't come to its defence. Wiser that it shd. adhere to Congo, esp. if that can be done peaceably.'[17]

Any uncertainty Hammarskjöld felt about the operation was eroded on 10 September, when Irish UN troops in Jadotville reported that they could see Katangese forces setting up in the bush around them, preparing for a siege. The next day, he approved O'Brien's plan. Khiari supplied five arrest warrants for senior Katangese figures.

'Above all', said Khiari, 'no half measures.'[18]

On Wednesday 13 September 1961, O'Brien launched Operation Morthor as a police action to end the secession. It became a war.

# 15

# I AM PREPARED TO DIE FIGHTING IN MY OWN HOME

## Operation Morthor, September 1961: Part I

When the news came in just after dawn, Captain Roger Faulques was at his headquarters in a villa outside Elisabethville. White men in suits and Katangese in uniform traced their fingers over maps of the city. A radio unit hissed static in the corner. Faulques lit a Gauloise, the first of sixty a day, and blew smoke at the ceiling.

The news was bad. At four o'clock in the morning, UN soldiers had begun creeping through the dark streets of Elisabethville to their targets: the radio studios; the transmitter at the College of St Francis; the Chaussée de Kasenga tunnel bridge; the houses of Munongo, Tshombe, Kibwe and Mutuka-wa Dilomba. In the city centre, a phalanx of Gurkha UN soldiers was trotting up to the post office, Swedish and Irish armoured cars rolling alongside them. The UN was taking over the Katangese capital.

A tall, limping 37-year-old with a short thatch of grey hair and a face like a well-loved dog toy, Faulques had spent most of his life in one warzone or another. As a teenager he had joined the Maquis to fight the Germans. In Indochina, he was a Foreign Legion officer struggling to keep the *tricolore* flying over a colony that wanted independence. Faulques earned the Légion d'Honneur before the Viet Minh got its hands on him. Paris negotiated his release and he went straight back into the jungle. The Frenchman liked to tell people he had so many bullet holes he would sink if he went swimming.

Trinquier picked him for the Katanga mission because the two men had grown close in Algeria, bonding over counter-revolution and torture. The colonel got himself expelled from Elisabethville and Faulques became top man in the French mercenary contingent. Faulques knew some of his fellow soldiers from Algeria and the Légion; others were new faces. They gathered around him in the villa.

The UN has moved against Katanga, Faulques told them. Get ready to fight back.

The post office, angular and modernist in white stone, sat between two roads on the edge of a public square. A pair of radio antennae rose high from the roof. Golden metal letters spelt 'Poste' and 'Telephones' above the entrance. A skeletal clock crowned the building. Inside, twenty black gendarmes crouched by the windows in the dark.

Gurkhas deployed around the square, lit by the headlights of armoured cars. An interpreter held up a megaphone. In French, he ordered the Katangese to leave the building. No response. He tried Swahili. No response. A group of Gurkhas moved up to the post office's double doors. Apart from the firefight near Kabalo during April's Operation Conga, the UN had avoided violent confrontation with Katangese forces. Swedish conscript Tommy Nilsson remembered the most dangerous part of his tour occurring when he flew home in June: 'Some cargo wasn't secured enough and one box hit the roof so strongly it made a small hole in the outer surface. It was a scary experience and most of us were ready to say goodbye.'[1] That was all about to change.

As the Gurkhas pried at the post office door, a sniper bullet knocked an officer to the ground. Then the gendarmes inside the building opened fire. Bullets smashed into concrete and ricocheted off armour plating. The Gurkhas ran for cover.

An Irish armoured car rotated its canon and blasted in the post office doors. Red tracer fire streamed across the white frontage. A gendarme was shot out of an upper storey window and fell to the pavement, his guts hanging out. He scooped them up in his hands and ran off crying. A wounded Swedish driver crashed into a wall.

The noise of machine guns woke journalists in the Hôtel Léopold II. David Halberstam's first thought was for his clothes in a laundry on Post Office Square. Then the reality of the situation sank in and the *New York Times* reporter joined the other half-dressed foreign correspondents running through Elisabethville's streets towards the sound of gunfire. A handful of journalists remained at the Léopold II to ring the post office switchboard.

'We in the Post Office, M'sieu, are about to die,' said senior operator Emmanuel Kasamba.[2]

Gurkhas entered the post office entrance hall, thick with masonry dust and gun smoke. Rifle fire cracked inside. A Gurkha shot Kasamba dead before heading off into the smoke. The Katangese fought from room to room. It was five in the morning when the last defender, swinging an empty rifle, fell off the roof and slapped into the pavement.

Two days earlier, Victor Rosez had been happy. His school, Elisabethville's International Institute, had sent everyone home and locked its doors until the situation with the UN was resolved. The Belgian schoolboy, a few days from his sixteenth birthday, walked cheerfully home towards the Chaussée de Kasenga with his friend Jean-Claude. No lessons, no homework.

Rosez's father worked for the railways. After years of chugging around Katanga behind a steam train in a wagon with beds and its own petrol-powered refrigerator, the family had settled in Elisabethville. Victor missed the sounds of the jungle but liked the excitement of the city. General Muke lived nearby in Uvira Square and Victor made friends with his son. Every morning, the general's chauffeur picked up the two boys in his Chevrolet Impala and dropped them off at school.

Rosez enthusiastically supported the secession. He helped his mother sew Katangese flags for the first Independence Day celebrations and joined a mob of Munongo's followers raiding the Belgian consulate to protest Charles Muller's visit. Later he spent evenings and weekends in a Union Minière factory making bombs for the Katangese Air Force. Victor pasted glamour shots of Belgian models from magazines on his bedroom walls, revered President Tshombe and got the barber to cut his hair like Marlon Brando.

Rosez and Jean-Claude were walking past the Kasenga tunnel, where the road dipped beneath the railway while train tracks continued overhead on thick concrete legs. It was home to an Irish UN roadblock. The two schoolboys saw a mercenary strolling towards it, unaware. Jean-Claude gestured to him and pointed at the peacekeepers. The mercenary ran off. He and Victor were still laughing about it when Irish troops opened fire.

'The Irish UN group in position on that place fired at us and my schoolmate Jean-Claude was deadly wounded,' Victor said. 'I could escape and ran home using backyard ways ... I could not help my friend ... the shooting didn't stop.'[3]

His friend was dead.

The tears were barely dry by 13 September. When he heard about the assault on the post office, Rosez raced to the general's house. Muke was at Camp Massart organising a defence. Victor, still mourning Jean-Claude, became a soldier.

'I wore immediately an old uniform of the general (a brushstroke camo with three captain stars, because one year before this the general was only a captain, quickly promoted to general chief commander),' Rosez said:

Nobody gave any comment, the soldiers whom knew me very well, accepted what I did. We went to the 'base terrestre' not far from there, me and four soldiers, and came back with as much ammo as we could carry. I had a bag with nearly 2,000 7.62mm rounds, I think around 40kg.[4]

Together with two teenage friends (one Belgian, the other Dutch) and ten Katangese soldiers, the 16-year-old captain secured the house, guns poking from every window. They waited for the United Nations.

Within a few hours, all UN teams had secured their targets. Kibwe was in custody. Munongo and Mutaka-wa-Dilomba were on the run. Tshombe evaded troops sent to arrest him by climbing over the wall of the presidential palace in his dressing gown. He found shelter with the British consul Denzil Dunnett.

'We did not discuss politics,' Dunnett said later.[5]

Tshombe had telephoned the UN at 4.30 a.m., while fighting raged in the post office, to request a ceasefire. O'Brien strung out negotiations while trying to get permission from New York to send troops into the British consulate. Hammarskjöld refused. At 6 a.m., Tshombe made a half-hearted agreement to negotiate with O'Brien in person, then broke contact.

UN functionary Michel Tomberlaine went by car to collect him from the presidential palace. The Frenchman drove up to the gate and waved at the guards. They opened fire. Tomberlaine accelerated away, tyres screeching, his windows shot out. The Katangese president, now hiding in a cottage in the palace grounds, had changed his mind about negotiations.

'I am prepared to die fighting in my own home,' he told a journalist.[6]

Reports had reached him about the Radio Katanga murders. Indian troops, supported by Irish and Swedes, had occupied the building after bloody fighting. They took twenty-five Katangese gendarmes prisoner. The Indians pushed them into a small room, some gendarmes so scared their knees knocked together, and threw in a hand grenade. An Indian soldier walked through the smoke and blood and dismembered body parts, shooting survivors in the head.

An Irish soldier at the scene tried to make an official complaint but was ignored. A Swede advised him to forget what had happened.

'I kept my mouth shut,' said one Irishman. 'We all did. But we could hardly talk at the time because of what we'd seen. It was murder – pure murder. We were a peacekeeping force. But you would think we were a nation at war.'[7]

The bodies and severed limbs were shovelled into a grave behind the building.

Across town, outside the post office, Gurkhas had laid out the corpses of the building's defenders on the street; a bloody, ragged line of black bodies with faces smashed open by rifle bullets. A crowd of African and European civilians on the other side of the square watched Indian soldiers casually bayonet the corpses as they walked past. The crowd groaned every time a bayonet went in.[8]

'Katanga's secession is ended,' Conor Cruise O'Brien announced to journalists at his early morning news conference. 'It is now a Congolese province run by the central government in Léopoldville.'[9]

As the sun rose, Roger Faulques outlined the situation to his men. Orders had come through: the Katangese government was authorising its armed forces to fight back. Muke was already with his gendarmes in Camp Massart organising resistance.

Faulques established teams, jabbed at maps on the walls and allocated targets. His mercenaries, most French but spotted with Belgians and other nationalities, would lead paracommando units against buildings occupied by UN troops. Groups outside Elisabethville would target larger towns. Faulques was keen to capture an Irish camp near Jadotville run by 42-year-old Commandant Pat Quinlan.

As the Frenchman was giving orders, Pat Quinlan was receiving a call from UN headquarters telling him that Operation Morthor had been a success. The Katanga secession, the voice on the telephone told him, was over. Quinlan felt relief.

The Irish occupied villas in the bush, up the road from the bus station and a Union Minière building. Sent to Jadotville with orders to clear local roads of Baluba ambushes, Quinlan's men were more worried about a Katangese attack. Gendarme units had been moving through the bush around the Irish for the last few days and the residents of Jadotville, black and white, were viciously hostile. The Irish positioned their armoured cars, which looked like siege engines mated with vintage cars, and cut trenches into the ground around their billets. The success in Elisabethville was good news for the UN, but Quinlan told his men to remain alert.

'We're all going out together,' Quinlain had promised the 34th Battalion in Ireland, 'and we're all coming back together.'[10]

In scrub grass near the villas, French mercenary captains Michel de Clary and Henri Lasimone marshalled their gendarmes. De Clary was a wealthy aristocrat who loved war more than the playboy life he could have enjoyed with his family inheritance. Lasimone, a dark 41-year-old born in Chad, had escaped the Rumpunch roundup with the help of an ID card from the Katangese Ministry of Information. Local gendarme chief Tschipola was supposed to be in charge but the real boss was Major Makito, a witchdoctor with an army rank.

Over the previous days, Makito had organised crowds of locals from Jadotville to protest near the Irish base. '*À bas l'ONU!*' (Down with the UN!)[11] The pair urged de Clary and Lasimone to attack as soon as possible. The two Frenchmen waited for orders from Faulques.

At 7 a.m. gendarmes in Elisabethville began firing at UN vehicles driving through the city, unnerving the peacekeepers. An hour later, a Katangese police jeep near the post office was fired on by Gurkhas and crashed, killing two men and injuring another. Dietrich Mummendy, a German photographer, snapped away as Gurkhas shot up the ambulance that arrived several minutes later. Nearby, Vandewalle watched from the Belgian consulate.

In a different part of town, Roger Jaspar, his teenage son Michel and a friend called Doctor Kousenetov had just left Jaspar's house on avenue Mandariniers. They wanted to get Radio Katanga back on the air. At the Ministry of Information they found Jaspar's office door riddled with UN bullets and the room wrecked.

'If you had been there', said Guerrero, his Portuguese editor, 'you would have been dead.'[12]

Jaspar had never seen combat this close up. Born in Hanoi, where his father was Belgian consul, he had bounced between the Far East, Léopoldville and Paris before the war, mixing occasional work as a radio broadcaster with a steadier sales job for Lever Brothers. He was in the Congo when German tanks rolled into Brussels. The Force Publique sent him to London. Millions heard Jaspar's voice as he announced the liberation of Paris in August 1944.

When the war was over, Jaspar went back to college and studied agronomy. He was putting his education to use in the Congo when Tshombe asked him to employ his radio skills for another cause.

The trio loaded Jaspar's car with as many documents as they could recover and set off for Radio Katanga on avenue Delvaux. The place was temporarily empty of UN soldiers. Jaspar used his cinecamera to film unspooled magnetic tape in pools of blood. They were investigating a grave in the garden behind the radio station when a UN armoured car came down the road.


United Nations troops remained in their isolated strongholds: the seized targets in Elisabethville, the Swedish camp to the east, the HQ near the airport, the Lido, Hôtel Léopold II, Prince Léopold Farm. Radio reception was bad throughout the city, drowning voices in static. Gendarmes jumped up from behind walls to spray bullets at convoys travelling around the city.

'Morthor was beginning to go off the rails,' thought O'Brien.[13]

Journalists asked awkward questions. O'Brien could not admit that Operation Morthor had been an attempt to end the secession by force; the UN was supposed to be a peacekeeping organisation. He told the press that Morthor's aim had been to arrest more mercenaries and gave an excuse about a provocative fire at a garage. No one believed him.

O'Brien was lucky his excuses were slow to reach the rest of the world. The post office telex had been destroyed in the fighting and journalists had to file their stories from Northern Rhodesia. Some drove themselves, others paid couriers. In Ndola, just over the border, newsmen caught out of the country by the fighting queued by Charlie Bloomberg's car-hire firm. Bloomberg, a neat man with a toothbrush moustache, charged high fees. He might never see his vehicles again.

Lionel Fleming, the BBC's diplomatic correspondent, drove one of Bloomberg's hires into Katanga with a colleague from the *Chicago Herald Tribune*. Gendarmes at a checkpoint on the road to Elisabethville demanded their identification. One spotted the phrase '*Irlande du Nord*' in Fleming's British passport.

'You are Irish!' the guard shouted. 'You are members of the UN!'[14]

The Katangese dragged the journalists into a guardhouse and beat them. They were rescued by Peter Younghusband, a passing South African reporter for the *Daily Mail*, who pleaded their loyalty to Katanga. The newsmen loudly praised Tshombe as they climbed into their cars, bruises already swelling yellow and purple.

By late morning, Elisabethville had quietened down and only the occasional crack of a sniper shot disturbed the streets. The Union Minière chimney smoked over the city. UN patrols of armoured cars and jeeps drove down deserted boulevards. The occasional silhouette of a Belgian civilian with a rifle in his hands appeared at a window or a rooftop.

Attack groups of Faulques' Katangese paracommandos crept silently through gardens, over walls, dashed across side roads.

'We knew the town like our own house,' said one French mercenary.[15]

Captain Paul Ropagnol led his group towards the College of St Francis in a sharp grey suit, his working clothes from the Union Minière desk he had been hiding behind since Rumpunch. Lieutenant Antoine 'Tony' de Saint-Paul was at his side.

O'Brien continued to tell journalists that Operation Morthor had succeeded. In Léopoldville, Adoula announced that the Katangese army would be integrated into the ANC and asked the UN to declare a state of emergency in the province. Kasa-Vubu despatched Egide Bochely-Davidson, former high commissioner in Gizenga's Stanleyville government, to replace Tshombe. The Katangese president had fled to the mining town of Kipushi, near the Rhodesian border, and set up base in an unfinished house with wooden crates for chairs.

Elisabethville waited for the bullets to start flying.

1 Nurses of the Union Minière du Haut Katanga and their Congolese assistants, April 1918. Katanga province was sixteen times bigger than Belgium. Its reserves of cobalt, copper, tin, uranium and radium made it the economic powerhouse of the Congo. (Wikimedia Commons)

2 Moïse Tshombe, President of Katanga, talking with United Nations officials, 1961. (Lars Carlsson)

3 Godefroid Munongo, Katangese Minister of the Interior and power behind the throne, with United Nations officials, 1961. (Lars Carlsson)

4 The 'Welcome to Free Katanga' sign near Elisabethville airport. (Tommy Nilsson)

5  Major Guy Weber (right) salutes the new Katangese state. (Daniel Despas)

6  Swedish UN soldier Tommy Nilsson out on patrol, early 1961. (Tommy Nilsson)

7 Irish pipers in Elisabethville, early 1961. (Tommy Nilsson)

8 Moroccan UN soldiers in Elisabethville, early 1961. (Tommy Nilsson)

9 UN troops confront Katangese gendarmes and their Belgian officer in the bush, early 1961. (Tommy Nilsson)

10 Katangese and Belgian civilians take cover as the bullets fly during fighting in Elisabethville, 7 December 1961. (Corbis)

11 Swedish UN soldier Tommy Nilsson poses by a termite hill. (Tommy Nilsson)

12 Weapons inspection in camp. (Tommy Nilsson)

13 Bush march. (Tommy Nilsson)

14 At Post Älgen. (Tommy Nilsson)

15 Captain Richard Browne, British mercenary commander of the Compagnie Internationale. (Leif Hellström)

CAPTAIN RICHARD BROWNE
. . . off to his home at Half-way House.

16 Two members of the Compagnie Internationale arrive back in Johannesburg after their capture by UN troops at Kabalo in April 1961. (Private source)

17 The Lido swimming pool in the west of Elisabethville. (Tommy Nilsson)

18 The post office in Elisabethville, scene of fierce fighting in September 1961. (Tommy Nilsson)

19 The Chaussée de Kasenga tunnel bridge in the east of Elisabethville. (Tommy Nilsson)

20 *Below left:* Teenage Belgian volunteer Victor Rosez (left) with two friends in Tshombe's forces, 1961. (Victor Rosez)

21 *Below right:* Pierre Magain, the Belgian pilot who flew a Fouga jet fighter against the United Nations, 1961. (Leif Hellström)

22 South African navigator and political operator Jerry Puren, in shorts, with ground crew and police at a Katangese airfield, 1961. (Leif Hellström)

23 A UN truck destroyed during the September 1961 fighting in Elisabethville. (Jean Kastergat)

24 A cannibalised roadside corpse in Elisabethville, 1961. (Stig von Bayer)

25 The Radio Katanga building in Elisabethville after the September 1961 fighting. (Jean Kastergat)

26 A mass grave, September 1961, twenty-five soldiers 'assassinated by O'Brien … Through the blood of these soldiers Katanga will live!'

27 Polish pilot Jan Zumbach, with sunglasses and cigarette, at Kolwezi airfield, 1962. (Leif Hellström)

28 Katangese
gendarmes in
Kishiale, eastern
Katanga. (Tommy
Nilsson)

29 Belgian volunteer
Christian Tavernier
(right) in Kongolo,
1962. (Leon Libert)

30  French mercenary Bob Denard (centre, with moustache and map) somewhere near Kolwezi during the collapse of the secession, January 1963. (J.-C. Laponterique)

31  Belgian civilian Albert Verbrugghe, a miner, who has just seen his wife and a friend die in the firestorm, begs UN troops to stop shooting during the last days of the secession, 3 January 1963. (Corbis)

32  The final days at Tshombe's villa in Kolwezi, January 1963. (Jean Kestergat)

33  Stamps issued to celebrate the first anniversary of Katanga's independence on 11 July 1961. 'Congo' is crudely overprinted. The issue became invalid in February 1963.

# 16

# KATANGA AGAINST THE WORLD

## Operation Morthor, September 1961: Part II

The fighter jet came in low over Jadotville. The Fouga was thin as a rocket, a two-seater trainer painted red and white with pods at the end of each wing and a tail angled upwards like a bird in flight. Katangese mechanics had armed it with a machine gun and a bomb delivery system held together with rope and solder.

Most Katangese air power had been seized by the UN during Rumpunch. The Fouga's pilot and his aircraft had dodged the round up by hiding out in Kolwezi, the only major town free of peacekeepers. On the afternoon of 14 September, the pilot was out for revenge.

Twenty-five-year-old Pierre Magain sat in the perspex cockpit, hands on the joystick, scanning white figured dials on black: tachometer, altimeter, airspeed, rate of climb, oxygen regulator, g-meter, flap position. Magain, a short Belgian with glistening black hair swept back over a face that looked older than it should, kept an eye on the fuel gauge. The Fouga's armaments slowed down its usual 423mph speed and ate into the two hours it could spend in the air.

Jadotville's houses rushed away beneath the jet. The faded green of the bush, the bus station, the UMHK building, then the Irish villas and trenches and armoured cars. Magain had reached his target.

The Irish had been under siege since the opening morning of Morthor. The first mortar shells fell as they celebrated an outdoor mass. Irishmen dived into slit trenches, fumbling with their rifles as a wave of Katangese gendarmes came at them through the bush. Armoured car crews hosed the attackers with long bursts from Vickers machine guns.

Lars Fröberg, a moustached and frowning Swedish interpreter attached to Quinlan's men, stood by the window of his office mocking the poor accuracy of the Katangese artillery. An incoming mortar shell whined loudly then faded away. Fröberg turned to his Irish companions.

'That was certainly not meant for—' he said.[1]

The shell detonated outside and caved in the window. Glass fragments sliced through the room. A concrete slab deflected most of the blast and saved Fröberg's life. One shell-shocked Irishman lost his voice for thirty minutes.

Quinlan's men held off the first attack and the gendarmes fell back into the bush. The Irish waited in their trenches as vultures circled over sprawled Katangese corpses. One of de Clary's mercenaries rang the telephone in Fröberg's office. In French he threatened, lied, swore, promised good treatment, demanded surrender. Another voice came on the line and calmly told Fröberg to give up before the Katangese Air Force arrived.

Quinlan knew his men were surrounded and did not have the strength to break out. They would have to hold their positions until a relief force could reach Jadotville.

In Elisabethville, rooftop snipers wiped the sweat from their foreheads as they waited for a target to break cover. All UN locations in the city were ringed by an invisible halo of Katangese gendarmes, paracommandos and mercenary officers. UN troops only risked the open in armoured columns that rolled through town delivering supplies and changing guards.

The rest of the city lived a distorted normality. Locals went to work, sat outside cafés and walked babies in prams a few streets away from mercenaries giving orders to gendarmes. Journalists in the Hôtel Léopold II bar chatted as others typed up copy. Conversation would abruptly stop when a firefight erupted somewhere in the distance. Crackling rifle and sub-machine gun fire, the tubular pop of mortar rounds, gendarmes shouting as they tried to force their way into a UN stronghold. Then the noise would die away.

'The whole atmosphere was unreal,' said American journalist Smith Hempstone. 'It was almost like a stage set with people going through the act of war mechanically. And then you saw that the blood on the men brought into the casualty stations was real. It almost surprised you.'[2]

The next day, O'Brien asked New York for permission to seize Tshombe's presidential palace and the gendarme stronghold at Camp Massart. Hammarskjöld refused. The Katangese fightback had unnerved the Security Council. Morale dropped further when newspaper stories contrasted UN rhetoric about self-defence with the reality in Elisabethville. Katanga's supporters spat venom in the international press.

'What has happened today is the law of the jungle,' said Rhodesia's Roy Welensky. 'The right of the biggest to impose his will on the smallest ...

A government that is out of step can be made to toe the line. If not it can, upon a pretext, be taken over by the Secretariat of the United Nations.'[3]

The Security Council ordered UN troops to act only in self-defence. O'Brien felt Hammarskjöld and Khiari distancing themselves from him. Things got worse. UN troops skirmished with gendarmes in Albertville. At Kamina military base, Chief Kasongo Nyembo's Baluba warriors, loyal to Tshombe, attacked Swedish and Irish defenders. Fighting raged along the miles of runway, around the new built barracks, the hundreds of villas. Radio communications from the base ceased in the late afternoon.

In Elisabethville, Kibwe finessed his way out of custody by claiming that Belgian ultras controlled Tshombe. Only he, Kibwe said, could persuade Tshombe to stop the fighting. O'Brien, under serious strain and having trouble seeing the Katangese as anything other than Belgian puppets, allowed the vice president to leave. Kibwe seemed cheerful as he drove away. His biggest complaint was that Indian soldiers had put too much sugar in his tea.

Roger Jaspar and his son had escaped the UN armoured car at the radio station after a wild dash through Elisabethville's back gardens. On 14 September, they tried to get Radio Katanga back on the air with the help of an elderly amateur radio enthusiast living on the Chaussée de Kasenga. As machine guns fired in the distance, the Flamand invited them to take his transmitter.

'I have been here more than thirty years,' he told Jaspar. 'I am more Katangese than Belgian. Now is not the time for me to abandon this beautiful country.'[4]

In the house of another sympathiser in the Bel Air district, Jaspar and his son ate a late breakfast listening to Michel Tomberlaine broadcast the UN version of events. At three o'clock that afternoon, the transmitter powered by a generator in the garage, Jaspar went on the air reading a bulletin supplied by a Belgian ultra:

> This is Radio Free Katanga. We have a message from President Tshombe. Contrary to the information from foreign radio stations, the Katangese government proclaims that the President can be found among his people. He is neither imprisoned nor on the run and is personally directing the operation of total war against the United Nations.[5]

Few people heard the broadcast. But Captain Paul Ropagnol, Lieutenant Tony de Saint-Paul and their Katangese paracommandos were about to boost Tshombe's propaganda efforts by seizing the radio station at the College of St Francis.

A two-storey flat-roofed modernist construction in concrete, wood and glass, the College was located in an upmarket residential avenue where green lawns fought a losing battle with red Katangese soil. Irish troops had occupied the building in the early morning. At 14.30 a local Belgian woman sent over her husband with boiling water for them to make tea. He returned at 15.00 with another man in civilian clothes: Tony de Saint-Paul. The Frenchman spoke good English and tried to persuade Lieutenant Ryan's Irishmen that Ropagnol had them surrounded.

'I'm here to save your lives,' said de Saint-Paul. 'You stand no chance.'[6]

Ropagnol ramped up the pressure with a phone call to the Irish. A priest translated as the Frenchman threatened to overrun the building. Lieutenant Ryan went outside to talk with him, leaving de Saint-Paul a hostage. Ryan was shaken when Ropagnol barked an order and nearby buildings bristled with Katangese soldiers aiming their FN FALs. The twenty-three Irish UN soldiers surrendered. Will Vermeulen, a colleague of Roger Jaspar, used the Radio College transmitter to get on the air and broadcast Tshombe propaganda.

Outside, Ropagnol and de Saint-Paul had to pull the lead tight to stop their paracommandos executing the prisoners.

'We aren't angels,' Ropagnol told them, 'but we are still soldiers.'[7]

The Katangese glared and rubbed their thumbs along their bayonets.


The Fouga jet made its first attack at Jadotville that afternoon. The Irish troops heard a whining noise high in the sky and saw a black dot approaching. As the jet got closer, the whining widened to a scream.

Pierre Magain had joined the Belgian Air Force as an 18-year-old and got out in 1959 after a five-year contract. He knew Katanga from his training days at Kamina airbase. One of Marissal's men approached him with an offer in early 1961. Magain signed the contract and joined the secession.

Magain had a bad temper. After a few drinks he would curse the UN, the Americans and anyone else within range. Sober, he was more cautious, avoiding newsmen and refusing to be photographed. Magain's fellow pilots in the Katangese Air Force (Avikat) thought him strange but talented. When three Fouga training jets arrived to join Avikat's fleet of light aircraft and a pair of battered DC-3s, Magain was one of the pilots chosen to fly them.

Rumpunch decapitated Tshombe's air force. Its commander, Belgian Victor Volant, and his pilots headed home, leaving most of their aeroplanes in the hands of the UN. Captain Ngosa, a recently trained Katangese pilot, took command of the remainder. Chain-smoking Belgian José Delin, officially Ngosa's advisor although everyone thought he was really in charge, fuelled up the remaining Fouga and ordered Magain into the air.

On his attack run over Jadotville, Magain's machine gun chewed up the Irish trenches, spraying red dirt on the defenders. His bombs burst sewer pipes leading to the villas. Then the Fouga whined away, heading for Elisabethville, where Magain bombed the Lido and a Baluba refugee camp.

The Irish situation got worse when de Clary shut off water and electricity to the UN villas. Quinlan ordered all available water to be stockpiled in containers, baths and sinks. It turned stagnant. Overflowing toilets swarmed with flies. The Irish burned in the sun and stank in the heat. Quinlan radioed Elisabethville, asking for details of the relief column.

Morale increased slightly when two Belgian mercenaries, Michel Paucheum and Pierre van der Weger, stumbled into the Irish front lines. Fröberg interrogated the pair and found them bitter at a Frenchman who had directed them, deliberately they said, into UN positions. The whining of the returning Fouga interrupted the questions. Fröberg and the mercenaries scrambled under a table as Magain strafed the villa.

Conflict between French and Belgians was not the only problem facing the attackers. The Katangese had taken heavy losses and strains were showing. A mercenary called Wrenacre, a veteran of the Free French and then the Foreign Legion, which he joined after killing his wife's lover, had died near Jadotville. Other mercenaries suspected he had been killed by a Katangese officer in a row about command.

De Clary stalked through the bush trying to boost gendarme morale, claiming that victory was near. Lasimone organised his men around the road from Elisabethville, waiting for the UN relief column.

At nine o'clock on the evening of 14 September, listeners rolling the radio dial for a Katangese station heard Will Vermeulen broadcasting from the Radio College. '… and therefore, President Tshombe has beaten the United Nations. Here is Radio Katanga, here is President Tshombe …' Then some confusion, static. 'We are obliged to stop our transmission. But it is not impossible you will hear us again soon.'[8]

An Irish car patrol had rolled along avenue Wangermee near the Radio College, the whole street blacked out by a power cut, to check on Lieutenant Ryan's men. Tracer fire and anti-tank rounds erupted from gendarmes at the side of the road. De Saint-Paul knocked out an armoured car with a bazooka as the other vehicles accelerated away. The car's crew, led by Commandant Pat Cahalane, scrambled out, deaf from the explosion, and surrendered.

As bullets spat across the avenue, the armoured car suddenly lumbered into life. Two Irishmen remained inside, one badly wounded. Bullets bounced off its hide as the car accelerated down the avenue and disappeared into the night. It would be discovered the next day lodged in a drainage ditch at the side of boulevard Elisabeth surrounded by 9mm shell casings. The UN recovered one

body but the driver, Trooper Patrick Mullins, had disappeared. He would never
be seen again. An abandoned gendarme position was near the scene. Local
whites muttered that Baluba were not the only cannibals in Katanga.


On the afternoon of 15 September, Lieutenant Bob Denard arrived at Faulques's
HQ wrapped in bandages and carrying papers identifying him as a Belgian civilian injured crocodile hunting. The Katangese were using ambulances, and even
hearses, to get past UN patrols on the long drive from the Rhodesian border.

'Sometimes I drive ambulances and sometimes they contain automatic rifles
and not people,' one man told journalist Reg Shay.[9]

Denard ripped off his bandages and went to find Faulques. He found him
among barking walkie-talkies, maps and cigarette smoke. For once the chain-
smoking Frenchman seemed happy to see Denard. He waved at a map of Katanga.

'The peacekeepers are losing the battle,' Faulques said.[10]

It seemed that way. The Katangese had Jadotville and Kamina under siege,
UN posts in Elisabethville surrounded, the Radio College in their hands and
Kibwe free. The vice president had joined Tshombe and Munongo in Kipushi.
From the mining town, Munongo contacted O'Brien to demand the release
of the two Belgian mercenaries captured at Jadotville. O'Brien ignored him.
He was more worried about Faulques.

'The French are brave, resolute, and fanatical,' a UN official said to a journalist. 'Most of them are Algerian extremists of the type who think de Gaulle is a
communist. They're tough babies.'[11]

Faulques was lucky the UN could not see the chaos on the Katangese
side. Journalists spotted white mercenaries screaming with rage as their black
troops refused to follow them into battle. Hastily promoted Katangese officers
floundered in combat, undertrained and overconfident. De Clary was reporting
insubordination and even mutiny among gendarmes in Jadotville.

'Their relations are like those between labour and management, with military decisions subject to negotiation,' said a visiting journalist. 'Moreover,
when an attack is under way, the Katangese will move forward as long as their
officers do. But as soon as an officer gets hit, the whole unit is apt to retreat
in panic.'[12]

Faulques sent Denard to join Ropagnol's unit, fresh from its triumph at
the Radio College. Elisabethville's streets were deserted, its jacaranda trees
splintered from shrapnel. Abandoned UN armoured cars littered the streets
where their crews had run from ambushes. Denard joined Ropagnol and de
Saint-Paul in an attack on a group of Irish UN troops in a nearby villa.

Katangese troops moved around the perimeter to make their numbers appear
greater. They shot out the windows and de Saint-Paul called on the men to

surrender. The Irish emerged with their hands up, fooled into believing they were facing a larger force. The Frenchmen made a point of sharing their food, getting scarce by this time, with the Irish. The paracommandos watched, fingers on triggers.

Commandant Pat Cahalane, the senior Irish officer taken prisoner after the Radio College ambush, and another twenty-five Irish prisoners were sitting in a remote farmhouse 40 miles outside Elisabethville. Faulques drove over to see them and made a good impression by ordering the gendarme guard to return the Irishmen's watches. He failed to draw them out about the UN military situation, not helped by his poor English (Mobutu was a 'blacking fuck bastard'), and demanded Cahalane sign a statement condemning the Radio Katanga massacre.[13] Cahalane refused. Faulques turned aggressive but the Irishman would not change his mind.

Munongo had a better use for the prisoners: he wanted to exchange them for Katangese. His gendarmes stopped journalist Hans Germani, a Wehrmacht veteran and well-known secession sympathiser, as he crossed the border from Rhodesia in a Citroën 2CV. They asked him to tell the United Nations that Munongo would execute Cahalane unless all Katangese prisoners were freed.

Germani drove into Elisabethville through the slag heaps of the Union Minière district in the south. He found Captain Art Magennis, brother of an Irish journalist he knew, in the Hôtel Léopold II. Magennis passed on the message to O'Brien on the one remaining telephone line at the post office. O'Brien ordered him to deliver a reply personally to Munongo: the UN would not negotiate.

Germani blindfolded Magennis and the pair drove out of Elisabethville to make contact with Faulques' HQ.

'We were only about a kilometre out of the city when a smell of burning started coming from the bloody car,' said Magennis. 'I said that the clutch was burning and Germani turned to me and asked, how did I know? I looked at him and said "What the hell do you think the smell is?" The next thing the clutch burned through and the car stopped.'[14]

They borrowed another car but only made it as far as a nearby farm occupied by mercenaries, who promised to pass O'Brien's reply to Munongo. They seemed confident of victory.

On Saturday 16 September, Magain's Fouga attacked a DC-3 transporting wounded UN personnel out of Kamina then bombed the airfield and went on to strafe the Irish at Jadotville. Later he attacked Elisabethville airport, preventing American Globemasters carrying supplies for the UN from landing. The Fouga blasted out all the glass in the departure lounge and destroyed a number of aeroplanes.

'I always believed in air power,' said UN administrator Wayne Fredericks, 'but I never thought I'd see the day when one plane would stop the United States and the whole United Nations.'[15]

As the bullets kept flying, the UN overcame its initial reluctance to amplify the fighting. It requested Ethiopian Sabre jets to stop Magain's Fouga. Rhodesia threatened to shoot them down if the Sabres entered its airspace. Emperor Haile Selassie sent them anyway but the British impounded the jets in Uganda for alleged technical reasons; Harold Macmillan's government could not afford to lose the support of Katanga-sympathising Tory MPs. The Fouga continued to control the skies. A helicopter managed to deliver supplies to the Irish at Jadotville before Magain's jet whined out of the clouds and chased it away. Quinlan's men had little ammunition and less water.

Two UN companies set out from Elisabethville to relieve the Irish. Lasimone's men ambushed them on the road. The battle lasted most of the day. Magain's Fouga dive-bombed the UN troops. Eventually the relief column turned back.

In the late afternoon, Quinlan authorised Lars Fröberg to negotiate a ceasefire.

By now, Elisabethville's civilians had learned to stay indoors. The city had only sporadic electricity and water. Guests in the Léopold II brushed their teeth with Simba beer. Prisoners had escaped their camps in Elisabethville and were looting the suburbs. Nervy UN troops were trigger-happy. Anyone on the streets was at risk.

Roger Jaspar and his teenage son Michel were driving through the deserted streets of Bel Air when a UN patrol opened fire. Jaspar was wounded and the car crashed. Michel dragged his father to cover. A friend following behind managed to load them into his vehicle and they sped off, blood pooling on the floor mats. Jaspar would spent the rest of Morthor in a hospital awaiting repatriation to Belgium.

Jim Biddulph, a Rhodesian journalist, couriered other journalists' copy back to the border.[16] A Swiss financier linked to Tshombe's government, with a suitcase of bearer bonds, grabbed the passenger seat on Biddulph's last trip out of Elisabethville. Swedish UN troops turned an anti-aircraft gun on them and blew the car apart. They claimed it had failed to stop at a roadblock. The Swiss was killed and Biddulph so seriously injured that surgeons had to slice bone off his hip to patch the hole in his skull.

On Sunday, Magain's Fouga attacked Kamina, still holding out against Chief Kasongo Nyembo's Baluba warriors, and fired on the control tower. At midday, Magain reappeared and bombed the runway, burning a DC-4 into a metal skeleton and wounding two airmen. Shortly after, news came from Jadotville that the Irish had surrendered to de Clary's troops. The brief ceasefire Fröberg had organised broke down when Irish troops blew the leg off a mercenary approaching their lines. De Clary demanded surrender. Quinlan had no choice.

'More than two hundred prisoners,' Faulques said to his staff. 'They have an exchange rate better than gold!'[17]

Munongo was more restrained but pleased that O'Brien would now have to negotiate.

'We are trying to find a solution,' he told journalists at Kipushi airport. 'We think it will not be too difficult.'[18]

Victor Rosez celebrated when he heard the news. For the last four days he had been fighting in the streets of Elisabethville. The UN had not approached Muke's house so the teenager and his crew set out in search of them. They dodged around Elisabethville firing on any peacekeeping vehicle they saw.

'All the way along there was a heavy shooting that didn't stop,' said Rosez. 'We broke some Second World War records in using (light) ammunition.'[19]

At midnight, the British consul contacted O'Brien with the news that Tshombe wanted to discuss a ceasefire. Hammarskjöld got the message in Léopoldville while listening to an Indian military band playing a Scottish funeral dirge. Advised by British diplomats, he agreed to meet Tshombe in Ndola, Northern Rhodesia on 17 September.

Ground crew at Ndjili airport prepped a DC-6B for the Secretary General's flight to Rhodesia. It would never reach its destination.

# 17

# THE LAST FLIGHT OF THE ALBERTINA

Dag Hammarskjöld's Mysterious Death, 18 September 1961

For one egotistical moment, Jerry Puren thought the crowds were waiting for him. Then reality hit and he was just another passenger descending the mobile stairs of a South African Airways passenger jet, its engines still cooling, into the crowds of reporters, UN officials and Katangese politicians swarming Ndola airport. A newsman stopped him for a quote on the situation in Elisabethville.

'I am ready to fight to the end for Katanga,' said Puren, 'and to avenge many of my colleagues who have been killed during the fighting'.[1]

Tall and bald, with a neat moustache and legs thin as cigarettes, Puren was a used car dealer from Durban in his late thirties. He joined the South African Air Force as a navigator during the war, flying over North Africa and the Middle East. After Germany's surrender, he transferred to the RAF and spent the next decade transporting British soldiers around what was left of the empire. Then back to civilian life. Puren married, had two daughters and a dull job. His marriage cracked up. By early 1961 he was a divorced businessman telling war stories to cronies in Durban bars. He directed any spare energy into a private airfield built by locals, reminding himself of the old days.

'The call to arms came casually, almost accidentally,' he said. 'A contact in the South African Defence Force HQ mentioned in passing that a Belgian chappie was in the country recruiting for someone called Tshombe in a place called Katanga. Would I be interested?'[2]

The Belgian chappie was Carlos Huyghé, then helping Russell-Cargill set up the Compagnie Internationale. Puren became a lieutenant and escorted a cohort of South African volunteers to Elisabethville. He was lucky to be in the capital when Malaysian troops swooped at Nyunzu. An officer without a command, he used his RAF experience to get a job as a bombardier with the thirty aeroplanes in four squadrons that made up Volant's Katangese Air Force.

Puren pushed through the Ndola crowds into the airport lounge and found Katangese officials deep in conversation with Max Glasspool and Gurkitz the Hungarian, two Avikat pilots. They explained the circus outside. Dag Hammarskjöld was on his way from Léopoldville to meet Tshombe. A cease-fire was possible.

Katanga had given the UN a bloody snout. A deal now could secure the country's future.

At 16.51 on Sunday 17 September, a Transair Sweden DC-6B took off from Ndjili airport. Nicknamed the 'Albertina', it had enough fuel for thirteen hours in the air.

There had been some alarm on the tarmac that morning when engineers found a bullet hole in one of the engine exhaust pipes picked up on an earlier flight over Elisabethville. Engineers replaced the pipe and cleared the aeroplane.

Captain Per Hallonquist, an experienced pilot and head of Transair's navigation division, headed the Albertina's six-man crew. American Sergeant Harold Julien provided security with a three-man team. They had searched the Albertina's interior before allowing Hammarskjöld and his retinue on board.

Hammarskjöld should have been in New York.[3] His flight home, scheduled for the end of the previous week out of Brazzaville, had been cancelled when Abbé Fulbert Youlou could not guarantee its safety because of the fighting in Katanga. The Secretary General stayed in Léopoldville. Then Conor Cruise O'Brien passed on Tshombe's offer of peace talks. The Irishman volunteered to accompany Hammarskjöld to Northern Rhodesia but was told he would not be needed. The Secretary General already had a five-person entourage, including Alice Lalande, a Canadian-born secretary, and advisor Heinrich Wieschhoff, still hoarse with the bronchitis that had nearly kept him home.

The aeroplane took off. Hammarskjöld opened a book while the others busied themselves with paperwork or small talk. The Secretary General was working on a Swedish translation of Martin Bubber's *Ich und Du*, a German book of religious philosophy published back in 1923 and given to him by the author.[4] The Swede was a deeply Christian man, a throwback in a country that regarded itself as coldly rational. The 56-year-old had kept his views quiet through a long career as a civil servant. His reputation as a competent, apolitical technocrat got him elected UN Secretary General in 1953 after Norwegian Trygve Lie resigned.

Some believed Hammarskjöld kept more than his religion quiet. Conor Cruise O'Brien liked to gossip that the Swede was homosexual, a diagnosis based on Hammarskjöld's dislike of women.

'At one of my last meetings with him – in New York, before I left for Katanga – he had flown into a rage because there was a large picture of Jacqueline

Kennedy on the front page,' said O'Brien.'The attention the media were paying to "that woman" was, he thought, preposterous. His normally pale face turned red and his voice shook. This was the only time I had ever seen him manifest emotions about anything.'[5]

Thousands of feet above the bitchy rumours, Hammarskjöld wrote in flowing handwriting on a yellow legal pad. The theme of *Ich und Du* was that all human relationships eventually bring us into contact with God.

The Albertina set course for Ndola.

Jerry Puren was only in Northern Rhodesia because of a roadblock in Elisabethville twenty-one days earlier. In the early morning of 28 August, he had been making his way to the capital's airport in a borrowed car for another bombing mission. Gurkitz dozed in the passenger seat.

Puren's first duties when he joined Avikat had been to shower the area around Elisabethville with pamphlets announcing Tshombe's release. Then it was raids on Baluba villages, the bombs falling from the makeshift racks welded to the underside of his aeroplane. The Belgian commanders assured Puren that it was necessary war work. Later, in smoky Elisabethville bars, he heard stories of bloody women and children crawling into Katangese guard posts begging for help.

It was four in the morning when Puren drove out to Elisabethville airport, hungover from too many Simba beers the night before. The streets were empty. He passed Moïse Tshombe talking with a crowd of gendarmes outside the post office. The president looked tense. A UN checkpoint blocked route Don Bosco. Irish troops hauled the pair out of the car and pushed them into a lorry. Operation Rumpunch had begun.

'For my part, I was quite calm,' said Puren. 'It was as if all the tensions and conjectures of the past months were destined to end this way. Arrest by the UN. It was almost a relief that the situation had been crystallised; the battle lines finally and irrevocably drawn.'[6]

Under guard at Kamina airbase, he discussed escape with Jan van Risseghem, commander of the Katangese Air Force's Combat Squadron and one of the few pilots apart from Magain able to fly the Fouga. The Belgian mercenary had little enthusiasm for the idea.

'The surrounding tribes are hostile, this base alone is huge and crawling with UN troops,' he said. 'Besides, why escape? Just accept, the party is over.'[7]

Puren recruited a Belgian pilot called Verloo who had a fiancée in Elisabethville. They slipped out of the barracks on the third night and headed for freedom. Kamina base was so huge that it took them two and a half hours to reach the perimeter fence. Early next morning, they emerged from the bush and headed for the nearest town. The local Sûreté man gave out fake identification and priest costumes, which got them south to Kolwezi, a scab of red dirt and smoky white factory chimneys.

Puren received a letter of thanks from Tshombe and two weeks' leave in South Africa. He arrived in Johannesburg on 12 September. Morthor interrupted his holiday. Five days later, Puren was in Ndola airport lounge waiting for Hammarskjöld to arrive so connecting flights could resume to Katanga.

Gurkitz told him he should not have bothered escaping. After being expelled to Brussels by the UN, the Hungarian had flown straight back to Rhodesia. The Belgians made no attempt to stop him.

The secession had transformed Ndola, a mesh of colonial bungalows and copper mine scaffolding, into a transport hub. It had road and air links to Kipushi, a Katangese town so close to the border half its airfield sat in Rhodesian territory. Anyone wanting to visit the secession flew in from Salisbury and caught a ride north.

The company of light infantry who guarded the border ignored the daily parade of journalists and mercenaries. They only stirred when armed groups crossed the border the other way.

'We soon learned that any nervously chattering, disorganised and white-or light blue-helmeted group we encountered were likely to be Swedes or Ethiopians,' said Brigadier John 'Digger' Essex-Clark. 'The French mercenaries would remain stock still and threateningly quiet in their camouflaged uniforms, as would the Indian Army Gurkhas.'[8]

The Rhodesians stayed away from the French after they enlisted a mercenary doctor to help one of their own, hurt in a shooting accident. The Frenchman's primitive surgery, learned under a flickering bulb in a tunnel at Dien Bien Phu, did not save the patient. The incident strained their sympathies for Tshombe's regime. A Union Minière emissary turned up and tried to bribe the entire company to join the Katangese Gendarmes with a suitcase of cash. Essex-Clark told the man ('obsequious, mousy and shabby') to piss off and not come back.[9]

The inhabitants of Ndola had fewer scruples about helping Katanga. The landlord of the Elephant and Castle Hotel, Len Catchpole, a cheerful cockney who ran the place with the help of his boss-eyed brother Ken, the local hangman ('Met me bruvver? 'E jerks them to Jesus!'), made good money smuggling weapons over the border to Katanga.[10] Catchpole, a former mayor of Ndola who once lost a drinking competition with an elephant to promote his pub, was a born entrepreneur. He put up mercenaries in his hotel, arranged transport and, on one occasion, smuggled weapons into Elisabethville in a lorryload of coffins.

'I do know that no one – no one – was going to search the wheels of either Len or his brother when they crossed the border either way,' said John Trevelyn. 'It was just not done. Both men had close relationships with police officers in Ndola at Superintendent and Special Branch level. It was really an extension of what used to happen back in the UK in those days – the unspoken word – the wink and nod.'[11]

The town's status as a back door into Katanga meant plenty of mercenaries hanging around the airport on 17 September, among them former Compagnie Internationale commander Richard Browne. He was missing his moustache and had grey dye in his hair, the remnants of a disguise adopted in a failed attempt to re-enter Katanga in June.[12] Every time he slipped over the border, UN troops scooped him up and repatriated him. Browne protested that he only wanted to collect his personal possessions and sort out back pay. Carlos Huyghé sat with him in the Ndola airport lounge. The Belgian had been kicked out of the country on 5 August with barely enough notice to sell his possessions in the newspaper small ads: 'Expelled by the UN; refrigerator for sale.'[13]

On the other side of the lounge, Puren, Glasspool and Gurkitz huddled together and talked about the significance of the peace talks.

'History is unfolding,' said Puren.[14]

At 21.02 Léopoldville time, after four hours in the air, Captain Hollonquist contacted Salisbury Flight Information Service for a weather report. He also asked for the estimated time of arrival of a DC-4 carrying Lord Lansdowne to Ndola. The 58-year-old Lansdowne, British Joint Parliamentary Under-Secretary of State for Foreign Affairs, had flown ahead of Hammarskjöld on the orders of the British government to smooth arrangements for the meeting with Tshombe.

Hollonquist gave his estimated time of arrival as 23.35 (00.35 Ndola local time). The Albertina had another two and a half hours in the air, flying wide to avoid Katangese territory. The pilot made contact with Salisbury twice more. At 21.35, he announced that the Albertina was over the southern end of Lake Tanganyika and received the information that Lansdowne's aeroplane had just landed at Ndola. During the last communication, at 22.32 Léopoldville time, Salisbury handed over to Ndola control tower. There were a number of communications between tower and aeroplane over the next half hour. The ETA changed to 00.20 Ndola time.

It was close to midnight when the Albertina approached the North Rhodesian airport. At 23.57 Ndola time, Hallonquist requested permission to descend. At 00.10, the aeroplane made visual contact with the airfield. It was a clear night hazed with mist from a local cobalt refinery.

'Your lights in sight, overhead Ndola, descending,' Hallonquist told the tower. Ndola asked him to report when the Albertina reached 6,000ft.
'Roger.'[15]

Jerry Puren was among the crowd waiting at the base of the control tower in the chilly night. They had been there for several hours. Someone said they could hear an aeroplane engine and conversation died as the crowd strained to listen. High in the air above Ndola the red anti-collision light at the top of the DC-6B's tail fin flashed and the approach began.

At 00.30, Lansdowne's pilot contacted the control tower to request permission to take off. Lord Lansdowne, a veteran of the Royal Scots Guards with a Croix de Guerre, had orders from the British government to be on his way to Salisbury before Hammarskjöld arrived. London wanted to keep its role in the peace talks discreet. The tower admitted it had lost contact with the Albertina twenty minutes previously. Five minutes later, it gave permission for take-off and the DC-4 headed for Salisbury with a worried Lansdowne on board.

Airport manager John Williams discussed the overdue aeroplane with Lord Alport, the British High Commissioner for Rhodesia. Alport seemed unconcerned. 'The reason for breaking off contact with Ndola', said Alport:

> might be that Mr Hammarskjöld's plane had been informed by one of the United States attaché's planes on Ndola airfield that Lord Lansdowne had only just taken off and that, in view of Mr Hammarskjold's expressed wish, the Léopoldville plane had gone off for a short time to allow a definite interval between Lord Lansdowne's departure and Mr Hammarskjöld's arrival.[16]

He also suggested Hammarskjöld was transmitting a message or phone conversation from the Albertina and would not land until it had finished. Williams agreed with his distinguished guest. No need for alarm. The group at the base of the control tower, including Jerry Puren and Glasspool, numbed by the cold and tired of waiting, made their way to the nearby Savoy Hotel. Tshombe waited in his room at a local villa for the telephone call that Hammarskjöld had landed.

As the time crept towards one o'clock in the morning, Lord Alport, now less sure, suggested that Hammarskjöld might have diverted his flight. At 01.15, Williams telephoned the local police and asked if any explosions or crashes had been reported in the area. None had. He contacted the crew at Salisbury tower and asked if they had any information about the Albertina. They did not.

By 01.50, Williams had woken from Alport's spell and sent a priority signal to Salisbury asking for information on flight SE-BDY's whereabouts. Salisbury tried to contact Léopoldville for information, sending the request via a Johannesburg teleprinter, but got no answer. Ndola issued an INCERFA – an alert indicating concern about an aeroplane and its passengers. Williams hung around the cold and empty airport for another hour. At 03.00, he went to his bed in the Rhodes Hotel and ten minutes later the airport shut down for the night.

As Williams was drifting off to sleep, two policemen knocked at his door. One of their colleagues, Assistant Inspector van Wyk, had seen an aeroplane fly overhead at twenty past midnight. It flew out of view then a flash had lit up the sky. They had patrols in Land Rovers looking over the area. An exhausted Williams told them there was nothing that could be done until daylight and went back to bed. Police patrols driving through the bush in the African night found nothing.

Ndola airport reopened just before six o'clock on the morning of 18 September. A little before seven, Williams sent another INCERFA alert to Salisbury with additional information about the flash of light in the sky.

At 06.53, Salisbury finally woke up to the seriousness of the situation and issued a DETRESFA – the aeroplane in distress signal. They copied in Ndola, Elisabethville and Johannesburg. At 07.44, Salisbury made contact with Léopoldville by radio. The Congo capital had no knowledge of the Albertina's location. Salisbury ordered the Ndola police to start an official search by air and ground.

The first aeroplanes did not take off until 10 a.m., flying north and south of the airport. Police searched the bush in Land Rovers and on foot as the sun rose in the sky. Some time after 14.30, an African charcoal burner called Mazibisa contacted the authorities. He had seen an aeroplane wreck out in the bush.

At 15.10, a search aeroplane spotted a plane wreckage west of the airport. Almost simultaneously, Rhodesian police reached the site on the ground. It was the Albertina. Seventy per cent of the aeroplane was molten metal. Papers, smashed tree trunks and personal possessions, including the charred remains of a pack of cards, littered the ground. Only the American Harold Julien survived the crash. He had serious burns and had been lying in the sun since dawn. The other six crew and nine passengers were dead. Their smashed wristwatches put the crash time at between 00.11 and 00.13.

The police found Dag Hammarskjöld lying on his back near the wreck with a fistful of grass in his hand, dead from massive internal injuries.

The only people ever charged in connection with Dag Hammarskjöld's death were Ledson Daka and his friend Moyo, two black Rhodesian charcoal burners who investigated the Albertina's wreck with Mazibisa. They looted Alice Lalande's cryptography machine, thinking it was a typewriter. The local police caught them trying to sell it in a local market. A judge gave them two years.

The DC-6B had crashed as it turned to begin its approach. Its landing gear was down. During the turn, the Albertina came into contact with the treetops, banked slightly to the left and slid at a low angle into the trees. Propellers thrashed branches into wood chip. The left wing got ripped away and the amputated stub smashed into the ground by a 2.5m termite hill. The nose cone jammed into the hill and the aeroplane cartwheeled over.

Five tons of fuel poured out of the broken engines and caught light. Ammunition and flares inside the aircraft exploded. A gas tank blasted high into the air. Hammarskjöld was thrown free of the burning wreckage, probably because he had been standing at the moment of first contact with the treetops. His was the only corpse not burned. The final resting place of flight SE-BDY was a clearing smashed in the trees 9½ miles west of Ndola airport.

Harold Julien lasted five days in intensive care. He drifted in and out of consciousness. In rare moments of lucidity, he muttered about a crash and then an explosion, or an explosion and then a crash. Hammarskjöld saying 'Go back!' The pain … Morphine. Then he died, leaving investigators barely more informed.[17]

'It wasn't such a big deal, as planes crash all the time in Africa and I had no idea who Dag was,' said John Trevelyn. 'The general opinion at the time from people who were at the wreck is that it was a simple pilot error.'[18]

The UN and Rhodesian Federation investigators who swarmed Ndola in the aftermath were less sure. But the DC-6B did not carry a flight recorder and the crash site offered no conclusive evidence. Some investigators thought the Albertina could have been brought down by catastrophic mechanical failure, atmospheric conditions or pilot error, possibly involving mistaken altitude. They thought it significant that the Ndola page was missing from the Albertina's navigation manual. Others believed one of several mutually contradictory conspiracy theories: failed hijacking, ground-to-air rocket, bomb on board, interception by another aircraft. Magain's Fouga was top suspect for the last scenario, with the narrative of Katangese air superiority fresh in everyone's minds. Whatever brought down the Albertina, it happened so suddenly the crew had no time to even begin a distress call.

Locals came forward to report what they had seen, confusing investigators with blends of truth and fiction. Northern Rhodesians were agitating for independence and some stories seemed designed to embarrass Salisbury. Investigators noted that a local leftist union organiser with no love for imperialism, coincidentally also a Swede, was encouraging black Rhodesians to approach the authorities. His motives were questioned. For every local who claimed to have seen two aeroplanes in the sky, another swore a squadron of Rhodesian government jets had taken off from Ndola to shoot down Hammarskjöld or that a group of uniformed paramilitaries had blown up the Albertina after it hit the ground.

Even apparently reliable witnesses had their stories picked to pieces. An African charcoal burner called Buleni claimed to have seen a smaller aeroplane directly behind Hammarskjöld's DC-6B on its approach.

Investigator:'Could you clearly see this other aircraft above the big one you saw?'

Buleni:'Yes we did. It was a small aeroplane.'

Investigator:'Did it have lights on?'

Buleni:'Yes, it had lights.'

Investigator:'What kind of lights?'

Buleni:'Actually, I saw one red light.'

Investigator:'On the smaller plane?'

Buleni:'Correct.'[19]

Experts claimed the charcoal burner was describing the DC-6B's anti-collision tail fin light.

Other theories failed to stand up. A hijacking? Bullets found in two Swedish security men turned out to be their own ammunition, which had exploded in the heat. All bodies had been accounted for and the Albertina had no extra passengers. Pilot error? The Ndola page of a navigation information manual was missing from its loose-leaf binder because it had been removed for closer study and then burned up in the crash. Mechanical failure? All engines were running at the time of the crash and had been increasing power. The altimeters were correctly set. Rocket, bombing, interception? Despite the suspicions of Transair's chief engineer Bo Virving, the Albertina had not sustained any combat damage. Magain's Fouga did not have the range to reach Ndola and return to Kolwezi, and the Belgian never flew at night. Other pilots claimed it would have been impossible for another aircraft to intercept the DC-6B in the dark African night sky. Most importantly, no one had a motive for killing Hammarskjöld.

'I never made any secret of the fact that my sympathies were with Tshombe,' said Rhodesian Prime Minister Welensky:

> but I would say that if there were two men in Central Africa, who had need for Hammarskjöld to stay alive, it was Tshombe and myself, because I have always believed that the thing that sparked off the attack on the post office and really brought about the bloodshed that developed, were the attitudes

of two men: C.C. O'Brien and Khiari the Indian representative. Neither Tshombe or I had any reason for wanting the death of Hammarskjöld.[20]

The Rhodesian investigation established that the Albertina had crashed because it was flying dangerously low. The final report suggested that someone in the cockpit misread the altimeter and did not realise how close the plane was to the ground, or that a ridge had temporarily blotted out the airport lights, disconcerting Hallonquist enough for the aeroplane to rapidly lose height. Perhaps the stress of flying a distinguished passenger around a warzone had got to the pilot.

The Rhodesian Board of Investigation officially adopted a verdict of pilot error. It was the least unconvincing option. The UN agreed. Bo Virving protested. No one really accepted the verdict except for Carl von Rosen, Hammarskjöld's regular pilot, who missed the final flight because of illness. He re-flew the Albertina's route and blamed Hallonquist.

On 19 September, Moïse Tshombe drove over the border into Katanga. He sent a message to the UN through British embassy staff. He still wanted to negotiate a ceasefire.

Back in Ndola, the airport slowly returned to being a staging post for mercenaries, arms dealers and journalists. No one was paying much attention in late September, when a short, tubby Flemish Belgian burned brown as tree bark from years in the sun walked down the metal stairs of a passenger jet and lit a cigarette. Jean Schramme was just too late for the fighting in Elisabethville.

# 18

# *UN AFRICAIN BLANC*

## Jean Schramme and Temporary Peace in Katanga

He did not look like a warlord. Shy, unassuming, weak around the mouth, thinning light hair brushed back. Jean Schramme came from a well-off Bruges family, his father a lawyer, his uncle something to do with administration in the Belgian Congo. A stuffed leopard that guarded the staircase at his uncle's home was the start of an enthusiasm for Africa, its stiff fur a tactile connection to a country thousands of miles away.

In 1947, 18-year-old Schramme left Bruges's canals and barges, its medieval churches spiking the clouds, men in mackintoshes trudging through the rain, houses rising out of the river. He went to the Congo.

His family had secured an apprenticeship with an old planter near Léopoldville. Schramme stepped off a Sabena airliner and fell in love with the land where mornings sprang up in fiery purple and the nights fell like a black-out curtain. The oppressive humidity sapped the spirit of some settlers but Schramme found it invigorating. He proved a quick study and at 22 bought his own plantation at Bafwakwandji, Orientale province, where he grew crops, processed oil and looked down on the Belgian merchants and government employees who managed only a few years in the Congo before flying home with full pockets and a suntan.

Military life gave the first sign of steel beneath Schramme's doughy exterior. He proved a good soldier during compulsory service with the Force Publique and tested himself further by transferring to the paracommandos, where he leapt out of aeroplanes over the unending green of the jungle, wind frothing the treetops.

Back at the plantation, he reorganised the estate on military lines. His hundreds of black workers now had to drag themselves out of bed at six in the morning to the sound of a bugle call. Their day was carefully timetabled. Schramme worked hardest of all, inspecting all corners of his huge plantation until the early hours before snatching a few hours' sleep and starting all over again.

Like many colonists who invested heart and soul in the Congo, Jean Schramme thought he knew the country better than the natives. For him, the *évolués* were betrayers of ancient tribal traditions, their western suits and ties worn to flatter white men by impersonating them. Schramme was unashamed to be a paternalist. His workers called him *père*. He called himself *un Africain blanc* (a white African).

In the months before independence, tribal drums kept him awake as they beat messages through the night. During the day, parties of Lumumba propagandists tried to politicise Schramme's workers. He welded metal sheeting to his lorry as makeshift armour and hid a sub-machine gun in the door panel. On 30 June 1960, Schramme gave his workers two days off then carried on as usual. Ripples from the army mutiny soon reached him. It started with trespassing on his land and the return of Lumumba's MNC men, but quickly escalated to sabotage and roadblocks. Schramme was arrested and dragged off to the local police station, only released when a mob of his estate workers forced the police to let him go.

The local Belgian administrator had fled to Uganda the day independence was declared so Schramme took on the responsibility of ferrying anxious settlers across the border. During one trip, he was arrested again, beaten and dumped in the holding pen. During his weeks there he claimed he saw eight white men hanged by the new Lumumbaist authorities.

'*Mon dieu, mon dieu …*'[1]

Maybe it happened. Not everything Schramme said could be trusted. Beneath the Belgian's mild shell beat the heart of a megalomaniac who would take credit for the sun rising in the morning if he could and never missed an opportunity to exaggerate the evil of his opponents.

Schramme bribed a guard, returned to his estate and made a successful break for Uganda at the end of the year. His cousins found him among the refugees in the British colony and begged him to return to Bruges. Schramme refused. In Uganda he had belatedly discovered Tshombe's declaration of independence for Katanga. Here was Schramme's Africa: blacks and whites fighting on the same side. With whites giving the orders.

Schramme made his way to Elisabethville, the streets full of stray dogs set free by fleeing Belgians, and enlisted as a second lieutenant. He did not impress many people, being remembered only as a quiet sycophant. In turn, the Belgian had little respect for the foreign mercenaries he met: 'The mercenaries seemed ridiculous to us, with their bullying looks.'[2]

In early spring, he joined Groupe Mobile E: sixty black and ten white soldiers under Lieutenant Robert Hugh Chalmers, a 28-year-old Scot who

called himself Louis Chamois, spoke terrible French and claimed to have fought
with Castro's revolutionaries in Cuba. Grubby, big-nosed, shaven-headed, his
uniform spattered with old blood stains, Chalmers set up camp in Niemba
village with his black sidekick, a deserter from the Royal African Rifles in a
dirty red fez.

'At first glance I saw I was dealing with a doubly crazy drunk,' said Schramme.
'He pretended to be an officer but was interested in nothing more than the
bottle and his revolver.'[3]

Chalmers' Groupe Mobile had a thuggish reputation. Frans Heymans, a
48-year-old Belgian settler from Bunia who had fought in Korea, tried to trans-
fer out in May 1961 and complained to the Katangese Sûreté of 'brutalities … at
the hands of Chamois and his men' he had suffered in the process.[4] Schramme
tried to ignore the chaos and do his job. Then Operation Rumpunch came along.

'The United Nations had imposed their orders on Tshombe,' said Schramme,
'not a single White in the Katangese administration or army. You cannot imag-
ine a more racist decision … We were being expelled based on the colour of
our skin.'[5]

Schramme was arrested by Swedish UN soldiers near Kongolo in the north
and flown to Léopoldville. The Swedes wanted to investigate Andre Cremer's
claims that Chalmers's men were hunting UN soldiers for Munongo. They
found no evidence and deported Schramme and his fellow mercenaries on
17 September. The Belgian preferred to tell people he had escaped from custody and smuggled himself onto a Brussels-bound Sabena jet with the help
of a priest.

Schramme spent several weeks under the grey skies of Bruges listening to
his family beg him to stay. He flew back via Rhodesia, picking up a copy of
*Quotations from Chairman Mao* in Salisbury. Know your enemy.

By the time he returned, Operation Morthor was over.

The fighting in Elisabethville had stuttered on for another day and a half
after Hammarskjöld's death. Magain made the most of it. On the morning of
18 September, the Fouga attacked Conor Cruise O'Brien as he stood talking
to journalists outside UN headquarters in Elisabethville. Journalist Sandy Gall
thought the Fouga 'about as dangerous as a wasp' and took his time finding
cover, but O'Brien dived into a trench and was crushed by a *Time* journalist
who landed on top of him.[6]

'That was the best shot of the war,' said a Congolese colonel, laughing down
into the tangle of legs and angry faces.[7]

Magain had already fired on a UN DC-3 at Kamina airport and come in low
over Kolwezi's long straight avenues to blow up a Union Minière fuel dump. The

attack on O'Brien was his last appearance over Katanga. A British MI6 officer called Neil Ritchie, posing as attaché to the High Commission in Salisbury, persuaded Avikat that grounding the Fouga would help peace talks along.[8]

Khiari and Tshombe met in the control tower at Ndola airport. The talks continued through the night. At 15.45 on 19 September, they agreed a provisional ceasefire for midnight the next day. The fighting in Elisabethville died down in anticipation. One of the last shots fired hit Frenchman Paul Ropagnol in the leg. The ceasefire held and peace was massaged from temporary to permanent, helped along when the UN declared itself neutral in the fight between Léopoldville and Elisabethville.

'Katanga's secession is purely the internal affair of the Congolese,' said Khiari.[9] He signed the official ceasefire document on a table draped with the Katangese flag.

A *Time* journalist estimated the dead from Morthor: forty-four UN troops, 152 Katangese police and soldiers, seventy-nine African civilians and fourteen European civilians.[10] Tshombe grinned for the cameras but was luckier than he knew. Before the peace deal was made public, President Kennedy had authorised the dispatch of American jets to take down Magain's Fouga. The fighting stopped before they set off.

Life in Elisabethville remained dangerous. Balubakat Jeunesse broke out of a chaotic UN refugee camp in the east of the city, set up to protect local Baluba from Munongo's police, and invaded nearby Bel Air, a suburb of small cottages in neat hibiscus gardens. The locals fled. Cars with mattresses strapped to their roofs, African servants balancing bundles on their heads, white men with hunting rifles patrolling barricades near the stadium. Smith Hempstone, *Chicago Daily News* reporter, was attacked in his car by a Baluba mob with machetes. Nearby Irish UN troops watched without interest as he barely escaped the blades.

Swedish UN troops eventually secured Bel Air. The bodies of locals, hacked apart by *pangas*, lay in the streets. The Swedes raided the home of the refugee camp strongman, a witchdoctor called Montefu, whom they blamed for the rampage. They found him standing over a bucket of amputated fingers, noses, ears and penises used for *dawa*, the magical charms many Congolese believed brought them luck or invincibility.

'These Jeunesses are very wicked people,' said the Swedish officer who led the raid.[11]

By late September, a kind of normality had returned to Elisabethville. The pavement tables outside the Palace Tavern filled up in early evening as the sun cooled in the sky. Young whites drank aperitifs, older ones café au lait. Katangese stuck to Simba beer. The Tavern's patrons stared across the square at the bullet-holed, sand-bagged post office, its clock run down at 6.55. Gurkhas stared back at them along their rifle barrels.

White mercenaries swaggered through the bars, a Simba beer in hand, boasting they had defeated the United Nations.

'The Irish and the Swedes make a lot of noise about being wonderful soldiers,' said a Belgian mercenary. 'But they're not worth a damn. All the Ethiopians are former criminals. The Gurkhas aren't human. They're not black and they're not white. They're macaques. Kennedy is a doubly filthy macaque. He's not only American; he's Irish too.'[12]

After a few more drinks the victory march turned sour. They complained that civilians seemed ungrateful, that Tshombe encouraged his officers to take credit for the victory, that jauntily arrogant gendarmes claimed 'Muke the Victorious', not Faulques, had stopped the peacekeepers.[13] Yav started wearing a colonel's uniform to Cabinet meetings.

The mercenaries did not understand that senior Katangese felt humiliated that their country owed its survival to white men. A Belgian medic with friends in high places told Faulques that the Cabinet had discussed sending the French mercenaries home, a course of action encouraged from the shadows by Vandewalle and other Mistebel leftovers. Tshombe was already investigating ways of reducing his dependence on whites. A scheme to recruit Zulu warriors from South Africa fell apart but hundreds of Lunda tribesmen from Northern Rhodesia crossed the border to join the gendarmes, encouraged by Tshombe's funding of local politician Harry Nkumbula's anti-imperialist African National Congress.[14]

Official control of the mercenaries passed from Faulques to Lieutenant Colonel Robert Lamouline, a Minaf Belgian who had volunteered to stay on after Rumpunch. Faulques was smart enough to seek protection from General Muke. He flattered the Katangese army chief and those around him, including Victor Rosez.

'After the cease fire I got some nice compliments of the General,' remembered Victor Rosez:

> I think I was the youngest Captain in history at that moment. Of course they asked me kindly to remove the stars from my uniform but the General gave me a nice compensation. I was sent to Kamina, Kolwezi, and Kipushi base to have a quick airborne formation. Bob Denard [probably Paul Ropagnol – the two men looked similar] gave me a nice breast pendant: a parachute with dagger and the words: *qui ose gagne* (who dares wins). I think he got it from Colonel Faulques.[15]

The plan worked. Muke made the chain-smoking Frenchman a colonel in October. Faulques tightened his control of the paracommando schools and began training the best Katangese troops at Kolwezi.

Other Frenchmen found it harder to accept the situation. The gendarmes remained a mess, all chaos and personal empire building. Senior Katangese officers refused to listen to mercenary suggestions for reform. Faulques' increasingly autocratic manner did not help. Many of the French contingent, including Badaire, de Saint-Paul and the injured Ropagnol, returned to France. Belgian mercenaries also went home, glad to put Morthor behind them.

'Many live in fear of being shot in the back by their black troops,' wrote New York-based journalist Andrew Borowiec.[16]

One French mercenary switched sides. Henri Lasimone had emerged a hero after Jadotville and got a place in the operational general staff. He fell out with Faulques, convinced the senior man disliked him for not fighting in Algeria. In a drunken rage, Lasimone beat up his UN worker girlfriend, a good-looking Polish woman. She took shelter in the organisation's headquarters. The Frenchman sobered up and defected to the UN to get her back.

He spewed a lot of bile about his enemies in the process, claiming Faulques was surrounded by French fascists who regularly carried out war crimes against civilians. Conor Cruise O'Brien, under pressure from the UN hierarchy and media over his handling of Morthor, was happy to publicise Lasimone's smears. The fascism claim was hard to prove but the Irishman found it easy to believe the rest. On one occasion, UN troops had followed mercenary-led Katangese troops through a village in the north to find Baluba bodies hanging from trees. And Jerry Puren had seen a clearing near Elisabethville full of the rotting corpses of Tshombe's political enemies.

Lasimone did not tell O'Brien that he had previously fought for Kalonji in South Kasaï but been expelled for war crimes of his own in May 1961.

'The Congo?' said Lasimone. 'It's a brothel.'[17]


Jean Schramme arrived back in bullet-holed Elisabethville in late September to find the city bickering with the UN over the ceasefire. After a few weeks instructing Rhodesian mercenaries, he headed for the Kasaï border to retake Kisamba from the ANC with a small group of soldiers. Schramme's men ambushed the town in camouflaged jeeps. A bazooka shell hit an office, destroying it in a cloud of smoke and shredded paper. ANC troops ran in panic. Schramme's machine guns cut them down. He radioed his commanding officer to tell him Kisamba had fallen.

'That's impossible, Schramme. You had two battalions against you.'

'If you don't believe me, come yourself,' said Schramme. 'Send some occupation troops to relieve us. We are a little tired.'[18]

He made lieutenant.

This time Mobutu was to blame for the fighting. On 16 October, the cease-fire was fixed in Elisabethville. Prisoners were exchanged. Katangese forces reoccupied garrisons in Albertville, Niemba, Nyunzu and Jadotville, 'free to undertake whatever movements are necessary to discharge their functions'.[19] In Elisabethville, the Katangese took back the Lido, the hospital, the radio station, the post office and the Chaussée de Kasenga tunnel bridge. There would be joint control of the airport. The UN agreed that the Katangese could take military action against any threat from outside their borders.

Everything looked good for Tshombe until four days later, when Mobutu's ANC, hoping to take advantage of the secession's weakened state, crossed into Katanga from Kasaï. They threw back gendarmes, burned villages and sent thousands fleeing south. It was the first time Mobutu's men had taken military action against Tshombe. Separately, Stanleyville ANC troops invaded from the north. The two armies should have been allies but Antoine Gizenga had quit his position as deputy prime minister in September and returned to the east, where he again promoted himself as Lumumba's successor.

Tshombe's gendarmes regrouped against the two-pronged invasion and counter-attacked. Mobutu's men fell back to Luluabourg in chaos, where they arrested hundreds of whites and raped fifteen women. Gizenga's men were more successful, capturing Albertville, Kabalo, Nyunzu, Manono and Nyemba with the help of local Baluba. Albertville's entire white population fled over the lake to Tanganyika when they saw the Jeunesse approaching.

UN officials were still debating how to react to the incursions when news arrived of fresh horror in Kivu province. On 11 November, a UN supply plane landed at Kindu with supplies for local Malaysian troops. A mob of Stanleyville ANC shot the thirteen Italian crewmembers and hacked them to pieces. Their body parts hung in a garage until the next day. Townspeople paraded through the streets holding severed limbs. Smoked flesh turned up for sale in Kindu market.

'Look here, we have fresh meat,' called the market traders, 'meat of the white man, this extra tender meat.'[20]

UN investigators reported that there was little chance of arresting the killers.

Pantanaw U Thant, a 52-year-old Burmese diplomat and amateur radio enthusiast from a family of rice merchants, inherited the chaos when he replaced Hammarskjöld as Secretary General on 3 November. 'Ever since the unhappy chain of events in Katanga in September', he said, 'everyone is asking what next for the UN in the Congo, is there a next step that can be taken, or has a dead end been reached for the UN?'[21]

The new Secretary General shared Hammarskjöld's belief that ending the Katangese secession would bring peace to the Congo. Even some of Tshombe's strongest supporters in UMHK were beginning to feel the same. The mining company had not expected Tshombe to put its operations in the front line of a war. Its president, Monsieur Robiliart, said:

> Like any private enterprise anywhere, we need peace and order, not war and strife, to conduct our operations smoothly. Those who accuse us of military adventuring assume we are ignorant of our own self-interest. It is preposterous to suppose that a private company would engage in activities that would invite harm to its personnel or its properties.[22]

Privately, the company admitted trouble getting its people in Katanga to carry out instructions 'in the spirit they were given'.[23] At the end of September, the board brought home Maurice Van Weyenbergh, their senior man in Elisabethville, for showing more loyalty to Tshombe than UMHK.

U Thant pruned his own tree by removing Conor Cruise O'Brien, using the excuse of the Irishman's messy divorce. Forty-two-year-old UN veteran Brian Urquhart replaced him. O'Brien went home bitter and quit his job. Urquhart got a taste of the tension in Elisabethville a few weeks later, when gendarmes kidnapped him from a dinner party in front of US senator Thomas J. Dodd, a Katanga supporter. Urquhart spent two bruised hours in their company before Tshombe ordered his release.

'Better beaten than eaten', Urquhart said when rescued.[24]

Whatever peace there had been between the UN and Katanga evaporated. An Indian soldier who had been searching for Urquhart turned up dead in an alley.

Journalists headed back to Elisabethville, sure that another battle was approaching. Britain secretly supplied UN jets with bombs to use against Avikat planes, prepared to risk domestic backlash as long as it cut short the fighting and minimised any danger of Rhodesia getting involved. On 24 November, the UN Security Council again authorised the use of force to drive out the province's remaining mercenaries. Many, like John Trevelyn, had already shrugged off their sweat-crusted uniforms and left Katanga, contracts finished. Two hundred remained.

'Let us prepare for it,' said Tshombe, who had been reading Winston Churchill's wartime speeches:

> Let Katangese fighters arise at the given moment in every street, every lane, every road, and every village. I will give you the signal at the appropriate time. Not all of you will be able to have guns and automatic weapons, but we still have our poisoned arrows, our spears, our axes.[25]

White heat emptied Elisabethville's streets at midday. Gendarme roadblocks went up around the city. Katangese brains boiled in their skulls and trigger fingers twitched. The province was an oil spill ready for a spark.

# 19

# THE WORK OF AMERICAN GANGSTERS

Operation Unokat, December 1961: Part I

Captain Gurbachan Singh Salaria lay in tall grass near boulevard Baudoin. Insects chirped around him. Sun bleached the grass and faded the message 'Welcome to Free Katanga' painted in Swahili, English and French on a wooden hoarding near the airport.

The 26-year-old Sikh, a professional soldier with a serious face and neat moustache, had joined the army to escape a life of farming in the Punjab. The military gave him parades, officer training school and an aeroplane ride to the Congo. In the early afternoon of 5 December, he was waiting for a company of Gurkha Rifles and two Swedish armoured cars further up the road to attack a Katangese roadblock.

He slid his *kukri* knife from its scabbard. When the action started, Salaria's platoon would move in and cut off the defenders' retreat.

The roadblock had gone up a few days earlier. On Saturday, a group of gendarmes had got belligerent with workers at Elisabethville airport. Indian UN troops had intervened. Nearby Katangese soldiers had opened fire but were too drunk to shoot straight. The Indians arrested everyone. News of the incident reached town. Katangese patrols had taken to the streets carrying bottles of Simba beer big as artillery shells. An Italian driving Baluba hospital workers back to the refugee camp was beaten at a roadblock. Ten UN men were abducted in central Elisabethville.

'Please attack the United Nations dogs!' said the Radio Free Katanga announcer, and introduced the next record.[1] The station crackled from wirelesses all over Elisabethville that December, broadcasting scratchy 45s and propaganda. Its tone had got more radical since Tshombe left to visit his son in Paris, leaving Munongo in charge.

The Katangese drizzled petrol on the flames. A company of paracommandos shut off a roundabout on boulevard Baudoin with armoured cars, closing the main road to the airport. Three Belgians in civilian clothes supervised the placing of 6omm mortars.

'We have shown great patience, gentlemen, as I believe you can testify,' Évariste Kimba told foreign journalists as they sipped free champagne at the daily news conference, 'but there are limits to that patience, above all when the life of our country, Katanga, is at stake.'[2]

On 3 December, a Swedish soldier who tried to drive through another roadblock in the north of town had been shot in the guts. He crashed his car into a palm tree and died with pints of blood pooled in his lap. The backlash shook Kimba into agreeing to remove the boulevard Baudoin roadblock. Muke went down to the roundabout the next day but the time for conciliation had already passed. If he made any attempt to withdraw his men, they were in no mood to listen. The roadblock stayed up.

On Tuesday morning, Brian Urquhart told journalists he had discovered a Katangese battle plan to assault the United Nations. Munongo denied the plan existed. U Thant ordered Operation Unokat (shorthand for United Nations Operation Katanga): UN troops would dismantle Katangese roadblocks and swarm the city.

The Indians were in the north of Elisabethville, near the airport; the Swedes and Irish to the east near the tunnel, the gendarme camp and Baluba refugees; and the Ethiopians were in the west at the Lido, across the river from squawking Elisabethville zoo. Brigadier K.A.S. Raja, commander of the UN forces in Katanga, told them all to get ready for action. They had lost Morthor. This time they would win.

Salaria lay in the elephant grass waiting for the signal to attack.


The Swedish armoured cars rolled forward, the Gurkhas running behind them. The attack smashed through the Katangese roadblock before the defenders could get their range and sent Tshombe's men fleeing down the tarmac. Salaria's group came out of the grass and advanced towards the boulevard Baudouin to cut them off.

As Salaria reached the road, a concealed Katangese position opened fire. He waved his *kukri* knife and shouted '*Ayo Gorkhali!*' (The Gurkhas are here!).[3] His men charged the ambush, sending gendarmes running and armoured car crews boiling out of their vehicles in panic. Machine gun fire hit Salaria in the neck. Spraying arterial blood and waving his *kukri*, he urged on his men. The Katangese retreated.

Munongo declared war:

We are all here, resolved to fight and to die if necessary. The United Nations may take our cities. There will remain our villages and the bush. All the tribal chiefs are alerted. We are savages; we are Negroes. So be it. We shall fight like savages with our arrows.[4]

As he spoke, a radioteletype in UN Elisabethville headquarters chattered out U Thant's orders from New York: take any further military action necessary. Fighting had already begun near the airport.

Gurbachan Singh Salaria lay down on the boulevard Baudoin and bled to death, the only UN casualty that afternoon. Forty Katangese died.

Early next morning, Swedish Saab jets attacked Kolwezi airstrip. They destroyed a DC-4 on the runway, leaving it vomiting oily black smoke, its back broken. The airstrip's fuel storage tanks exploded in orange mushroom clouds. Jerry Puren ran through the heat and flying dirt to find his girlfriend Julia in a gun emplacement feeding belts of .50 calibre ammunition into a machine gun.

A graduate of Liège University, Julia was the daughter of a Belgian electrical engineer. Puren first knew her as a soft voice on the gendarme radio network. Her instructions guided Puren's aircraft over northern Katanga during operations. Only 22, she fell for Puren at their first encounter. Slim, blonde and doll-like, she was a fervent Katangese nationalist. As the machine gun scanned the sky, Puren knew there was no point telling her off.

'My father doesn't mind me being here for the same reason you shouldn't,' said Julia. 'Katanga needs soldiers, of any sex. So save me your gallantry.'[5]

The air strikes continued all day. Swedish Saabs were joined by Indian Canberra jets. A storm of rockets incinerated four more Katangese aeroplanes on the tarmac. Smoke coated the airfield. One Katangese gendarme was dead, others injured. Puren and Julia curled up in a trench and watched the last Saab perform a victory roll over the devastation as it flew off.

'Where were those brave Swedes,' said Puren in the sudden silence, 'when they should have been fighting Hitler?'[6]

UN troops pulled back from the streets and took shelter in their bases, flinging mortar shells into Elisabethville city centre. Brigadier Raja planned to hold his positions until he had enough reinforcements to sweep through the city. Shell fire from Irish UN troops hit a Catholic cathedral in the African district to the south-east and the Prince Léopold Hospital, causing Ruth Tshombe, the President's wife, to have a miscarriage. Rogue UN mortar shells blew apart a Red Cross truck as it evacuated civilians, killing two children. A UN officer suggested to journalists that gendarmes were shelling their own side 'in an effort to inflame the population against the United Nations'.[7]

Henriette Cardon-Sips and her family spent the first two days of the fighting hiding in their bathroom, the only room with a concrete ceiling. Exhausted from lack of sleep, Henriette risked a night in her own bedroom. She woke the next morning to find the room's windows blown in, the curtains tattered with bullet holes and the stuffing slashed out of furniture by flying glass and shrapnel. She had slept through the whole thing and had no idea if the attackers were UN or Katangese.[8]

'U Thant says this is only local action to protect UN troops and keep communications open,' said British Prime Minister Harold Macmillan to his Cabinet, not sure if he believed it or not.[9] Fat US Globemaster supply aeroplanes with bright orange nosecones blotted out the sun as they flew in low on their way to the airport. President Kennedy had authorised American support for Unokat the minute the first bullets started flying. Belgian ultras accused Washington of being the hidden hand behind the fighting.

'Look, look at the work of the American gangsters!' shouted a Belgian driver to foreign journalists in Elisabethville.[10] In the back of his car, a stunned African woman held a dead baby in her arms.

Gendarmes under the Globemasters' flight path sprayed gunfire into the sky. Victor Rosez was among them.

'I started to shoot at the planes with a FM FN .30 in the Square Uvira, near to the road to the airport of Elisabethville,' said Rosez, 'screaming to a few gendarmes "*kumpiga naye* ..." [hit him] and they started to shoot too. A few seconds later we heard dozens of other gunfire in the neighbourhood ... finally we saw some smoke coming out the aircraft but it managed to land.'[11]

The peacekeepers had twice as many troops as the Katangese but depended on airlifted ammunition and supplies. The road from the airport was already insecure, mortar shells falling like hail along its tarmac. Raja remained confident his plan would work.

'To arms, Katangese!' said an announcer on Radio Free Katanga. 'Drive all UN personnel out of Katanga! Let each Katangese choose his Gurkha, his Swede, his Irishman, his Norwegian. We know that there is enough for everyone.'[12]

The anonymous voice at the condenser microphone promised victory music to inspire the troops. Cha-cha and Cuban jazz were popular in Elisabethville.

Locals stayed off the jacaranda-lined avenues and listened to the distant thud of mortar shells smacking into buildings. Bands of red bereted paracommandos and Katangese soldiers in jungle camouflage jogged down shuttered boulevards towards the action, quart bottles of Simba beer clinking against loose cartridges in the pockets of their combat trousers. Up on the roof, sunlight gleamed on the rifle in the hands of a white civilian in short sleeves.

In the city centre, Roger Faulques orchestrated Katangese action from a sandbagged room in a villa near the Hotel Léopold II. His command post stank of cigarette smoke. Squawking walkie-talkies hung from roof beams.

'Two companies of Ethiopians with armour support on Route 126. We have no rockets left and two injured … heavy pressure … instructions … over.'[13]

Maps of the city overlapped on the walls, covered in a rash of pins and pencil marks. Faulques was running the same game plan as September: isolate UN units in their strongholds, overwhelm them. Telephones rang constantly as soldiers and civilians reported the latest sightings of enemy troops. The Frenchman barked orders into receivers and stuck another pin in a map.

The forty mercenaries, most Belgian, in Elisabethville went to war in shifts, fighting during the day then falling into bed, or living like vampires, never seeing sunlight. Off duty, they hit the Hôtel Léopold II dining room, stuffing down veal steaks and *pommes frites*. Out in the streets, they and their men would be lucky to get a handful of maize a day. Belgian civilians fought a more casual war, sniping at UN positions from their own apartment windows or dragging themselves away from a meal in Michel's Greek bistro, one of the few still open, when the sound of gunfire came close.

The Katangese lacked the morale boost of seeing Magain's Fouga in the skies. Engine trouble had grounded the fighter jet. But on the evening of 6 December, a twin-prop Dove light aircraft that had survived the Kolwezi carnage appeared over Elisabethville airport and Jerry Puren began dropping bombs from its doorway. The attack did little damage but rattled American pilots. Globemaster supply flights were suspended until Ethiopian Sabre jets could be found to escort them.

On the wireless, Radio Free Katanga announcers worked themselves into a frenzy before dropping the needle on the next 45rpm record.

'Bring out your guns, spears, knives, axes and clubs, and kill all the UN to combat the murder campaign of Secretary General U Thant and his international minions!'[14]

Then a vinyl hiss before the bouncy trumpet and maracas of a cha-cha single.

Tshombe arrived back in Elisabethville on 8 December. He visited the wounded in Prince Léopold Hospital to shake hands and reassure.

'Your wounds are not in vain,' he said to a soldier mummified in white bandages.[15]

He pointed out shell holes in the hospital roof to the journalists following him around the wards. Back in the presidential palace, he seemed calm and flashed the occasional smile. In private, rumours that UMHK was negotiating with Léopoldville after damage to its mining facilities at Kolwezi got him so angry he threatened to burn down the company's facilities unless it showed more loyalty.

'This day will be marked with a white stone by the capitalist bourgeoisie to mark the story of its decadence,' he said.[16]

Elisabethville received reinforcements when Jean Schramme and his mobile column of 150 men from Kisamba entered the city on an unguarded southern road, a giant armoured snake of jeeps and lorries. Schramme sat in the leading vehicle. Faulques gave him control of the northern sector around Albert I Stadium. One of Schramme's soldiers went through the town acting as spotter, phoning in the location of UN troops from private houses and cafés. Schramme fired off mortars while the voice on the telephone adjusted his aim.

Also in the city was Bob Denard, now a captain in the Katangese army. He had spent the previous few months in Kongolo as part of a Groupe Mobile under Major Kimwanga, visiting Baluba villages to hand out cigarettes and toothpaste, trying to buy loyalty. During negotiations with barefoot local chiefs, it was important not to stare at their missing toes, lost to jiggers, the parasitic chigoe flea that laid eggs in human flesh.

In Elisabethville, Denard commanded thirty men, a dozen white, the rest Katangese, who raced around Elisabethville in a convoy of jeeps. They would pull up near UN strongholds, lob a stream of mortar shells and speed away before the enemy could respond.

'If the Blue Helmets were ordered to crush us at all costs', Denard said, 'they could do it with the loss of a hundred dead. But their leaders were too concerned about international opinion to risk lives. So we continued to attack them with impunity.'[17]

UN troops abandoned the Lido but fought for the Chaussée de Kasenga tunnel, the main gateway to the city from the eastern suburbs. The Katangese pushed them back as bullets ricocheted off the concrete lip of the railway tracks. In the north-east, Belgian civilians living near the UN headquarters fired 3,000 rounds in one afternoon.

Victor Rosez joined Major Mbajo's unit at the presidential palace. The teenager found himself sharing foxholes dug in the palace garden with Tshombe's presidential guard, a collection of soldiers dressed in plumed brass hussar helmets, green tunics with red trimmings and white jodhpurs, all bought in bulk from a Parisian theatrical outfitter. Before the fighting, they rode around on retired racehorses, picked up cheap in Rhodesia.

Journalists outside the palace asked the British consul if there had been any attempt to arrange a ceasefire. The consul shook his head.

'Nobody seems to want it.'[18]

After three days of fighting, Katanga's oppressive December heat softened with sporadic tropical rainstorms that filled trenches and flooded bunkers. In breaks in the rain, Tshombe's men appeared from behind their barricades to wildly spray bullets at UN positions. The peacekeepers would admit to only ten dead, with estimates for the Katangese at five times that.

Late on Friday 8 December, UN troops secured the road from the airport. George Ivan Smith and Brigadier Raja made their way to the headquarters in Elisabethville for the first time since the fighting began. They departed just ahead of a Katangese assault on the airfield led by a converted bulldozer that looked like a medieval siege engine but was knocked out by the first bazooka shot. The attack failed, as did an air raid on the gendarme camp by UN fighters whose bombs missed every target. A UN air strike on the post office by Canberra jets, flying so low they clipped treetops on their approach run, failed to disrupt Katangese military communications but angered the foreign press who used its telex.

In Brussels, a mob shouting 'Kennedy to the gallows!' attacked the US embassy on Monday.[19] The Belgian parliament unanimously approved a speech from Foreign Minister Paul-Henri Spaak that called Operation Unokat 'intolerable'.[20] As columns of black smoke rose above Elisabethville, Brian Urquhart made ceasefire suggestions. Tshombe ignored him.

UN supplies and reinforcements continued to arrive in American Globemasters, now escorted by fighter jets. With Avikat a mess of blackened metal ribs, the only Katangese aeroplane in the air was Puren's Dove. The South African bombed Elisabethville airport by night on Monday and Tuesday, causing panic but little damage. At the end of the week, the Dove crashed in Northern Rhodesia when Glasspool preferred to stay in a Kolwezi bar rather than operate the airfield's landing lights. The Katangese Air Force no longer existed. Globemasters continued to land.

As his forces grew in strength, Brigadier Raja got ready to spring the trap that would crush the Katangese gendarmes in Elisabethville.

# 20

# CLEAR VICTORY

## Operation Unokat, December 1961: Part II

It rained hard at the Chaussée de Kasenga. The water flooded mortar barrels, drenched clothes, turned dirt to mud. The Katangese defenders sheltered in railway carriages and watched their commander, a Swiss-Italian mercenary called Jean de Luigi, crouching in a puddle by the bridge's low concrete wall.

Until a few months ago, 43-year-old Luigi had worked in Salisbury as chef for the Earl of Dalhousie, Rhodesia's Governor-General. It was a prestigious if unexciting job. Then his wife left him for a man who was, in Luigi's words, 'a glamorous person'.[1] The Italian went to Katanga to find his own glamour. He commanded the bridge by day and drank in Michel's bistro at night. Over Simba beer, Luigi talked earnestly with journalists about fighting for civilisation alongside his gang of mercenary friends who called themselves 'the Idealists'.[2]

Luigi looked down at the Chaussée de Kasenga as it dipped below and under the railway. It was Saturday 16 December and the Irish were out there in the rain, waiting to attack. A week of fighting had exhausted Katangese soldiers and eaten up ammunition. Elisabethville had no electricity or water. On 12 December, Ethiopian troops seized control of the new hospital, the tallest building in Elisabethville, dislodging mortar spotters from the roof. The shells kept falling. The man from *Time* magazine watched two Belgian civilians amble into a used car lot, set up a mortar and bombard the UN HQ five blocks away.[3]

A propaganda war ran parallel to the street fighting. UN spokesmen briefed journalists about Katangese shells killing Baluba in the refugee camp; Red Cross vehicles being used to transport soldiers; and gendarmes murdering a Goan civilian they mistook for a Gurkha. Tshombe's men blamed Ethiopian soldiers for the deaths of three middle-aged Katanga Red Cross volunteers whose corpses turned up in a quarry near Kasapa Police Camp; the deaths of UMHK director Guillaume Derricks and his 86-year-old mother; and

Henrietta Baratella, a 36-year-old French woman shot in the face at a road-block on the avenue d'Uvira.[4] No one knew who to hold responsible for Jean George Olivet, the Swiss Red Cross representative, found by Schramme's men in a shallow grave with two other bodies near UN headquarters. A gutted ambulance stood nearby.

On Friday 15 December, President Kennedy sent a personal communication to Tshombe, requesting a ceasefire. For the first time, the Katangese leader seemed willing. Tshombe offered to meet Adoula in a neutral French African nation.

It was too late. Brigadier Raja had enough reinforcements to launch his offensive.

On Friday evening, Gurkha troops attacked over the golf course in the north-west and came up against white mercenaries dug in among the bunkers and greens. The UN soldiers fought their way across the course in eight hours and pushed into the city. The next morning, Ethiopians waded across Kiboko creek to take the Lido area, fighting mercenaries in the bush around Elisabethville zoo while animals howled in their cages. A group of Ethiopians broke into the house of a 70-year-old British widow, slapped her around and looted her possessions.

It was still raining when Irish mortar shells fell on Jean de Luigi's Katangese gendarmes at the Chaussée de Kasenga. Luigi and his men fired at the Irish troops creeping up the road below them. Another UN group flanked the Katangese and came along the railway tracks. Luigi's men shot dead Lieutenant O'Riordan as he led the charge, then killed a radio operator trying to recover the body. The gendarmes were driven out of their train carriages but they clung to the bridge's concrete walls. Charlie Raleigh, a young soldier from Wexford, fired on them from the Chaussée de Kasenga with an anti-tank gun that sent a shell straight through the bridge. Luigi's men fled in clouds of concrete dust. The Irish pushed towards the centre of the city.

Luigi was last seen with a dirty bandage wrapped around a head wound trying to rally his men as they retreated through Elisabethville. A mercenary with less commitment trotted into the Hôtel Léopold II in battle dress and trotted out wearing civilian clothes.

Schramme's men put up a fight by Albert I Stadium against waves of UN troops heading towards them from the north, blasting machine guns at figures looming out of the gun smoke. Schramme ordered a retreat before they were overwhelmed. As they fell back, his men took out some UN armoured cars, leaving iron skeletons to burn with greasy black smoke.

In the east, Swedish soldiers reached the gates of Camp Massart. Led by lieutenants Kamstedt and Gullstrand, schoolteachers in civilian life, the Swedes waded through the Kampemba River, Ljungman AG-42 rifles held over their heads. At the entrance to the gendarme camp on Kasenga road, two stone columns the colour of giraffe skin held up a white-painted sign: Camp de Police. Hand-to-hand fighting with Katangese soldiers started in the late morning. Buildings burned. The Swedes controlled the camp by the end of the day.

Tshombe and Munongo decided to abandon Elisabethville. They gave orders to General Muke.

'*LA CAUSE DU KATANGA EST JUSTE,*' said the headline on the single typewritten page of *Katanga Libre,* the closest thing Elisabethville had to a newspaper in December.[5]

Displaced civilians packed the Hotel Léopold II, sleeping on floors and corridors. The lobby was a sea of exhausted bodies. Beer had run out and food was limited to two sandwiches a day. Outside the hotel, Katangese paracommandos and Belgian settlers set up mortars for a last stand while abandoned dogs barked in the street.

Muke found Faulques in his villa near the hotel and gave the order to retreat. The Frenchman was angry: he still believed he could defeat the UN.

'It was at that moment that Faulques and Muke had a fight (with words),' said teenage paracommando Victor Rosez, who left his post at the presidential palace, untouched so far by the fighting, to join the other gendarmes. 'Faulques used to drink a lot and once he was drunk his (French) vocabulary was horrible … but he was a nice guy beside that and one of the best strategical officers I ever met.'[6]

The two men rowed in front of their subordinates. Muke stuck out his chin and told Faulques to follow orders: 'I have supreme command over the Katangese armed forces.'

'I wouldn't even use you as ammunition,' said Faulques.[7]

But he obeyed, planning the final retreat to the sound of falling rain and the thud of mortars. The UN had squeezed the Katangese into the city centre. Faulques's men would have to escape to the south through the last unoccupied streets, like sand falling through an hourglass neck. They had to move fast. UN pincers were only blocks away from sealing the route.

A river of jeeps, lorries, armoured cars and hundreds of walking men flowed toward the slag heaps and smoking chimneys of the Union Minière district. Stragglers, deserters and officers with lost commands emerged from hiding to join them. Jean Schramme pushed his men south, glad the order to retreat had come: 'We had so few troops to put in the front line it was welcome …'[8]

Behind them, Bob Denard's flying column bought time. The Frenchman's bazooka shells sent UN scouts diving for cover. By the time the scouts had leapfrogged their way up the boulevard from doorway to doorway, Denard was in another street firing another bazooka. When the UN pincers finally met, the Katangese had already slipped through, a demoralised but whole army.

The defence of Elisabethville was over. Faulques set up temporary HQ in the Union Minière hospital and watched his men march out of the city before joining the retreat himself. The last dregs of the rearguard exchanged fire with Ethiopians near the Lido before abandoning their mortars and heading into the bush. The Ethiopians occupied the UMHK district the next day, moving along red mud roads through factories and mine works, shutting down the mining complex as they went. The destruction of a 40mm Bofors gun in the area by UN air strike on Sunday 17 December signalled the end of the fighting.

An informal ceasefire was agreed. By Tuesday the UN controlled the entire city; only the presidential palace and Radio Free Katanga remained unoccupied. Both were silent. Tshombe escaped to Kipushi and agreed to talks with the Congolese government. War-weary civilians, black and white, cheered Swedish armoured vehicles rolling through the battered streets of central Elisabethville.

'This is a dead city, a battlefield where vultures circle overhead and the smell of panic is stronger than the stench of the unswept, palm-fringed boulevards,' wrote *Time* magazine's man on the spot.[9]

Henriette Cardon-Sips was able to walk the streets in daylight for the first time since the fighting began. At the height of Unokat she had moved her family into a house opposite the hospital, where nurses collected rainwater in buckets. Cardon-Sips had hoped the red cross painted on the hospital's roof would offer some protection from UN mortars. A storm of 2,000 shells fell in one night with a noise so loud it would have woken a marble statue. With no electricity, Cardon-Sips baked bread in an old petrol stove and her husband begged food from nearby priests. They gave him an entire antelope.

The UN suffered twenty-one soldiers dead, four of them Irish, and 100 wounded. At least half the dead fell before 12 December.[10] Katangese casualties were a minimum of 141 dead and 401 wounded.[11] The Katangese claimed eighty-three of the dead were civilians, fifty-four of those African. Black soldiers made up the majority of Katanga's combat deaths, with only eight whites killed in action, two being Belgian settlers who joined the Katangese armed forces and the rest mercenaries.[12] At least thirty Baluba refugees were killed and 140 wounded by Katangese mortar shells. On 19 December, Swedish troops tried to hold back a mass breakout from the camp. The Baluba who got past them looted private houses and stocked up on weapons. Civilians who resisted had their throats cut.

Tshombe's forces regrouped near Kipushi. Jean Schramme went north to find new recruits for his unit. Bob Denard left for Brussels on 21 December to have shrapnel removed from his arm, travelling on a fake Belgian passport in the name of Albert Demol, a 'commercial agent'. Jerry Puren reappeared in Kolwezi. The Rhodesians had deported him to South Africa after his crash. He was surprised to be given help by the South African security services to re-enter Katanga. The government spooks wanted information on Tshombe's movements and assured the navigator they had the secession's best interests at heart.

Puren found José Delin in Kolwezi. The moustached Belgian, cigarette wedged in the corner of his mouth, was packing his bags. He had already left Avikat once. His testimony at the Hammarskjöld enquiry in Rhodesia during the autumn had cleared Katanga of involvement but gave away too many military secrets. He had been encouraged to resign but hung around the secession and rejoined during Unokat.

'Why are you so keen to leave?' Puren asked.

'Three reasons,' said Delin. 'The UN has told me to go and go I will; half the bloody Katangese Air Force pilots and mechanics have stationed themselves at Kipushi with all the aircraft and won't come back, and finally, I'm just bloody tired of all this chaos.'[13]

Puren replaced him as Avikat chief of operations. All he had to command were hunks of blackened metal and a Fouga with a damaged engine. Airpower had been decisive in the battle. Raja could not have launched his counter-attack without reinforcements brought in by American Globemasters. UN jets had destroyed Avikat on the morning of 6 December and left Elisabethville without air cover. Only the UN's desire to avoid civilian casualties had stopped it reducing the town to rubble.

'United Nations troops exercised a remarkable measure of self-restraint,' wrote the anonymous author of the UN White Paper on the Congo issued in January, 'and adhered strictly to their limited military objectives. Strict orders were given to confine fire upon civilian objects to the minimum necessary to silence the attackers; UN troops were forbidden to enter houses at all unless fired upon from them'.[14]

Despite the UN's self-congratulation, the victory was ambiguous. The tiny state of Katanga had again held off the United Nations, this time for almost two weeks, despite being outmanned and outgunned. And Raja's plan to destroy Tshombe's army had failed.

'It is evident that ONUC [Opération des Nations Unies au Congo] is not in a position to win a clear victory,' said an internal UN report.[15]


On 20 December, the Americans oversaw peace talks between Tshombe and Adoula at a hospital in Kitona, a sticky, hot airbase under UN control near the mouth of the River Congo. Nigerian soldiers provided security. The two Congolese leaders greeted each other with a hug.

'Hello, you old rascal,' said Tshombe.

'How've you been?' said Adoula.[16]

American ambassador Edmund Gullion and returning UN representative Ralph Bunce tried to get a meeting started but Tshombe announced that he was tired and took a nap in a hospital bed. Adoula and his entourage went sightseeing. That evening they met up for a meal, drank whisky and told jokes. Negotiations started the next day behind closed doors. UN soldiers heard raised voices and watched tray after tray of beer being delivered. Talks collapsed around midnight with Tshombe and Adoula heading for their respective aeroplanes.

On the tarmac, Bunce begged the men to reconsider and reminded Tshombe of the consequences of walking away. At 2 a.m., Tshombe finally agreed to what the UN called the Kitona Declaration. He accepted a united Congo, Katangese armed forces under Léopoldville control and the repatriation of all European mercenaries. Gullion and Bunce congratulated each other. The Katanga secession was over.

At Kitona air base the Katangese President prepared to leave for Elisabethville, smiling and shaking hands. Just before boarding his aeroplane, he handed Gullion and Bunce a letter. It repeated his support for the Kitona Declaration but added: 'I would however draw your attention to the fact that the haste with which my journey was made did not allow me the time to consult the competent authorities of Katanga so as to be authorized to speak on their behalf.'[17]

Out on the tarmac, the door of Tshombe's aeroplane swung shut.


Any hope of Katanga accepting the Kitona Declaration vanished in the last days of December, when Gizenga's ANC occupied Kongolo in the north of the secession. Tshombe's gendarmes executed fifty civilians in the town's prison before they retreated. Soldiers under Major Daba took over the town. The town was looted, women raped, men killed. Most whites had fled but a Catholic mission remained behind.

On New Year's Day, drunk and stoned ANC soldiers shot nineteen priests, a doctor and a Belgian merchant.[18] Balubakat youth, their leader a shoeless man in a pinstriped suit and antelope hide mask, hacked the bodies into chunks and threw them into the Lualaba River for the crocodiles.

On 4 January, the Katangese legislature rejected the Kitona Agreement. Gullion and Bunce felt sick but were not surprised. Tshombe padded the blow by promising to remove mercenaries from Katanga; he hinted that negotiation over Léopoldville's authority was still possible. In Elisabethville, he turned on the charm and gave a friendly speech to Irish soldiers: 'When you leave

Katanga, I hope that you will come to say goodbye to us. I also hope that for some of us this goodbye will be no more than *au revoir.*'[19]

The next day, Tshombe visited Gurkha commander Colonel Mitra. During the reception, Mitra got carried away and declared he would become blood brothers with the Katangese President. He produced a *kukri* and both men made cuts on their wrists while onlookers applauded.

'It is going a little too far,' scribbled U Thant on his copy of a report on the incident.[20]

Behind the public relations exercises, Tshombe did what he did best. He hired more mercenaries. As the gun smoke slowly dispersed over his capital, the secessionist leader put the task of reconstructing Katanga's air power and re-equipping its army into the hands of two foreigners. One was a Polish pilot, smuggler and womaniser who worshipped money more than God; the other a Trinidadian arms dealer and unstoppable self-publicist who once crashed the Emperor of Abyssinia's private plane into a tree. Within six months, one of them would be rich and the other in prison.

# 21

# MR BROWN FROM POLAND

Jean Zumbach and the Rebirth of the Katangese Air Force

In January 1962, a 45-year-old man with dark pomaded hair and a jutting chin sat in an upscale Geneva hotel suite looking at his watch. Jean Zumbach did not appreciate lateness. The charm of being fussed over by pretty African secretaries in their knee-length skirts had worn off two hours ago. Zumbach was in Switzerland to discuss a contract with Moïse Tshombe but had spent more time waiting up here on the third floor of the Hôtel des Bergues than on the aeroplane that brought him from France.

Zumbach gave Tshombe five more minutes and watched the second hand on his expensive wristwatch sweep round the dial. In the final minute, a door opened, a secretary waved and Zumbach strolled into the suite's drawing room. Tshombe jumped up from a crowd of African bodyguards and flunkies, beaming his usual ear-to-ear grin. Greetings, handshakes, apologies. Drinks were ordered from room service and a member of the President's entourage fetched a glass ashtray for the chain-smoking Zumbach. Soon they were discussing money.

Tshombe's contacts in Paris had assured him that Zumbach, an ex-RAF pilot who would do anything if the price was right, was the man to rebuild his air force.

Paris police knew Zumbach as a nightclub owner with a murky history, the kind of operator who kept a pistol in his desk drawer and arms dealers' telephone numbers in his pocket book. They had a lot of men like that in the files, but few had such an upscale background.

Jan Eugeniusz Ludwig Zumbach's family had its origins in Switzerland but had settled in Poland as landowners by the time he was born in 1915.

Brought up on an extensive estate near Brodnica, northern Poland, he spent his youth hunting game, skipping school and getting farmers' daughters pregnant. Zumbach seemed fixed to be an aristocratic country squire until a local air show lit the flame on a lifelong love of flying.

'Everyone was spellbound by the cool elegance of these heroic challengers of the laws of nature,' he said. 'I swore by all the saints that I must, I would, be a pilot.'[1]

He joined the Polish Air Force, after some subterfuge involving his birth certificate (his family had hung onto their Swiss citizenship), and became a fighter pilot. In hospital after a training crash when German troops rolled over the frontier on 1 September 1939, Zumbach hobbled after his retreating unit on crutches before getting the job of locating missing army units in a beaten up civilian plane without a radio. He spent the last days of the invasion checking abandoned dug outs as the Germans advanced on the horizon.

After the fall of Poland, Zumbach made it to France, then had to flee again when the Germans occupied the country. He escaped to Britain in the summer of 1940 and joined 303 Squadron, a Spitfire interception unit based at Northolt. The Battle of Britain was at its height and Zumbach and his fellow Poles were flung into the maelstrom of aerial combat over the English coast. It was a time of daily battles, blasting German planes out of the sky with streams of machine gun fire, then listening with artificial insouciance as the list of dead friends was read out at the next morning's briefing. Zumbach notched up eight kills and drowned any finer feelings with all-night drinking sessions at the Orchard Inn, followed by a few hours in a borrowed bed with a local girl.

'Sexual freedom was long overdue in a country where Victorian respectability had outlived its usefulness,' Zumbach said.[2]

Drink and sex kept his mind from the grim reaper at his shoulder. During one mission, he parachuted from his burning Spitfire over the Channel, destined to drown until a freak wind blew him back across land and within inches of a live power cable. He landed in a minefield, where British soldiers mistook him for a German and shot at him. The next day he was back in the air.

When the Luftwaffe's back finally broke in late 1940, Zumbach was a 25-year-old veteran with a chest full of medals. He made Wing Commander and watched the tide of war turn from behind a desk. By 1944, his time in the air was limited to occasional flights into Allied-occupied Europe. On one flight, a fellow Pole with a brother in Belgium asked him to deliver a package. In the back room of a Brussels tenement building that stank of piss and garlic, Zumbach watched the brother spill a pile of diamonds from the package, glittering under the bare light bulb. He made £500 for his trouble. It was the start of a profitable sideline in smuggling.

When the war ended, the RAF gave Zumbach £200, a demob suit and the strong hint that he and his fellow Polish exiles should go home. The pilot was smart enough to see the USSR's fingerprints all over Eastern Europe and stayed in the west. Fellow Poles who returned were thrown in jail.

Zumbach moved back into the smuggling racket with the help of a Paris black marketeer, a French Jew who had lived out the Nazi occupation with the help of a fake ID and a talent for buying low and selling high. The pair linked up with British ex-RAF friends of Zumbach who ran an air charter company. Soon the group was running currency, real and counterfeit, across the Channel and bringing in Swiss watches stuffed into the cockpit seats. The gang diversified into gold from Switzerland and cigarettes out of Tangiers. Zumbach was not sentimental about his wartime home and flew Jewish guerrillas into Palestine, then under British mandate.

'Men with strange bulges under their armpits stood about on [Tel Aviv] street corners while patrolling British soldiers seemed to take no notice,' he said. 'My passengers were heartened by the sight.'[3]

By the start of the sixties, Zumbach had retired from the smuggling life and was a prosperous forty-something based in Paris, known to everyone as 'Jean'. A girl called Gisèle, a young and blonde teacher of English at a local language school, seemed to have tamed him. The Swiss-Pole owned a smoky cellar discothèque near Étoile and an upscale restaurant on rue Quentin-Bauchart. His waistline bulged from rich food and his face was pale as milk from living at night. Zumbach had become a stock figure familiar from a thousand thrillers: the rakish lounge lizard with a mysterious past.

In January 1962, adventure came knocking on a door that seemed to have closed forever in the form of some French arms dealers with whom Zumbach had crossed paths previously. There was talk of good money for a ferrying job, flying aeroplanes to Katanga. Not illegal, the dealers said, but not really legal either. On 8 January, Zumbach met Tshombe and his entourage in Geneva.

'Rather a small man, with a large head,' said Zumbach.[4]

The Pole was more interested in the long hours Tshombe spent at 3 rue de Petitot, premises of Imefbank and the nominal address of a new, supposedly Swiss corporation called BNKSA with a huge bank balance and no other assets. Tshombe's stake in the corporation may have been connected to Katanga's 1961 budget deficit of several hundred million Belgian francs. His link to Imefbank came through Viscount Oliver-Robert de Ferron, the bank's vice chairman, a Swiss (some said French) aristocrat and the Icelandic consul in Geneva. Ferron turned up in Elisabethville during the early days of the secession with a plan to run the entire economy. The Belgians squeezed him out when they suspected his plans would mainly benefit Imefbank and the Bank of Lagos, a shadowy set up also under the viscount's control.

The Katangese government kept in contact with Ferron. During the Morthor fighting, he helped the Banque Nationale de Katanga convert 34 million Belgian francs to Swiss currency and tuck it away in Zurich's Crédit Suisse. On 19 December, the Banque Nationale du Katanga began liquidating its remaining Belgian accounts. Some of the cash went into French franc and Portuguese escudo accounts. Some went into Imefbank.[5]

Tshombe told the Katangese assembly he was safeguarding the country's financial future. Zumbach assumed that Imefbank was a retirement fund. He could not criticise his new employer for that. After watching Poland being handed over to the USSR, the pilot transferred his allegiance to something greater than the fate of nations: money, preferably in non-consecutive, unmarked bills.

Smuggling, nightclub management and supplying a secessionist air force were all the same to Zumbach, as long as he got paid. And Tshombe was prepared to pay well to keep himself out of Léopoldville's hands. By early 1962, both Lumumba's political heir and the Congo's only other secessionist leader were in prison facing treason charges.

On 1 March 1961, Albert Kalonji declared himself chief of chiefs for all Baluba in Kasaï. As the new *Mulopwe*, Kalonji was supposed to sacrifice a family member to ensure invulnerability, take his pick of local virgins and allow villagers to eat dirt from beneath his feet. He disappointed local witchdoctors by agreeing only to the dirt eating.

Kalonji told his friends that traditionalist-minded tribal chiefs had pushed the position of *Mulopwe* on him. His critics, including South Kasaï prime minister Joseph Ngalula, thought Kalonji had suggested the whole thing as part of a plan to become dictator. Ngalula complained so loudly that he was exiled to Léopoldville, the *Mulopwe* having bought the co-operation of Kasa-Vubu and Mobutu with profits from his diamond mines. The UN had banned the export of conflict diamonds but Kalonji smuggled the stones across the River Congo to Brazzaville, where Youlou pretended he had dug them up himself.

Rich and worshipped, the *Mulopwe* underestimated how much Léopoldville hated his secession. By the end of the year, Ngalula had persuaded the Congolese government to revoke the parliamentary immunity that had kept Kalonji safe during earlier visits to the capital. Mobutu's men arrested the *Mulopwe* in Léopoldville on 30 December.

The cell doors slammed on Antoine Gizenga a few weeks later. Parliament had stripped the deputy prime minister of his position after Stanleyville ANC troops invaded north Katanga at the end of 1961. On 8 January, Kasa-Vubu ordered him to return to the capital. Gizenga refused. A more charismatic man could have caused trouble but Gizenga spent his time in clammy introversion by the river. Not even his troop of female bodyguards, pearl-handled revolvers on each hip, made him look like a leader. Stanleyville fell apart while he brooded, and his supporters turned on him.

'We have had enough of the anarchy and terror that reign in our province,' said one of Gizenga's soldiers.[6]

International support had also faded away. American money persuaded previously loyal African leaders to abandon Gizenga. The USSR preferred to focus on Germany, where the construction of the Berlin Wall had increased tensions between east and west. Moscow's interest in exporting the Cold War to Africa faded further when Afro-Asian nations refused to back Khruschev's post-Ndola plan to replace the post of UN Secretary General with a three-pronged system that would have boosted Soviet influence. The suitcases of cash stopped arriving in Stanleyville.

'[Gizenga's] group has become disillusioned with Russian promises which never materialized,' cabled US ambassador Clare Timberlake to Washington.[7]

In his damp villa, Gizenga issued daily orders that no one followed. The few cars limping along the roads outside were wrecks and the roads themselves not much better. General Victor Lundula declared his allegiance to Kasa-Vubu, carrying most of the Stanleyville ANC with him. Gizenga ordered the general's arrest but none of the 300 gendarmes still loyal would obey. Lundula moved on the evening of 12 January. A gun battle left eight Gizenga loyalists dead in the streets at the cost of six attackers. Gizenga's all-female bodyguards never fired a shot. UN troops moved in and disarmed the remaining gendarmes.

Gizenga sent a cable to Adoula: 'PUT MY OFFICE AND RESIDENCE IN ORDER. INFORM THE COUNCIL, THE PARLIAMENT AND ALL THE PEOPLE.'[8]

When he arrived in Léopoldville, the police arrested him. The only international protests were a few sparsely attended marches in the Soviet bloc. No one seemed to care when Gizenga was imprisoned on Bula Bemba Island off the coast.

The South Kasaï and Stanleyville rebellions were over. Tshombe was the last man standing.

In the Hôtel des Bergues, Jean Zumbach's main concern was a previously unmentioned clause in his contract that required him to remain in Katanga training new pilots. As discussions went on, it became clear that this was bait for a bigger role. The money was good ($3,000 a month) and after some haggling the Pole signed up. Zumbach was now a colonel in charge of rebuilding and leading Avikat's combat squadron. He chose the name 'Mr Brown' as his *nom de guerre*.

Zumbach might have hesitated to sign the contract if he knew what was happening in Kipushi, a town near the Rhodesian border, where Tshombe's top mercenaries were hiding from the UN. Many had not been paid since the fighting began in December and morale was low.

'It was fine while it lasted,' said a mercenary pilot, 'but now it's not worth it. The few men who wanted to remain quickly changed their minds when they heard that the United Nations had established a special anti-mercenary unit to liquidate us.'[9]

Colonel Roger Faulques criss-crossed the town, spending each night in a different house. Avoiding UN snatch squads was the official line but some mercenaries thought he might have more to fear from the Katangese. Senior gendarme officers remained angry at Faulques's autonomy, high wages and the lack of respect he showed to Muke. I wouldn't even use you as ammunition.

On 19 January, Tshombe gave in to the critics and ordered Faulques to leave the country. The Frenchman crossed the border three days later, grumbling that he would never serve under an African again. Colonel Kiembe replaced him as Gendarme Chief of Staff. The remaining French mercenaries jostled for position: Major Bousquet, previously active in north Katanga, became Muke's aide; de Clary got the post of Tshombe's military advisor and chief of staff for mercenaries, despite rumours about links to the French secret service. Tshombe concocted some lies about Faulques being arrested but escaping with all the mercenary personnel files. The UN did not believe him.

In Geneva, Zumbach scrawled his signature on the contract. As he signed on with the secession, another of Tshombe's mercenaries was enjoying a smooth landing at Brussels International airport in the first-class cabin of a Sabena 707 passenger jet. 'The Black Eagle', alias 65-year-old Hubert Fauntleroy Julian, arms dealer, soldier of fortune and one of the first black pilots in the world, was on a mission to buy weapons.

# 22

# THE BLACK EAGLE

## Hubert Fauntleroy Julian, Arms Dealer

Hubert Julian's home overlooked the Harlem River in New York. The Bronx townhouse was crowded with elephant tusks, vintage rifles, Abyssinian medals, photographs of Julian with Marcus Garvey and Haile Selassie, souvenirs from Guatemala, books of newspaper clippings, a menagerie of parrots and a pet monkey. On Sundays his extended family turned up for inch-thick steaks flown in from South America, with African fruits for dessert.

Julian obviously had money – '[I'm] richer now than a yacht full of Greeks,' he told reporters – although how much was the subject of conjecture among interested parties.[1] An FBI report from the late 1950s claimed that he 'was subsidised by wealthy white women'.[2] Julian insisted he earned his cash. Both may have been true.

Julian had no objections to being supported by women, even when he had an income of his own. He proved it forty years earlier when he first arrived in America. The madam of a well-known Harlem brothel fell for his story of being a penniless medical student. She took Julian into her bed only to discover a few weeks later that her medical student had a suitcase full of cash and no knowledge of medicine. Julian was lucky she never discovered he had crossed the border from Canada in a plush McFarland touring car driven by a white chauffeur.

In early 1962, the Bronx townhouse was empty. Any FBI agents or angry madams looking for Julian, a towering athletic figure with his chin habitually held up at a forty-five degree angle to the rest of the world, would need a plane ticket to Elisabethville.

The Katanga secession was not big news in America. The papers ran regular pieces on Tshombe's adventures but there was no sign that their readers were paying much attention. Those who did read the foreign news sections tended not to like the Katangese leader.

Condemnation was fiercest in the African-American community. Malcolm X of the Nation of Islam called him 'a curse ... an insult to anyone who means to do right'.[3] Malcolm's fiery radicalism made him a divisive figure on most issues but his views on Katanga were strictly mainstream, shared by respectable organisations like the American Negro Leadership Conference on Africa (ANCLA), whose most famous supporter was Martin Luther King, Jr.[4] The ANCLA stood firmly behind President Kennedy's position of reintegrating the renegade province, by force if necessary. Even the politically inoffensive *Negro World* magazine described the men behind Katanga as 'white power interests'.[5]

The few white Americans who followed Katangese politics did not disagree. Liberals damned Tshombe as a tool of Belgian mining companies and the right blamed him for opening the door to communism. Support for Léopoldville from both sides was dampened but never extinguished by suspicions about the United Nations' role as world policeman.

Only a small but vocal collection of right-wingers supported Katanga. Michel Struelens, an expatriate Belgian on the Elisabethville payroll, was behind a torrent of press releases aimed at influential faces in Washington from Katanga Information Services on Manhattan's Fifth Avenue. Struelens was helped by Sid Hershman, who had ties to Cuban exiles in Miami, and David Martin, an administrative assistant of Senator Dodd. The Committee for Aid to Katanga Freedom Fighters was co-ordinated by Martin Liebman, a gay Jewish ex-communist turned PR man for conservative causes, out of his New York offices. Richard Nixon, who had recently lost the presidential election to Kennedy, was a member; so was Barry Goldwater, a major figure for conservative Republicans. In December, the Committee spent $6,000 on a full-page *New York Times* advert that declared: 'Katanga is the Hungary of 1961.'[6]

Other pro-Tshombe efforts included the film documentary *Katanga: The Untold Story*, made by the obsessively anti-communist John Birch Society, which told the truth without telling the full story and was shown at private events. Senator Thomas J. Dodd, recovered from his close shave with the Brian Urquhart kidnapping during his November visit to Elisabethville, continued a one-man crusade for Tshombe in the Senate. When he was not haranguing other politicians, Dodd appeared on William F. Buckley's syndicated television talk show to push the same point.

Philippa Schuyler, the pianist who played for Congo's leaders in June 1960, turned her experiences into *Who Killed the Congo?*, a vivid pro-Katanga account of the secession. She attacked the West for not giving Tshombe more support, painted his opponents as Marxists and claimed that democracy would never succeed in Africa. The book got good reviews from American conservatives and bad ones from liberals. By the time it was published, Schuyler had already left Africa behind. In Europe, she was calling herself Felipa Monterro y Schuyler, a pianist from South America or Portugal depending on her mood, and passing as white.[7]

Tshombe supporters were marginal figures in the America of the early 1960s but support for Katanga could sometimes sneak through disguised as populist anti-communism. Eighteen thousand New Yorkers cheered the words of William F. Buckley's brother-in-law, red-haired Yale man L. Brent Bozell, at 1962's Conservative Rally for World Liberation from Communism: 'To the Joint Chiefs of Staff: prepare an immediate invasion of Havana. To the Commander in Berlin: tear down the wall. To our Chief of Mission in the Congo: change sides'.[8]

Bitter words were exchanged between pro and anti-Tshombe camps. The ANCLA claimed Katanga's American supporters were motivated by knee-jerk anti-communism or ties to interested business. Martin Liebman and his friends argued that Katanga was a young nation whose struggle for independence had been aborted by UN bully boys and American hypocrisy. It was irrelevant that the John Birch Society made a virtue of failing to see both sides of the argument or that the only pro-Tshombe voice in the Kennedy administration, token Republican Douglas Dillon, had substantial investments in the Congo. And what made the ANCLA an expert on Africa? Léopoldville's US supporters had no clue about the role played by tribal conflict in the secession.

Liebman had a point. Slavery had rinsed away African cultural and ethnic affiliations from black Americans. The fratricidal nature of Congolese society, in which different tribes fought like cats in a sack, was as much a mystery to them as to their white counterparts.

It was doubly mysterious to Julian, a Trinidadian infused with British culture and brought up in middle-class comfort, but that did not stop him leaping into the situation feet first.

Julian was born in Port of Spain, Trinidad in 1897, to a family of comfortably well-off plantation managers. Like Zumbach, the flying bug bit early, when he saw an air show in 1913 and immediately discarded plans for a career in the family business. The death of American pilot Frank Boland after his biplane spiralled into the ground halfway through the performance did not faze Julian. He wanted to be airborne.

Family money subsidised a private school education, a pre-war trip to London and a few years in Canada learning French. It was there, in 1919, that the 22-year-old Trinidadian learned to fly. His mentor was William Bishop, a fighter ace at a loose end after the war, and one Sunday in November Julian completed a solo flight to become one of the first black pilots in the world.

The death-defying nature of early flying inspired Julian to invent a device to aid aeroplanes in trouble: a spinning blade reminiscent of a helicopter that opened a huge parachute canopy to bring the biplane gently to the ground. The money he made from the device (which never entered commercial production) funded Julian's trip to America.

Bishop gave him an introduction to a broad-minded pilot in New York State who would provide further training, and the Trinidadian set out to make a splash in Harlem society. He got his name in the newspapers with a series of parachute jumps over New York City, although the notices turned mocking after one jump saw him crash through a window miles off target and be immediately placed under arrest. Julian had landed in a police station.

Julian's achievements were remarkable in the face of fierce racial prejudice but throughout his life he made a habit of snatching defeat from the jaws of victory. American journalists made sure everyone knew when that happened. 'The Black Eagle' nickname invented by the *New York Telegram* newspaper was half-sarcastic.

In New York, Julian linked up with Marcus Garvey, another expatriate Trinidadian, and his United Negro Improvement Association (UNIA). To publicise Garvey's Back to Africa ideas, Julian offered to fly to Abyssinia in a seaplane and collected money from supporters to fund the trip. When the flight failed to happen, he was threatened with arrest for mail fraud and forced into an unprepared attempt from the Harlem River which dumped him into Flushing Bay five minutes after take-off.

UNIA washed their hands of him and Julian's career zipped through one scheme after another as he barnstormed for money, gave talks on self-improvement to railway porters, ran bootleg liquor and drugs for New York gangster Owney Madden, and tried and failed to start his own black American improvement association.

In 1930, as the Depression bit hard, Julian caught a break when an emissary of Ras Tafari, an Abyssinian leader about to be crowned Emperor Haile Selassie, requested his presence in Addis Ababa to organise an air display at the coronation. The Black Eagle lived well for several weeks, until he crashed Ras Tafari's private plane into a tree and was banished in disgrace. Back to New York ('I can state categorically that the Emperor and I were the best of pals when I left') and more money-spinning schemes until the Italian invasion of Abyssinia in 1935 returned him to Haile Selassie's side.[9] The Emperor refused him permission to join the air force and put him in charge of training ground troops.

The shoeless Africans were no match for the tanks, bombers and mustard gas of Mussolini's fascist legions. Julian was with his troops at the front, enduring shell fire with his usual buoyant self-confidence, but even he considered the Emperor's cause lost when he discovered the army's ammunition did not fit its guns. In November 1935 he gave up his colonel's uniform and left Abyssinia after a fist fight with another black mercenary, John Robinson, a Chicago pilot known as 'the Brown Condor' (the newspaper headlines in New York were predictable). On a final drive around Addis Ababa, Julian's car knocked down a pedestrian and a crowd of Abyssinians stoned him.

The Second World War was spent in relative quiet by Julian's standards. He fought for a week in Finland against the Soviet invasion of late 1939, then returned to New York as a Finnish military attaché, in which role he gave interviews but did little else. In 1940, he challenged Luftwaffe head Hermann Göring to a dogfight after hearing Adolf Hitler had made insulting comments about Africans ('I therefore challenge and defy you Hermann Goering as head of the Nazi air force to meet me Hubert Fauntleroy Julian at ten thousand feet above the English Channel to fight an aerial duel to avenge this cowardly insult to the honour of my race'), which Berlin ignored.[10] He failed to get into the Canadian Air Force. He sold used cars. Along the way, he picked up American citizenship.

It was after the war, when newspapers paid less attention to him, that things came good. He became an arms dealer. Selling weapons of death tends to bring out the worst in people. Julian had always cared more about his own well-being than doing the right thing but on entry to the high stakes world of international munitions supply, the Black Eagle's moral compass lost its north and began to spin.

He supplied weapons to the leftist regime of Guatemalan President Jacobo Árbenz Guzmán, finding time to chat with expatriate revolutionaries Fidel Castro and Ernesto 'Che' Guevara in Guatemala City's corridors of power. That bit of business did not stop him selling weapons to right-wing Cuban dictator Fulgencio Batista or repressive Dominican leader Rafael Trujillo, who had made himself godfather to every child born in his country.

Julian supplied Guzman's increasingly repressive regime right up until the CIA-backed invasion of June 1953, a contract which earned him a place in the agency's files on subversives. The file got thicker when he came close to a deal with Castro's regime after it overthrew Batista in 1958. That deal soured and Julian spent the night in jail after his pre-revolution dealings with Batista were discovered. Undeterred, Julian continued to sell weapons to whoever wanted them, regardless of politics or body count.

The road led to Katanga. Julian became interested in the Congo while on arms dealing business in Paris for Haiti's Papa Doc Duvalier in May 1960; news of the Belgian colony's impending independence was all over the French newspapers. With his usual impulsiveness, Julian flew off to Léopoldville, where he got an audience with prime minister designate Patrice Lumumba and convinced him that a Congolese Air Force with African, not Belgian, pilots was possible after independence. Lumumba was enthusiastic, but a day later sent a note to Julian's hotel calling off the agreement. Julian was the tall and elegantly dressed man whose presence at Lumumba's side had sent alarm bells ringing through CIA Congo station.

It was a year before Julian paid much attention to the Congo again and by that time Lumumba's body had been dismembered and burned, the prime minister's front teeth placed in the pocket of Gérard Soete. In October 1961 a new PR company, International Broadcasting System Inc (IBS) of New York, contracted Julian to be its representative in Africa. The company wanted to represent emerging African states on the world stage and had fixed on Katanga as its first client.

Julian flew into Elisabethville, where gendarmes on leave from the humid northern jungles were enjoying the dry heat and cold beer, and pitched the deal to Tshombe. Katanga's leader was enthusiastic about an American PR firm handling his battered public image and signed a $500,000 deal. It collapsed when the December fighting convinced IBS that the job was too dangerous. Julian resigned and signed on with Tshombe. The idea of a small state fighting for its freedom against overwhelming odds appealed to his romantic imagination, fed on very British tales of knights and dragons from his childhood. Tshombe's frequent boasts that money was no object also helped.

During Operation Unokat, Julian became a familiar figure to foreign journalists covering fire fights in the capital's streets. John Nugent, *Newsweek*'s bureau chief for Africa, saw him saunter, impeccably dressed, out of a building on rubble-strewn Avenue President Youlou and into a hail of mortar fire. Julian adjusted his tie and calmly hailed his limousine, whose driver was cowering behind the wheel further down the road. The Black Eagle waved to the crouching journalists, strolled to his car through flying concrete chips and rolling clouds of dust and headed off to another secret meeting.

For once, Julian's business was not weaponry. Tshombe asked him to recruit Caribbean medical staff for his overstrained hospitals. Staff shortages were so extreme that a Welshman in Elisabethville who claimed to be a doctor was sent immediately to the front line.

'Is it alright to cut penicillin with water, mate?' he asked a wounded mercenary with a bullet in his side.[11] The doctor turned out to be an unqualified British Railways dining car waiter.


Operation Unokat was over before Julian's mission of mercy took flight and Tshombe diverted him to another pressing matter: guns and ammunition. The Katangese war machine was scrap metal after the UN onslaught of December 1961. Brussels was nervy about providing more weapons and without a complete refit Tshombe was at the mercy of his enemies. Shortly before he left for Geneva to meet Zumbach, the Katangese leader asked Julian to rearm his ground forces. The Trinidadian agreed but, always a self-publicist, asked for a flashy title to go with his secret mission.

It was as Katangese ambassador-at-large that Julian went to Europe on a three-month $10,231,500 spending spree. Arms manufacturers in Belgium, France and Portugal were happy to make appointments. They pretended to believe Julian when he said the arms would be shipped to customers in South America. During his round of meetings with foreign bureaucrats at anonymous government offices, Julian failed to notice the United Nations had taken complete control of Elisabethville airport. Every new arrival was screened and searched.

Oblivious, the Black Eagle continued his deals. As he passed racks of black sub-machine guns at a Portuguese arms factory, he decided to take a sample with him when he returned to Katanga in April. What could go wrong?

# 23

# OCCUPATION: WARLORD

### The Rats Who Joined a Sinking Ship

The lorry stopped outside an African school in Kansimba and Captain Jean Schramme climbed out. Teenage boys abandoned their lessons and clustered around, prodding at his uniform, his gun, the badges on his beret. Schramme unlocked the lorry tailgate and waved the boys on board. Concerned teachers watched but said nothing. Laughing, the boys climbed in. Schramme closed the tailgate and got into the cab. The lorry drove off.

'It was a little curious as a recruiting method,' said Schramme. 'But I had no choice. War is war.'[1]

Schramme had arrived in Kansimba, a town near Lake Tanganyika in north-eastern Katanga, back in January with a group of eight white and twenty black soldiers, the remains of his unit from the December fighting. He began to recruit from the local schools.

'Sticking to the principle to which I had stayed true, I chose the very young as my soldiers, generally fifteen or sixteen years old,' said Schramme. 'Among the blacks this is the best age to make a warrior.'[2]

The boys only found out they had volunteered when the lorry pulled up outside Schramme's camp and a doctor told them to undress for a medical exam. He thickened his schoolboy army with white officers, like an emotional 22-year-old former paracommando from Brussels called Norman, and sad-faced former Louvain student René, who listened to classical music and cooked dishes with complex sauces. The commando grew into a battalion. Schramme had a cloth shoulder patch made of a leopard leaping over a map of Katanga.

'The natives had always called me Léopard since I lived in the Congo,' said Schramme, who looked more like a lemur than a leopard, 'so the commando naturally took the name of this animal and became Batallion Léopard.'[3]

The Belgian planter turned warlord had been reading *Quotations from Chairman Mao*. He put lessons from communist China's little red book into practice. The batallion moved through the Kansimba population like fish in the sea, patrolling the bush, helping locals, paying for what they took, repulsing ANC incursions. Morale was high. Schramme held court in crisp combat fatigues at a sprawling plantation house, the radio hissing static and garbled messages in the next room, the terraced lawns outside as manicured as a cricket pitch.

The Belgian was determined to keep Katanga breathing.

In the spring of 1962, anyone not sharing Schramme's optimism about the future could get good odds on Katanga not surviving the year. The value of the Katangese franc (KF) had plunged: in March 1961 $1 could buy 63 KF. A year later, anyone who still wanted Katangese currency could get 130 for their buck.[4]

The Unokat fighting had scared Tshombe's financial backers. The UMHK board in Brussels were holding discreet talks about reunification with the Congolese government. A group of London investors went further with a plan to forcibly divert UMHK's tax revenues to Léopoldville. The plan failed but had the covert support of the British government while it lasted.

Brussels also wanted to melt Katanga back into the Congo. Foreign Minister Paul-Henri Spaak even recommended the US deport Michel Struelens, the secession's man in Washington. The 33-year-old Struelens ('a charming chap' according to *Time* magazine) had been inflating Tshombe's ego with exaggerated accounts of American support.[5] Legal issues held up the expulsion and Struelens continued to unleash his lecture *The Basic Rights of Man Examined through the Tragedy in Katanga* on universities and rotary clubs.[6]

Spaak was experienced enough a politician to allow a little hypocrisy. He targeted Struelens but did nothing to stop the Marissal clan's mercenary recruitment.

That was little comfort to Colonel Adelin Marissal. His operation had been running smoothly until April 1962, sending Tshombe around 600 mercenaries, when disillusioned former helper Jean Charlier spilled his guts to newspapers and left-wing politicians. Marissal, terminal cancer chewing his bones, lived in fear of the clan being compromised. Some leftists were already trying to link him with Jean Thiriart, who had just been arrested supplying fake documents and safe houses to French OAS terrorists. It was a smear. Thiriart did not know Marissal and had given up on the secession over a year ago.

'When all these settlers returned from the Congo, surly, vindictive, speaking their minds,' said Thiriart, 'I thought they were sick, like me, at having lost an empire. I was very naive. The cause of their anger was much more mediocre: they were angry about losing the sun and no longer having a boy to do the dishes.'[7]

Others shared his disenchantment. Thiriart's former friend Count Arnold de Looz-Coswarem retreated to his family chateau to brood on the shortcomings of parliamentary democracy. Jean Gérard left the Katangese mission in Brussels. Only Colonel Cassart remained involved, fronting a German company that sold aeroplanes to Elisabethville at a healthy mark up.

Even Rhodesia and France were putting on pressure. On 8 January, police from Salisbury stopped a planeload of mercenaries heading for the border. They carried French passports. Toulouse police had already traced their recruiter to a hotel and were on their way to pay him a visit.

'Central Africa. Immediate work, good money, former soldiers (specialised or not), youths, free to serve, preferably have knowledge of Africa or the Tropics (drivers, radio operators, mechanics). Passport necessary.'

The advert was placed by a Monsieur Philippe, who occupied room seven of Toulouse's Hôtel Terminus.[8] He paid his bills on time and management pretended not to see the crewcut men queueing in the corridor. 'Philippe' was Paul Ropagnol, wounded in the leg at the end of the September fighting and preferring the south of France to saluting Faulques every day. Marissal's men had recruited him to restart French mercenary recruitment.

Tshombe needed all the soldiers he could get. UN troops occupied Elisabethville and other major towns throughout the country. ANC troops controlled many towns in the north and had retaken Manono, won by the Compagnie Internationale in spring 1961. Balubakat Jeunesse burnt villages out in the bush. Tshombe begged for international help and pretended all his mercenaries had left the country with Faulques.

'The affair of the mercenaries', he said, 'is like the tales about sea serpents or the abominable snowman'.[9]

He did not mention that hundreds of white mercenaries remained in Katanga, most in civilian clothes; that at least 600 Lunda from Northern Rhodesia were serving in the gendarmes; or that Elisabethville had budgeted 1,977.8 million Katangese francs for foreign help this year.[10]

Sixty of Ropagnol's recruits had already left for Katanga, with another 300 signed up, when the police kicked in his door. Ropagnol confessed everything about the operation, listing names and adding that of Faulques, unconnected to the operation, as revenge for some argument back in Elisabethville. Faulques cleared himself but Ropagnol got six months for illegal recruitment. The only happy ex-mercenary in France was Trinquier, who sued Tshombe for breach of contract in a Paris court and won 2 million KF. His critics muttered that he was lucky to get the money after his prediction of terrorism in Elisabethville had proved inaccurate.

Despite Ropagnol's arrest, there was no shortage of new mercenaries, some fresh faces, some returning veterans. Motives varied.

'I was somebody; all those people looked up to me,' said one. 'Even a Katangese major always tried to salute me.'[11]

'Plenty of lolly and plenty of fun,' said a South African masseur.[12]

'The Katangese didn't try to rape our wives,' said a bitter Belgian.[13]

The new arrivals joined one of the Groupe Mobiles set up after Unokat. Captain Tavernier, a giraffe-necked young Belgian, ran his 'Marsupilami' unit from Kongolo in the north. The son of a settler, Tavernier had joined a mortar platoon for Operation X-Ray, then made second lieutenant in the officer shortage after Morthor. He spent the rest of the year fighting the ANC in northern Katanga. In February 1962, Tavernier's Marsupilami unit went in with Colonel Kimwanga's paracommandos to retake Kongolo from the ANC. They found the bodies of 880 executed Katangese rotting around the town.

Captain Maurice Antoine, a Belgian soldier who had been kicked out of Katanga during Rumpunch but sneaked back in time for the December fighting, ran Groupe Mobile Noir in the Kilwa-Pweto-Mitwaba area and kept a low profile. Bob Denard went to Kabondo Diala; his Groupe Bison of twenty-five Europeans and fifty Africans contained long-time friends like Freddy Thielmans and Karl Couke, original *Affreux* including Charles Masy, and new recruits like Charles Gardien, a bulky Walloon ex-SAS paracommando with a moustache and a bad temper who hated communism, Germans, Frenchmen, the English and Apartheid equally. Denard pacified his sector so efficiently it was soon calm enough for his ex-wife Gisèle and son Philippe to visit. Gardien preferred local girls.

'White women do not mean anything to me,' he said to friends.[14]

While the mercenaries worked like ants trying to rebuild a crumbling hill, Tshombe was in Léopoldville hoping a heavy serving of charm would fool Adoula and the United Nations into believing he was serious about negotiations.

The Katangese President turned up in the Congolese capital on 18 March 1962 to discuss the agreement made at Kitona. The Katangese Assembly had already declared it void. Lunda traditional chiefs backed up that decision at a meeting in Jadotville. They blamed the recent violence on Adoula's government, the United Nations and US attempts to get hold of Katanga's copper. Tshombe, grinning ear to ear as always, claimed it was still possible to negotiate.

To everyone's surprise, Adoula and Tshombe sketched out an agreement that would have allowed substantial autonomy for Katanga in exchange for 50 per cent of the copper revenue. Hopes were raised but Jason Sendwe elbowed his way into the discussions and refused to accept anything short of reunification. Tshombe dropped the agreement, which may have been his idea all along. After that, the two sides remained so far apart that talks continued until the end of June with no result. Tshombe flew home. Adoula officially created a new province in north Katanga, run by Balubakat.

'There has never been and will never be a Katangese state,' he said.[15]

His words angered Tshombe enough to reach out to Lumumba loyalists and other discontents in Léopoldville. He made promises and formed alliances, hoping to bring down Adoula, whom he described as 'an American dog' kept in power through US money.[16] Katangese cash funded men who thought they could do a better job as prime minister.

'Without you', Jean Bolikango told Adoula, 'Katanga would have come back with no problems and without loss of human life or dispersion of the national inheritance.'[17]

The United Nations wearily restarted negotiations. Britain, Belgium, France and the USA came up with a plan for reconciliation, with enough options to boycott Katangese copper that UMHK would have an excuse to cease co-operation with Conakat. Washington suggested providing financial support to UMHK in case the Katangese turned nasty.

'It has perhaps been unrealistic to expect UMHK to stick its head in noose without any assurance of assistance and only slightly less so to ask this of Spaak,' noted a US State Department official. 'Although we can do little to protect UMHK personnel except through UN we can offer to share in some ways consistent with availability U.S. funds [to compensate] UMHK losses in destruction of plant and losses of operating revenue that would result from Tshombe's actions.'[18]

The plan was passed to U Thant, who smoothed off the rough edges and presented it as his own. Tshombe's team returned to the dance but made so many objections there seemed no chance of agreement. UMHK offered to put tax receipts in escrow until Tshombe and Adoula could agree on the division. Tshombe refused and made some threats about nationalisation.

'A bunch of clowns', U Thant said of Tshombe's government.[19]

There was nothing clownish about Tshombe's tactics: drag out negotiations until the UN gave up and went home. Money was running short in New York. Before 1960, the entire United Nations operation cost $100 million a year. Now the Congo military operations alone cost $500 million a year. The UN was $76 million in debt and only had enough money to remain in the Congo until March 1963.[20]

The clock was ticking and politicians in Washington wanted the secession settled before the cash ran out. President Kennedy believed Katanga could become the spark for an African civil war: Rhodesia, South Africa, the

Portuguese colonies of Angola and Mozambique, and Congo Brazzaville would support Tshombe; the rest of black Africa would support Adoula. Kennedy saw a continent-wide race war coming unless Tshombe was shut down.

No one believed in Katanga more devoutly than Jean Schramme, but even he could see morale dropping as 1962 rolled on. A joint operation planned with Bob Denard in the summer towards Kikondja, Mwansa and Klambi failed when a supporting Katangese company abandoned their positions rather than fight. Schramme preferred to blame the Frenchman.

'[Denard] had arrived in the Congo with the two red wool stripes of a corporal. I had been a little scandalised by his rapid promotion. To Sous-Lieutenant then Captain two months later, he burned through all the stages …'[21]

Denard got some of his promotions by writing gushing tributes to himself and sending the paperwork directly to Tshombe, knowing the president signed most things that crossed his desk without reading them. The former jailbird was on his way to becoming an important man in Katanga, with a salary to match.

For Schramme, Denard's rise symbolised the rot in Katanga's foundations. But other factors were at work. The losses and departures of the last year had made a mess of the chain of command. The revolving door of mercenaries with their rivalries and scams did not help. The quality of new Belgian mercenaries in particular had dropped after Colonel Marissal withdrew from the recruitment game in September, when articles in *Pourquoi Pas?* newspaper finally exposed his operation. Any military gains actually made were quickly undone by government corruption and backstabbing among Tshombe's entourage. It would be a race to see whether UN finances or Katangese morale collapsed first.

More problems were on the way. Jean Zumbach was in no hurry to take up his new job. And Tshombe's favourite arms dealer was facing the hangman's noose.

# 24

# THE FLYING HORROR

## Rebuilding the Katangese War Machine

On 19 April, Hubert Julian touched down at Elisabethville in a Sabena passenger jet. His briefcase contained paperwork detailing a deal for 5,000 pistols, 2 million cartridges, assorted mortars and shells, and 3,200 machine guns. A bag in the aeroplane's hold held two presentation pistols inlaid with silver, a submachine gun, an automatic pistol and 400 rounds of ammunition.

Julian found the tarmac crawling with blue-helmeted UN soldiers. An Indian officer searched his suitcase and uncovered a gas mask beneath a layer of silk shirts. Julian claimed the mask was for Katangese copper miners and might have got away with it but then the guns were found. More bluffing: 'The Sten gun is an excellent weapon for elephant hunting, you know.'[1]

The Indians put him under arrest. Julian was held for a month in a half-built Elisabethville hotel used by the UN as a prison. He suffered a suspected heart attack on 19 May and was moved to a Léopoldville hospital bed. Congolese prime minister Cyrille Adoula wanted him hanged, the UN wanted information and Washington worried his arrest would cause unrest among the African-American community.

Moïse Tshombe, still after weapons, tried other dealers, including Major Robert Turp, a former British Army officer with a colourful turn of phrase, an office in London's Queen Victoria Street ('not much more than a grenade's throw from St Paul's Cathedral') and a face like a plastic mask.[2] Turp did his best but the Katangese army needed more guns than he could supply. Tshombe approached the French arms dealers who had recommended Jean Zumbach. In discreet Paris offices they showed Katangese representatives leather-bound catalogues with pictures but no prices. The dealers charged whatever they thought the buyer could afford.

From his sick bed, Julian sent a jet stream of correspondence to congressmen, UN officials and anyone of importance who could keep the noose from his neck. Things looked bleak when the FBI discovered four B-26 aeroplanes registered in his name at Chicago and Newark airfields awaiting transportation to Katanga; but Julian was a survivor. His stream of denials and outright lies persuaded the UN not to hand him over to the Congolese government. He was deported in the autumn of 1962 with a warning to stay out of Katanga.

As Julian got his possessions together, he was approached by Robert Gardiner, the UN representative from Ghana, who had hero-worshipped Julian in his younger days but had strong views about foreign intervention in Katanga.

'This is one of the saddest days of my life,' Gardiner told him. 'I meet you in person for the first time as a mercenary willing to deliver lethal weapons to persons who care nothing for the lives of Africans and seemed determined to enslave us again.'[3]

Julian mumbled something about being misled by Tshombe but could not meet Gardiner's eyes. The Black Eagle was, for once, ashamed. But not ashamed enough to cancel a press conference in Brussels, where he announced he would be taking the United Nations to court.

'For my action before the International Court at the Hague I shall engage the best lawyers. It may cost $5 million but it is important the world should know what the Blue Helmets are worth.'[4]

He claimed to be absolutely innocent of arms trafficking.


As Julian lectured the press on UN dishonesty in an arrivals lounge at Bruxelles-National, Tshombe's other great hope for Katanga was at Kolwezi organising the new air force. Most days, there was a smile on Jean Zumbach's face. In the last few weeks he had become very rich.

His contract with Tshombe had started unpromisingly. The aeroplanes he was supposed to fly to Katanga, five Harvard T-6s supplied by Paris dealers without gun sights or bomb doors, had been delivered to an airfield in Geneva. What should have been a simple ferrying job became complicated when two men from the Swiss secret service told Zumbach to remove the planes in forty-eight hours. He flew the Harvards back to Belgium, then had them crated and shipped to Portugal.

A spider web of co-operation bound Portugal and Katanga. Lisbon liked the idea of a friendly neighbour to the north of its colonies (especially after Kasa-Vubu allowed Holden Roberto's Frente Nacional de Libertação de Angola exiles to launch violent guerrilla raids over the border) but did nothing for free. It took two months for Tshombe to provide enough cash to get the aeroplanes forwarded to Angola in wooden crates labelled 'agricultural equipment'. Local mechanics rebuilt the planes in Luanda, a town hot as a solar flare whose inhabitants spent every spare moment on the beach enjoying the ocean breeze.

Zumbach was joined by two London-based Polish pilots from his RAF days, 'Bucik' and 'Vanowski', while the French arms dealers brought in two Swiss flyers, Roger Pless and Jean Marc Pignon. In June, the group set off for Katanga. The last stop was Teixeira da Souza, a sweaty run-down border town in northern Angola. The Portuguese authorities were hospitable but Zumbach was anxious to move on after drowning cockroaches piled up around his feet in the hotel shower. It was the middle of September when the five men flew to Kolwezi and were greeted by Jerry Puren at the airfield.

Since Unokat, Puren had clawed together five aeroplanes (three Comanches, a Dove and a Dornier) which escaped the United Nations' bombs. He cleared charred aeroplane skeletons off the runways and prised his remaining crews out of local bars. The well-paid pilots, who rarely took home less than $1,000 a month, lived in Kolwezi's Hôtel Bon Auberge, an old colonial haunt that attracted a big crowd for its Saturday night dances. The patriotic owner let them run up a tab then spent months trying to collect his money. The pilots would graft anyone.

'All the pilots, with rare exceptions', said Puren, 'had some "deal" or racket working for them; some with government funds, some taking bribes from traders for extra air space freightage, some discreet and gentlemanly, some crude and violent'.[5]

The black Katangese ground crew looked on resentfully as the air crews counted their money and found excuses not to fly combat missions. Tshombe lost patience. In April 1962, Belgian advisors from the Travaux Publics tried to bring military operations under the authority of the civil air arm.

'Mister president, might I ask the reason for this rather sudden decision?' asked Puren.

'Commandant Puren, it is no concern of yours,' replied Tshombe.[6]

The ordinance was officially signed on 14 May 1962 but quickly reversed when the Travaux Publics grounded all aircraft for inspection, crippling supply efforts for Colonel Kimwanga's men in Kongolo. Munongo intervened and Puren won back his independence long enough to lose it to Zumbach in September. The Pole introduced himself as 'Mr John Brown', operational head of the combat squadron and highest-ranking officer around.

'Powerfully built, intelligent eyes,' Puren said. 'He had that authoritative, competent air so essential for commanding mercenary troops.'[7]

That view would change. Puren showed Zumbach around Kolwezi, a cool, quiet town of clipped lawns and whitewashed bungalows. The smoky cafés echoed with French, Belgian, Rhodesian and South African accents as the remaining mercenaries kept away from the UN authorities in Elisabethville.

Zumbach made regular trips to the Katangese capital for consultations with Tshombe and his Cabinet. His cynicism about the whole enterprise deepened when he realised General Muke used Michelin maps to plot his attacks and was under the impression a Belgian airlift was some kind of European elevator.

At Kolwezi airfield, the Harvards were turned into makeshift combat planes with machine guns bolted into their doorways. Zumbach's first mission, an inconclusive swoop over a rapidly scattered group moving along a jungle trail near Kongolo, was turned into a victory by the Katangese press. There was not much else for them to report that autumn.

'*Mon affreux volant*', Gisèle called him when he made a brief trip back to Paris. My flying horror.[8]

Zumbach took a ruthlessly capitalist approach to the secession. He convinced Tshombe that Avikat needed more aeroplanes and flew to Paris with a cheque for $75,000 in his pocket. There he wiped greedy smiles off the arms dealers' faces by insisting on a cut of any future business, paid into his Swiss bank account. After much negotiating, the dealers being men who bled through their wallets, and some veiled threats about taking Katangese business elsewhere, Zumbach got his money and Tshombe got his aeroplanes.

If the Katangese president knew about Zumbach's gouging, he did not care. 'Mr Cash Register', as the Belgians called Tshombe, took his own percentage from any arms purchases or business deals that caught his attention. Tshombe also bought military equipment from Europe through a chain store group he owned and sold it to his own government at a huge mark up.

'I can state as a rough and simple working formula', said dealer Major Robert Turp, 'that, where arms are concerned, the newer and blacker the country, the greater the graft.'[9]

The corruption was contagious. One afternoon, Turp met with one of Tshombe's cousins, a loudly dressed Scotch drinker, in a Brussels restaurant. The cousin wanted £100,000-worth of arms. Turp asked how much of a bribe the man needed to do business.

'Major,' said the man, 'I want you to know that I'm a patriot.'

'Yes?'

'Yes, a patriot. I want only 100 per cent for myself.'[10]

Zumbach took less than 100 per cent but it was enough. In the late autumn of 1962, he flew back to Kolwezi with the first of the new aeroplanes, a Lockheed Loadstar and a pair of Cessnas among them, and a group of pilots, most ex-RAF Polish but with a smattering of other nationalities. Zumbach's wife, the feisty Gisèle, came with him. She shocked locals by fighting with hotel managers ('let's get out of this brothel!') and exploring the local area in a Volkswagen with only a revolver for company.[11]

'If anything happens', a Belgian settler advised her, 'shoot the man first, then fire a couple of shots through the roof of the car. Then you can tell the police that you fired into the air to warn him off, but he forced you to kill him in self-defence.'[12]

Gisèle gave a Gallic shrug. Little bothered her, not even the tame hotel parrot in her room that squawked 'Bravo madame' whenever she took a shower.[13] She was self-reliant and had to be: Zumbach spent a lot of time back in Europe buying guns and planes. In his absence, the second-generation Katangese Air Force took shape. Mercenary pilots flew support missions for militia operations in the north, dropping bombs on columns of ANC troops along jungle paths.

On a rare visit back, Zumbach met Jean Schramme, whose Battalion Léopard had its zone of operations around Kansimba in the north-east. The Pole was impressed.

'He was the undisputed chief of a territory twice the size of a French department,' said Zumbach, 'which he administered for a meagre salary, and without firing a single unnecessary round'.[14]

Schramme had stamped his mark on his territory. His mortar attack on a UN camp in Mukato impressed the men in Elisabethville but some Belgian ultras around Tshombe disliked Schramme, thinking he was getting too powerful. Their gossip did not stop him making major and boosting the battalion with fresh companies of 17-year-old athletes.

At the end of October, elements of Battalion Léopard skirmished with ANC troops near Kiambi. The battalion attacked the ANC in strength with mortars and machine guns. The ANC ran, leaving their weapons behind them. René, the Louvain student with his marked-for-death look, was fatally wounded. He died in Schramme's arms.

Tshombe briefly had an ally against Léopoldville when Albert Kalonji made a surprise reappearance in South Kasaï on 7 September. Kalonji sneaked in from Rhodesia, having escaped custody in Léopoldville, and declared himself head of state again.

The *Mulopwe*'s second coming was short lived. On 29 September, his own troops launched a putsch against him. Kalonji blamed Joseph Ngalula, whom he accused of funding the violence using 13 million Congolese francs stolen from an account to build schools. Kalonji lived in his jeep for three days, riding around Bakwanga, rallying loyal followers. But the opposition was too numerous. He retreated to his residence, where bodyguards held off an assault by putschists while the *Mulopwe* slipped away.

Kalonji took a lorry across the Katangese border. After a brief stay in a Kamina villa, where Munongo refused to let him see Tshombe, Kalonji fled to

Paris. His partisans carried on a hopeless guerrilla war in the South Kasaï bush. Forminière representatives made their peace with Léopoldville and agreed to pay taxes to the central government.

'All through my reign', Kalonji said, 'I thought South Kasaï would survive for a long time.'[15]

The *Mulopwe*'s fall was overshadowed by world events. In October, America and the USSR came close to nuclear war over the placement of Soviet missiles in Cuba. Washington blockaded the island, Soviet ships tried to break through, and a U-2 spy plane got shot down. U Thant convinced himself the United Nations had played an important role in brokering the agreement that saved the world from nuclear holocaust. Ego inflated, the Secretary General became even less willing to allow Katanga to manipulate him.

Tough negotiating tactics bullied Tshombe into accepting the U Thant plan but no one was surprised that the Katangese president did his best to avoid implementing any measures. By November, the Belgians were pushing Tshombe to attend a conference with Adoula to make the U Thant plan a reality; Tshombe delayed, hoping Adoula's enemies in Léopoldville would bring down the government. When the Congolese prime minister proved stronger than expected, thanks to support from Kasa-Vubu and Mobutu, the Katangese scared UMHK's Belgian shareholders by promising a scorched earth policy if the UN took any military action.

'Every bridge, every road, every plant in Katanga will go into the air,' said Tshombe. 'Preparations have been ordered and made. I pledge that these steps will be taken whether I am here to order it or not.'[16]

In the winter of 1962, as Zumbach filled in his logbooks each night, the needle on his internal seismograph trembled. It was a sensation reminiscent of the tense weeks before German tanks rolled over the border in 1939: the feeling that made the hairs on the back of your neck stand up, that sent you snatching for your automatic each time you heard a noise outside, that made you stop and rub the cross around your neck as you climbed into the cockpit. The drums in the distance were coming steadily closer. Hubert Julian was lucky to have got out when he did. Zumbach and his fellow mercenaries were right in their path.

# 25

# CHRISTMAS IN ELISABETHVILLE

## The End of the Katangese Dream

On Christmas Day 1962, Katangese gendarmes fired at a UN helicopter flying overhead in Elisabethville. They hit something vital and the chopper fell out of the sky near the golf course. The crash killed an Indian second lieutenant called Kang. Gendarmes beat survivors lying in the wreckage.

'This is the last time,' said Brigadier Reginald Noronha, an Indian soldier decorated for bravery in the Burma campaign and current UN commander in Katanga. 'Next time there are going to be fireworks.'[1]

The Katangese and UN had been skirmishing since the summer. In July, UN jets shot down a DC-3 doing transport work for Tshombe; in September, a UN aeroplane was brought down by ground fire, killing two passengers; a firefight between Katangese and UN troops near Elisabethville the same month left two gendarmes dead; Swedish flyers refused orders to shoot down more Katangese aeroplanes in November but compromised by photographing the pilots, to Zumbach's discomfort; gendarmes in Elisabethville kidnapped Tunisian soldiers and arrested UN civilian interpreters for alleged embezzlement; mercenaries hijacked trainloads of UN supplies and diverted them to Kolwezi. More roadblocks, more antagonism, more Belgians spitting at the boots of patrolling peacekeepers.

Tommy Nilsson experienced the bitterness first-hand when he arrived back in Katanga with the 18th Battalion Swedish UN after a year at Malmö Police Academy. On an Elisabethville boulevard, he encountered a Belgian man with whom he had shared a friendly beer back in the first months of the secession. Nilsson greeted him and held out his hand.

'So', said the Belgian. 'You came back.'[2]

Then he turned and walked away.

'I should like this Christmas 1962,'Tshombe said in a radio broadcast,'to be a Christmas of unity and trust'. He advised the Katangese people to turn their eyes towards the star of hope.[3]

But there was little unity or trust in Katanga that December. Belgium and Britain were leaning on Tshombe to accept reconciliation, and UMHK already had a man in Léopoldville negotiating tax splits with Adoula. France was getting closer to Mobutu every day. Secretary General U Thant was making plans to cut Katangese rail, post and telephone links with the outside world. The UN chief had to work fast: money was running out and corruption seeping into his 12,000-man operation. An Ethiopian soldier charged with stealing 200 front doors told the court martial he had converted them into crates to ship home loot for superior officers.

In Washington, Kennedy got jumpy when agents reported that Moscow had approached Mobutu. The Soviets offered to invade Katanga within two months if the Congolese strongman broke with America and ditched Adoula, who had become so unpopular that he slept in a paratroop compound to avoid assassination. Mobutu remained loyal but Kennedy had to send a military mission under Lieutenant General Louis W. Truman, second cousin of the former president, to help plan the end of Tshombe's secession; in response, a mob of Africans and Europeans charged through Elisabethville carrying banners with the slogan 'No GIs in Katanga!'

The CIA supplied Mobutu with T-6 fighters and six Cuban pilots, all veterans of the failed Bay of Pigs invasion but officially employees of Florida-based Caribbean Aeromarine Co. The pilots decorated their Léopoldville office with signs showing the distance to Miami, counted their $800-a-month salaries and rehearsed attacks on Katangese targets while they waited for the T-6s to be armed with rockets for the real thing.

Through it all, Tshombe continued to believe that Katanga could survive if he bluffed the UN for long enough and held off the 7,000 ANC and Balubakat Jeunesse besieging his enclaves in the north. He played his opponents like a fish on a line, one moment loose, the next tight, never breaking the thread. Munongo encouraged him to keep UMHK obedient with occasional threats of fire and scorched earth.

'Everything will be destroyed,'Tshombe said. 'Everything.'[4]

But morale was starting to crack. In November, Major Jerry Puren watched two Belgians, red faced with anger under their mahogany tans, drag a mercenary pilot to a tree near the Kolwezi landing strip. They cocked their Uzi sub-machine guns. Colonel Kimwanga stood by.

'Colonel, please let's talk this over,' said Puren. 'You can't just shoot this man like that.'

'Why not?'

The pilot had been in northern Katanga on a mission to take Kimwanga and the mercenaries from Kongolo to M'Bulula. Instead, he flew his aeroplane all the way back to Kolwezi to avoid risking his life on the crumbling front against the ANC. Now he was shaking with fear against a tree.

'Damn it,' said Puren, 'he hasn't paid his hotel bill.'[5]

Colonel Kimwanga had a sense of humour. He let the pilot go. But everyone knew the 500 mercenaries in Katanga valued their skins more than the secession. Some had begun to slip over the border, first individuals then small groups, an exodus of rats the surest sign Tshombe's ship was holed below the waterline. Their departure infected the morále of the Africans they left behind.

When Puren made a supply run to M'Bulula's grass airstrip in late November, he found the Katangese garrison had pulled out, leaving only a local militia group under Chief Kitengetenge. Puren took command and led them towards the riverbank that formed the front lines. On the way, they ran into a retreating group of Katangese paracommandos.

'What's going on here?' asked Puren.

'1st Parachute Battalion from Kongolo. We are retiring.'[6]

The battalion's white mercenary advisors had vanished and the Katangese refused to man the front lines without them. After a stand-off, Puren let the paracommandos go and directed his men forward. He held the position for four days, watching ANC mortar shells smash the village on the other side of the bank, until paracommando commander Colonel Mbayo shamed his men back into the front line.

The Groupe Mobiles of Schramme, Denard, Antoine and Tavernier remained loyal. They chased the ANC out of their territories and back into the jungle; Zumbach's pilots flew in ammunition and flew out gendarmes with legs mashed by machine gun fire. But they could not save Kongolo and M'Bulula, which fell to the ANC on 5 December after a five-month siege. Even the ultras in Elisabethville realised that Katanga would not survive without compromise. Tshombe's Romanian advisor George Theodoru pushed him to hand over half the copper revenues to Léopoldville. The president was defiant.

'I have 30,000 men in arms,' Tshombe said.

'What you have is 30,000 uniforms,' said Theodoru, 'but that does not make an army. Do not let it come to a trial of strength.'[7]

Tshombe agreed to return to negotiations, not understanding that Léopoldville had no trust left. He made concessions but the Congolese government accepted only a few items, and then pressured Adoula into cancelling the agreement within days. The politicians in the capital knew the secession would be resolved using force, not words.

'No longer a statesman,' said Belgian Foreign Minister Spaak about Tshombe, 'but a powerful rebel'.[8]

On Friday 28 December, fighting began again in Elisabethville. Locals called it '*L'Affaire Simba*'.[9] Drunken Katangese gendarmes opened fire on innocent Ethiopian soldiers or drunken Ethiopians climbed the Union Minière slag heap and opened fire on innocent Katangese, depending on the allegiance of the storyteller. The shooting escalated and Elisabethville rocked to the noise of machine guns and mortars. Bullets flew past a Christmas tree standing in Post Office Square.

Electricity, water and telephone communications failed. Residents who had lived through Unokat had already filled baths for drinking water. They watched from their windows as United Nations troops drove into the capital. A journalist asked the UN's Robert Gardiner why his organisation was not doing the Christian thing and turning the other cheek.

'The other cheek has been held out long ago,' said Gardiner.[10]

Tshombe claimed that his gendarmes were innocent victims of UN aggression. Indian troops took him to the Elisabethville golf course to watch multicoloured Katangese tracer fire slash through the evening dark towards Gurkha positions. When Tshombe tried to leave, Brigadier Noronha physically stopped him and demanded the removal of all Katangese roadblocks in the city. Tshombe agreed to try but escaped to Rhodesia that evening in the back of a black Comet sedan. On the way, he ordered a ceasefire but his own men would not listen to him.

Gendarmes dropped mortar bombs on Ethiopians in the Lido and Gurkhas near the golf course. U Thant authorised the UN to take self-defensive measures. Bullets and shrapnel smashed the windscreens of parked cars. Some Belgian women braved the fighting to queue for bread and meat at the few shops still open. Others stayed in their apartments, huddled under tables with crying children, Christmas decorations still hanging on the walls. Residents of the Hôtel Léopold II slept in corridors, away from the windows. At night, the gunfire sounded like a rainstorm. With no Faulques and few mercenaries in Elisabethville, the resistance was chaotic.

'They are mad,' a Red Cross official said about the Katangese. 'They are killing their own men.'[11]

Belgian ultras took to the streets and handed out mimeographed leaflets supposedly from Tshombe, which stated: 'The Katangese people will defend themselves to the death. Everywhere the UN and its troops will be fought as our worst enemy. We shall resist them by every means until the total destruction, as we have announced, of our economic potential.'[12]

There was hand-to-hand fighting in trenches around the airport. Gendarmes set up mortar positions in the hospital gardens before a vicious firefight cleared them out, bullets smashing windows and hitting patients. Away from the fighting, Ethiopian soldiers shot dead the wife of a UMHK official as they searched her house for beer.

'This was the last time I wore a Katangese uniform, watching from a foxhole in the backyard of President Tshombe's palace,' said Victor Rosez:

> They were ready to attack us but finally they didn't … I think that this was the luckiest day of my life … 120 poorly armed guys against a full UN contingent … However the commanding officer Major Mbajo decided not to surrender … and after a few hours the UN withdrew … The same night I left the presidential palace and went to Ndola with some friends.[13]

The next morning, Major Jerry Puren discovered that the UN planned to bomb Kolwezi airfield. He and Zumbach had already dispersed some aeroplanes but most remained in their hangars. Puren assembled his pilots, chilly morning mist lying low on the runway.

'Gentlemen, we have received information that the airfield is to be bombed at dawn. That gives us exactly … one hour forty minutes to clear the decks.'[14]

He had six T-6s in the air before Swedish Saab jets came screaming in over the runway, shooting up Vampire jets, the remaining T-6s and a DC-3. The Cubans of Caribbean Aeromarine Co. would not be needed: most of Avikat's combat aeroplanes were destroyed on the ground. Puren jumped into a trench to fire a machine gun at the attackers, knowing it was useless.

'Perspiration, cordite, grease, frustration, noise and stifling heat: the old story.'[15]

Zumbach and Gisèle were in Angola with other Avikat aeroplanes at the time of the attack and decided not to return. Puren raged that the Pole had abandoned Katanga. The two men had never liked each other: Puren blamed Zumbach for spending his time in Europe when he should have been flying missions; Zumbach treated the lanky South African as a lackey and got his name wrong the few times they spoke.

Muke ordered Puren to Jadotville at noon. Puren drove past a flow of refugees on buses, bicycles and trucks, their possessions piled high in the back of their vehicles, children and barking dogs sitting on top. Swedish Saab jets buzzed over the refugee columns, sending civilians and soldiers scrambling into the red dirt of roadside ditches.

As he drove, the news came in. Elisabethville had fallen. At least fifty civilians had died in the fighting. UN troops occupied the presidential palace, issued ration cards and demanded Tshombe order a ceasefire. He refused.

'Everywhere, the UN and its troops will be fought with traps, with poisoned arrows and spears,' Tshombe said from somewhere in Rhodesia. 'We will resist by all means, including the total destruction of all our economic potential.'[16]

U Thant directed his peacekeepers take the rest of the country. He called it Operation Grand Slam.

# 26

# KATANGA '63

## Operation Grand Slam

Katanga was falling fast. UN armoured cars rolled into Tshombe strongholds across the country. Gendarmes, paracommandos and mercenaries abandoned their positions and fled. Kasongo Nyembo, the once-loyal Baluba chief, contacted Swedish soldiers to arrange his surrender. Tshombe reached out to other African leaders, even unsympathetic ones like Ghana's Nkrumah, for assistance. They refused. Munongo was in Mokambo with a hard core of ultras and mercenaries, issuing desperate orders for gendarmes to keep fighting.

Kipushi and Kamina fell on 30 December. Muke tried to organise a defence around Jadotville but the town was a whirlpool of lost commands and lost hope. Puren refused to send his T-6s into the sky against the faster Swedish Saabs. Christian Tavernier's Marsupilami group held off the UN by exploding a truck halfway across the main bridge into town. Then most of Tavernier's men deserted.

Évariste Kimba ordered Bob Denard to stop the UN advance, giving him command of a sector covering Elisabethville, Jadotville and Kolwezi. But Denard had been in Elisabethville collecting Groupe Bison's monthly cash payment and was separated from his unit when the UN troops took over. By the time a French friend supplied fake press passes to get through UN checkpoints, Denard's men were already falling back through the bush.

On 1 January, mercenaries and Indian UN troops fought a vicious gun battle outside Jadotville, leaving four peacekeepers dead. The Indians captured two mercenaries, a Belgian and an American army deserter born in Hungary. Their interrogations brought out talk of confusion, desertions and disgust with the Rhodesian and South African mercenaries who had abandoned them to the UN.

'Big bug-out artists', they said of their former comrades.[1]

Tshombe left Rhodesia and set up his headquarters in a redbrick Kolwezi villa. He contacted the UN for negotiations and authorised National Bank of Katanga staff to talk with Léopoldville about UMHK foreign exchange proceeds. Too little, too late. U Thant told journalists there would be no further negotiations.

The bridge blown by Tavernier had halted the UN on the other side of the River Lufira and U Thant issued orders to hold their position. For a moment it seemed Katanga might still survive. Tshombe ordered Schramme's Battalion Léopard to make the long journey from Kansimba to reinforce the town, but Indian troops ignored U Thant, claiming their radios were not working, and built giant rafts to transport their vehicles over the river.

Two hundred Belgians protested outside the US embassy in Brussels, blaming Washington for the fighting. They may have been right. Jonathan Dean, US consul in Elisabethville, had urged the peacekeepers to crush the secession.

'I was advised by our intelligence representative not to do this,' said Dean, 'but I felt that it was the right thing under the circumstances that there would be endless troubles if the Katangans were only pushed back a few miles and could continue the war against the United Nations.'[2]

Jadotville fell to the UN on 3 January. Tavernier's mercenaries blew the Union Minière control board at the mine, then headed for Kolwezi with Denard, Puren and the rest of Tshombe's forces. ANC troops and Bulabakat Jeunesse followed the UN, burning villages in the bush.

Even as his empire crumbled, Tshombe thought he could still win with charm and threats. On 8 January, he drove into Elisabethville to negotiate with the UN, the Belgian consul from Salisbury at his side, leaving Kimba and Kibwe in charge at Kolwezi. After a few hours of smiles and conciliatory phrases, Tshombe excused himself and drove across town to a press conference, where he threatened to destroy UNHK's facilities in Kolwezi if Operation Grand Slam did not halt: 'We have decided on a scorched-earth policy, we shall apply it thoroughly, and I think that it is not in the interest of ONUC or of Katanga to continue these useless acts of destruction.'[3]

Then he was smiles and co-operation again with the outraged UN negotiators. Despite the press conference, Tshombe had already changed his mind about scorching the earth, thanks to heavy pressure from British Consul Derek Dodson and Belgian advisors like Dr Joachi Frankiel, former rector of Elisabethville University, and René Clemens, the once-expelled head of the Bureau-Conseil. On 10 January, Tshombe escorted UN troops to Mokambo, where he calmed down Munongo and the ultras around him.

Down in Kolwezi, Denard took Tshombe's threats seriously. His Groupe Bison blew the bridges into town, wired up the Lufira power plant and the

Nzilo dam, which provided 80 per cent of Katanga's electricity, and planted explosives in every mining facility they could find. Local UMHK big shots were holding a board meeting when Denard's mercenaries barged into the conference room carrying dynamite and detonators.

'They went a little pale,' said Denard.[4]

Other Groupe Bison mercenaries were skirmishing with the UN outside of town. In the confused front lines a patrol drove their jeep into a pit near Gurkha positions. The peacekeepers thought they were Swedes and helped rescue the jeep until one of Denard's men spoke French and the bullets started flying. All but one of the patrol escaped, desperate not to be captured by Indian soldiers. Both sides expected the worst of each.

An English-speaking mercenary interviewed by a BBC radio correspondent explained the situation:

> If I captured any European UN troops, as they have behaved reasonably honourably throughout the entire conflict I would take them as prisoners and treat them as decently as possible until such time as I can have them repatriated. I certainly wouldn't like them to fall into Katangese hands. As for Ethiopian, Tunisian and Indian troops, who have behaved like animals out there, quite abominably, I would shoot them out of hand.[5]

And what treatment did he expect from the UN? 'From Europeans I would have a hard time, but I would probably live. From the coloured troops I would be tortured and shot very quickly.'

On 12 January, Tshombe returned to Kolwezi, where he discovered that UMHK had abandoned the secession. Company representatives had done a deal on taxes with Léopoldville but begged Tshombe to keep it quiet so as not to provoke the mercenaries, who still had their hands on the detonators. In Kolwezi's streets UMHK officials, pale and worried, told anyone who would listen that blowing the dam would cause a natural disaster. Outside of town, the mining men had tea with Brigadier Reginald Noronha, planning the best way to hand over Kolwezi without damage.

Most of the 140 mercenaries still in Kolwezi cared only about their wages. They lived separately from the gendarmes, preferring to spend their time in bars rather than on patrol. The 2,000 Katangese soldiers they once commanded lived in requisitioned school buildings, looted whatever they wanted and only reluctantly obeyed orders. Refugees swarmed the town. No one listened to Muke as he drove around trying to organise resistance. Journalists' press passes were useless.

'Passes won't do you any good,' said a white mercenary calling himself 'Jean Marie'. 'We are armed and we have trouble looking after ourselves.'[6]

The mercenaries were divided, Belgians distrusting French and Rhodesians distrusting Belgians, although they all admired 'Madame Yvette', the blonde Belgian wife of a mercenary who wore make-up and camouflage as she drove her ambulance. Rumours that Denard and his French friends had extorted 200 million francs from UMHK not to blow the dam curdled the atmosphere further.

In a flat near the Hôtel Bon Auberge, Jerry Puren proposed to his girlfriend Julia, then went back to interrogating Jean Zumbach's friends. He was working on a report about embezzlement: the Pole was rumoured to be in South Africa selling Katangese aeroplanes to cover his expenses.

Shinkolobwe, home to a long-dead uranium mine, fell to the UN. On 14 January, Indian UN troops found the single remaining bridge into Kolwezi and crossed it after a firefight with gendarmes and mercenaries. Their armoured cars halted at the city limits to wait for orders.

Tshombe contacted the UN in Elisabethville and officially ended the secession. Munongo angrily left Kolwezi for Rhodesia, promising to carry on a guerrilla war. He returned a few days later. Even he could see the night falling on Msiri's empire.

In the late afternoon of 17 January, Tshombe and Munongo were back in Elisabethville negotiating surrender terms with the UN. There would be an amnesty: gendarmes were not to be treated as prisoners of war, mercenaries were not to be prosecuted. Adoula and the UN agreed to the first two points.

Schramme's Battalion Léopard, packed into eighty lorries, twenty-four jeeps, eight vans and an ambulance, did not reach Jadotville before the UN took the town. He heard the news from pilot Jacques Demoulin.

'The UN broke the ceasefire and attacked Jadotville,' said Demoulin. 'The "volos" [volunteers, i.e. mercenaries] have retreated in disorder. It's all going to hell.'[7]

'What do you think?'

'We're lost. Good luck, Schramme.'

The Léopards headed south through Pweto, Mitwaba, trying to connect with someone. The radio was silent. Nothing from Elisabethville. A Katangese jeep collided with Schramme's car on a narrow jungle road. Schramme, aching and injured from the crash, kept trying to make contact. Nothing at Bunkeya. The civilians seemed demoralised.

It rained constantly, the roads turned to mud. It took ten days to drive 25 miles. In Lubudi, sad-eyed civilians wished them luck. Near Bukama, they passed Camp Mariel, where Schramme had started his Katangese adventure as an instructor. The battalion arrived in Kolwezi on 19 January.

'Where did you come from?' asked a tense Denard. 'We've been waiting for you for days and days.'[8]

'For days and days I've been expecting you on the radio,' said Schramme. 'Why were you silent?'

All senior mercenaries and gendarmes in Kolwezi were summoned to a meeting at Tshombe's villa. Over the last few days the Katangese president had been driving back and forth between Kolwezi and Elisabethville, convincing the UN that he would surrender, the mercenaries that they would get their back pay, and Katangese true believers that he would carry on the fight from over the border in Angola. Senior UN man George Sherry thought Tshombe seemed 'a tired and sad man', although he beamed his usual face-splitting grin for every camera.[9] In a crowded room at his villa, Tshombe announced that Katanga was finished.

'How many days at maximum can we hold?' he asked Schramme.

'No more than ten, Mister President.'[10]

Tshombe announced that the Katangese armed forces would pull back over the border into Angola. He and his Cabinet would stay. Schramme got a promotion: he would be in charge of the army in exile. Puren had to fly out what was left of the Katangese Air Force, along with supplies, fuel, weapons and the treasury. Denard interrupted.

'Mister President, we can't just be thrown out of Katanga without showing our real displeasure. We must do something.'

'Like?'

'Like blowing up the hydroelectric plant at Nzilo.'

Tshombe thought about UMHK and money and his future.

'That would be criminally irresponsible,' he said.[11]

Gendarmes, stripped to the waist in the sun, rolled barrels of fuel into aircraft, loaded boxes of weapons, crates of supplies. Other equipment left for the Angolan border by train. Belgian farmers shot their livestock. Tshombe's men sealed the Katangese cash reserves into wooden crates and flew them to Angola. The president's luxury DC-3, bought from a Puerto Rican millionaire and his French cabaret singer wife in August 1962, transported Katangese soldiers into Angolan exile. The Belgian pilot tried to sell it to cover his unpaid wages but Portuguese secret police got their hands on the plane first.

Rhodesian spies helped smuggle Katanga's gold reserves over the border. Kibwe had invested heavily in gold during the secession as a hedge against Katanga's foreign accounts being frozen.

Mercenaries, gendarmes and paracommandos prepared to leave for Dilolo by train and plane. Mortars and machine gun fire could be heard from the outskirts of Kolwezi as UN troops mopped up gendarmes in nearby villages and towns.

'I can tell you,' said Swede Tommy Nilsson, 'most of them were happy to go back to a civilian life with their wives and children. On one occasion, we disarmed 1,500 gendarmes, paid their salary and said goodbye to them. Not one single shot was fired – good for all of us.'[12]

Tshombe radioed the garrison at Baudouinville, still holding out against UN and ANC troops, and ordered them to surrender. Indonesian paratroopers rode the barge into Baudouinville at daybreak on Sunday to discover that the gendarmes and most of the population had fled. A pocket of gendarmes under Colonel Makito near Kongolo, east of the River Lualaba, finally surrendered to Nigerian and Malaysian UN troops.

Discipline broke down in the last days of Kolwezi. Two of Denard's men tried to steal Puren's jeep while he took a shower. He chased them down the street, wearing only a towel. One pulled a knife from his boot. Puren was saved by Verloo, the man with whom he had escaped from UN custody back in August 1961, who appeared with a sub-machine gun.

'Come on Jerry. Nothing personal', said Denard when he heard. 'We just need transport.'[13]

Late on Saturday 20 January, Puren and Julia were married in a white-walled Kolwezi church by a stammering American Methodist priest. The streets were deserted when they walked out. Denard and Schramme had already gone, heading a river of Katangese gendarmes, paracommandos and their families moving towards the Angolan border by train, lorry and jeep. The couple held a celebration in the Hôtel Bon Auberge for the few friends still left in town. At dawn the next day, the Purens left in a Tri-Pacer light aircraft from Kolwezi airstrip.

At 1 p.m., Indian UN armoured cars entered Kolwezi. The locals waved. '*Jambo, Jambo UN!*' they cried. Welcome, welcome UN.

The UN lost ten men in Operation Grand Slam, mostly Indian. In the chaos of the Katangese retreat no one was counting casualties, although a figure of 276 African dead, most civilians, was floated to journalists.


On 21 January, Tshombe signed an official declaration that the secession had ended. Along with Munongo, Yav, Muke, Kimba and Kibwe, he dined with UN officials in Kolwezi.

'Atmosphere friendly', a UN man telegraphed to Léopoldville, 'but throughout our conversation we felt Tshombe and Cabinet are extremely REPEAT extremely bitter about Europeans in general, Belgians in particular.'[14]

Munongo publically renounced any further resistance or guerrilla warfare. Tshombe announced that he was prepared to work with Léopoldville to solve the Congo crisis. On Tuesday, Joseph Ileo arrived in Elisabethville to take over the province for the central government and Tshombe returned to the presidential palace to await his fate. UN and Congolese flags flew over Katangese towns.

Since 1960, the UN had lost 135 men in the Congo, including fourteen Irish soldiers (nine of those killed by Baluba at Niemba), thirty-nine Indian, nineteen Swedish and forty-seven Ghanaian soldiers.[15] Only around half the total died at the hands of the Katangese. Baluba, the Léopoldville ANC and Gizenga's men killed the rest. On the other side, perhaps only thirty-two mercenaries were killed in action during the secession. No one counted dead gendarmes, but they must have been in the low thousands. Civilian deaths on all sides amounted to at least 10,000 and were probably much higher.[16]

In Léopoldville's boulevard Albert, 600 students chanted 'Tshombe to the gallows!'[17] Others stormed the British embassy as Congolese police sat in their jeeps and laughed. Léopoldville agreed an amnesty for Tshombe and his men. The UN soon discovered that the gendarmes were only prepared to surrender if no ANC men were in the area. Kasa-Vubu gave a speech:

> Officers, non-commissioned officers and men of the former Katangese Gendarmerie, in addressing myself particularly to you this evening, I do so on behalf of the entire country, the entire nation, to congratulate you and pay you a tribute for your patriotism because it was thanks to your understanding and to your refusal to use the murderous weapons placed in your hands by foreigners that the secession was ended, without too great a loss of human life or shedding of blood.[18]

On 25 January, the last of the Katangese armed forces crossed the border into Portuguese Angola. They would return, but to fight for a different cause and against a different enemy.

Katanga had failed as a country.

# 27

# *VERS L'AVENIR*

The Rise and Fall of Moïse Tshombe

It was 29 June 1967. The Hawker Siddeley 125 business jet was somewhere over the south coast of Formentera when Francis Joseph Bodenan came out of the cockpit holding a pistol. The jet passengers looked at him in disbelief: Moïse Tshombe, two Spanish bodyguards, a disbarred Belgian lawyer and his wife, and Marcel Hambursin, a Tshombe advisor who had proved his loyalty by being arrested years ago recruiting for the secession in France.

It took a moment for them to understand what was happening. They thought the meek-looking 43-year-old with combed-back dark hair and dead eyes was a businessman taking them on a trip to Ibiza. French police could have told them Bodenan was a former soldier, scrap metal dealer and convicted murderer.

The bodyguards came out of their seats and Bodenan fired two warning shots. A ricochet hit Hambursin in the foot. All resistance ceased. The passengers lay on the carpeted floor, face down, hands laced behind their heads. Bodenan returned to the cockpit and pointed his gun at the two British pilots.

'*En Algérie! En Algérie!*' he said. '*Comprenez-vous?*'[1]

They understood. Captain David Taylor junked his course to Ibiza and set a new one for Algeria. As the HS-125 turned in the sky, Taylor tried to work out who was behind this mid-air kidnapping. General Mobutu? Paris? The CIA? In the four and a half years since Katanga had collapsed, Tshombe had been a renegade, an exile and Prime Minister of the Congo. He had a lot of enemies.

When the UN inspected the Katangese treasury in January 1963, it found $116.28 rather than the $16.2 million it had been expecting.[2] In the last desperate days of the secession, Tshombe's ministers had smuggled suitcases of cash and bags of gold coins over the border. At least a billion francs had gone to a bank in Ndola, Rhodesia. Tshombe denied all responsibility.

'Never trust the whites,' he told an Indian UN commander. 'They're your worst enemies too. The Belgians led me down the wrong path.'

Léopoldville swallowed the loss, split Katanga into three provinces and welcomed back any secessionists prepared to accept Adoula's authority. No one was surprised when Évariste Kimba, who had been critical of Tshombe in the last months of the secession, took a government post, but Elisabethville's remaining ultras felt betrayed when Munongo switched sides. Tshombe would have been equally happy to serve the new regime but Adoula never asked. In June 1963, the former Katangese president managed to extract a diplomatic passport from Congolese Foreign Minister Auguste Mabika-Kalanda and flew to Paris.

Around 240 loyal Katangese gendarmes and sixty whites, like Jean Schramme and Jerry Puren, remained in Angola on several farms owned by Tshombe, calling themselves the Forces Katangaises Libres (Free Katangese Forces – FKL). As the days got longer and the wages more infrequent, the FKL's whites began to slip away. No new mercenaries replaced them. Marissal had died in February 1963 and his recruitment network was buried with him. Bob Denard headed to the Middle East, where he trained troops fighting to put the deposed Imam of Yemen back on the throne. British intelligence ran the Yemen operation, employing Roger Faulques to recruit additional mercenaries in London and Paris. An Egyptian fighter jet killed Tony de Saint-Paul on Christmas Eve 1963.

By the time Denard returned to France the next year, the remains of the FKL were back in the Congo. They had a new war.

The Simbas were a locust swarm of leopard skin, machetes and teenage hate from the villages of the east and north. They stripped the life from any area they touched. Former Lumumba loyalists like Pierre Mulele and Christopher Gbenye, operating from exile in Brazzaville, had stirred them up in late 1963 with Soviet money. The exiles wanted to overthrow Adoula and install a Moscow-friendly regime. Their new army cared more about spilling blood than class warfare.

Mulele led the Kivu section and Laurent Kabila a more organised group to the north-east, but neither man could control the Simbas, many of whom were *dagga* smokers who spent every day in a drugged haze. Tens of thousands of Congolese died (including Jason Sendwe, pulled from his car and hacked to pieces in June 1964), many tortured first. Special hatred was reserved for Europeans. Nuns and missionaries were favourite targets.

'It was anarchy, complete chaos,' said Pierre Matata, who tended gardens in Kasongo:

These guys came from the bush and they basically settled grievances against the outsiders, the Belgians, the Arabs, everyone who was not what they regarded as real Congolese. But it was not just whites they targeted. Any Congolese like us who lived in the town were a target for their hatred. They saw us as collaborators with the whites and they were cruel with us. They killed absolutely anyone connected with the white world, the modern world.[4]

Adoula's government collapsed. The UN had already left the country, the last troops pulling out in June 1964. New York decided that the Simba rebellion was not its fight. Mobutu and Kasa-Vubu seemed powerless. The ANC dropped their weapons and ran before charging waves of Simbas who, like the Baluba Jeunesse before them, believed magic made them bulletproof. They trusted in 'Mai Mulele' (Mulele's [magic] water) and muttered blessings from a witch-doctor in leopard skin and feathers. By 1964, the Simbas controlled most of Orientale and Kivu provinces. Cuba's Che Guevara hailed them as revolution-ary heroes and Peking sent weapons.

The Congo needed a new leader. Mobutu offered the job to Tshombe, then living in exile in Madrid. It had a crazy logic. The former secessionist was charismatic, with useful contacts in Belgium and a loyal army waiting in Angolan exile. Tshombe took the job. He did not tell Léopoldville that Simba leaders had previously asked him to lead their rebellion but had not been able to meet his terms.

Bombs set by Simba sympathisers were going off daily in Léopoldville when Tshombe arrived in June 1964 to become prime minister. He brought back old friends, like Godefroid Munongo and Albert Kalonji, and tried to negoti-ate with the Simbas, releasing Antoine Gizenga from house arrest and offering government posts.

'I explained that they should not destroy the schools and dispensaries,' said Tshombe, 'that they must not harass the whites, that our future did not lie in turning back and shrouding ourselves in tradition'.[5]

The Simbas, who barely listened to their own leaders, were in no mood to obey Tshombe. In August 1964, Stanleyville fell to the eastern rebels and became their new capital. Thousands of Congolese were publically tortured and hacked to pieces at the city's Lumumba monument, a life-size painted image set behind plastic like a cross between a Catholic icon and an advertising hoarding. Khanti Patel, the 10-year-old son of Indian shopkeepers, watched Simbas march near his home:

My father said don't go near the windows at all. And the Simbas were walk-ing past and some of them were about twelve, thirteen years old. And the older ones were all in the skins and palm tree fronds, and they just went 'Mai

Mulele Mai'. The next morning we found a dead body on the other side of the road, just opposite us.[6]

A few weeks later, he saw a group of teenage Simbas rape the mother of his Belgian schoolfriend in the street outside, then shoot the whole family dead.

Surrounding African nations refused to send troops to help. Belgium and America offered only advisors, including Colonel Frédéric Vandewalle. As the Simbas took more and more territory, Tshombe went back to his mercenaries. His decision owed something to Jerry Puren, the South African who had stayed by his side since the fall of Katanga. Puren believed that only white soldiers could bring order to the Congo and had a man in mind to lead them: Mike Hoare, the Irish-born mercenary he knew from his Compagnie Internationale days.

Hoare accepted the contract and set up recruiting centres in Rhodesia, Léopoldville and South Africa. He called his unit 5 Commando. Hoare's volunteers signed contracts (which promised, among other things, 600,000 Belgian francs for the loss of an arm) and trained hard. Discipline was tough, at first. Hoare shot the toes off a Belgian mercenary found guilty of rape. Soon his collection of South Africans with beards and bibles, hard-drinking Belgian dogs of war, white supremacist Rhodesians and adventurers from across the world headed into the jungle to fight.

Hoare's first attack on the Simbas was a disaster. An assault on Albertville left two German mercenaries dead and the unit fleeing for its life. The fiasco could have broken the authority of a lesser man but Hoare returned to base and reorganised 5 Commando with the help of American CIA officers who were secretly advising Tshombe. The Congolese prime minister supported Hoare but was disappointed enough by his failure to recruit more mercenaries, this time from France and Belgium. Former Katanga mercenary Bob Denard joined up with them and eventually became their leader.

Hoare's 5 Commando was all-white and Anglophone but Denard's men were French-speakers commanding black troops. Volunteers signed up in Europe through the Congolese embassies in Paris and Brussels, or via an American army officer who rented office space in the south of France. Some more exotic volunteers included Rafał Gan-Ganowicz, a fanatically anti-communist Pole who had escaped his home country one step ahead of a KGB firing squad by clinging to the underside of a train bound for West Berlin, and a collection of Italian far-right activists desperate for a chance to shoot 'Reds'.

Denard's men did not much like 5 Commando, and the feeling was mutual. The waters were further muddied by the arrival of Jean Schramme's private militia, the Battalion Léopard, who still hated all mercenaries, and a new outfit led by Christian Tavernier. The quarrelling commandos had no time to sharpen their claws on each other. Tshombe sent them after the Simbas. Out in the bush, all ideas of conventional warfare were abandoned. Katangese gendarmes, ANC troops and even former Balubakat Jeunesse went in alongside the mercenaries as a mobile column of jeeps and lorries, machine guns mounted on every surface, spitting fire at anything that moved. In the heat of battle, it was hard to distinguish civilians from combatants. Some mercenaries did not bother to try.

'If they caught you and you were black, you were dead,' said Brian McCabe, a young South African who ditched a clerical job for the mercenary life.[7]

The mercenaries were equally ruthless with each other. McCabe remembered a bullying sergeant, hated by his men, who was casually shot dead in a row over a card game.

Tshombe and Mobutu wanted 5 Commando to launch a direct attack on Simba bases in the north-east. Instead, Hoare sent his men on relief missions to besieged white communities deep in the jungle. Simbas were chased down and killed, and Belgian nuns and missionaries fell into the arms of mercenaries who stank of gun smoke and blood.

Female hostages had undergone horrific ordeals. Dr Helen Roseveare, a British missionary, was raped and tortured for weeks by a Simba gang. Only her religion kept her sane until the day a Rhodesian mercenary kicked open the door of the hut in which she was held prisoner and carried her into the sunlight. Roseveare survived to write a best-selling book about her ordeal. Her rescuer died two days later stepping on a land mine.

By late 1964, the Simba rebellion began to crumble but the rebels held onto Stanleyville and its inhabitants. The Belgian consul, Baron Patrick Nothomb, a dishevelled little man full of bravery, tried to protect the city's European residents. His phone number (2094) became the most dialled extension in town. Although he worked miracles as he dashed from compound to compound, begging and bribing favours from Simba commanders, he could only do so much. Europeans and Congolese began to disappear from their homes. In ranting monologues, Simba leader Christopher Gbenye threatened to kill every white person in the Congo.

Mike Hoare's mercenaries, Denard's men and Schramme's Battalion Léopard joined forces in a rescue column. Belgium agreed to supply paracommandos, all young men on their national service, for an airdrop by American aeroplanes. One of them was Victor Rosez, who had joined the Belgian army.

On 24 November 1964, the Simbas lashed out in a final round of murder when they heard aeroplanes droning overhead. American missionary Paul Coulson was among those shot dead in the street. Then Belgian paratroopers floated out of the sky and suddenly their red berets were everywhere as they took back the town.

Mercenaries fought Simba witchdoctors in the Stanleyville suburbs. African bodies lay in fly-swarmed piles along the mango tree-lined avenues. Thousands died. With the fall of Stanleyville, the Simbas retreated into their strongholds of north-eastern Congo. By the end of 1965, the Simba rebellion had collapsed despite reinforcements from Cuba, including Ernesto 'Che' Guevara himself, the symbol of Marxist revolution. The rebellion had killed at least 200,000 people.

'A poor man's Vietnam', said NBC's Chet Huntley in 1966.[8]

It should have been Moïse Tshombe's triumph. The Simbas defeated in a year and a half, the hostages rescued and peace returned to the Congo. Yet by 1966, Tshombe was again in exile.

It was a re-run of the dispute over Lumumba's rule in 1960. As Tshombe's popularity rose in the wake of his victory, President Kasa-Vubu turned against him and the resulting row paralysed the government. Mobutu, supported by America, stepped in and removed both from power. Tshombe remained in the Congo for several weeks, muttering threats about taking control by force. Mobutu charged him with treason and the former prime minister fled to exile in Madrid.

'The regime of General Mobutu cannot last,' predicted Tshombe. 'Law and order hang on the slenderest thread. It is by weakness that Mobutu has become a tyrant. He reigns by terror, his ultimate resource. It is inevitable that his regime must crumble before the rage of the people.'[9]

Mobutu declared himself sole ruler of the Congo. He sent Mike Hoare, the mercenary most loyal to Tshombe, back to South Africa. Hoare was replaced as leader of 5 Commando by John Peters, a tough Yorkshireman from the Merchant Navy who had no interest in politics.

Bob Denard, his Francophone men now rounded up into 6 Commando, swore loyalty to Mobutu. The Quai d'Orsay (France's Ministry of Foreign Affairs) had decided that the new Congolese dictator was a man they could do business with. They ordered Denard not to rock the boat. The Frenchman even located Stanleyville's gold reserves, which had been looted by the Simbas, and returned them to Léopoldville. His honesty made Mobutu suspicious.

Tshombe still had supporters. Katangese soldiers who had followed their leader from secession to defeat and back remained in the ranks of the Congolese army. Ostensibly loyal to Mobutu, they were in clandestine contact with Tshombe. Jean Schramme, the Belgian warlord who now ruled a corner of

the eastern Congo as if it was it his own private kingdom, also hated the country's new ruler. Denard soon showed his own signs of independence from Paris.

In July 1966, a unit of Katangese soldiers rebelled against the Mobutu regime.
Fighting broke out near Stanleyville. Mobutu called on America for help. With
US guns and foreign advisors, including Israeli army officers attached to the
CIA, the Congo's new ruler beat the Katangese across the border into Tanzania
and Rwanda. Captured rebels were tortured and murdered. It was an ama-
teurish attempt at a coup organised by Tshombe from his Spanish exile and
discreetly funded by UMHK, which saw its mines nationalised in the aftermath.

Tshombe's fatal mistake was to move without the support of his mercenaries. Denard had met with Tshombe a few months previously, while on leave
in Brussels, and warned him that the time was not right for revolt. The coup
came as an unpleasant surprise. A number of Denard's men were arrested by
Congolese troops on suspicion of involvement and some were killed. A massacre was only averted by Denard flying to Léopoldville and convincing Mobutu
that 6 Commando remained loyal.

Tshombe learned his lesson. Over the next few months, cables and letters
flew between Madrid and the Congo. Schramme and Denard agreed to help
him try again. John Peters declined to get involved (he was rumoured to have
murdered a Rhodesian mercenary who wanted him to align 5 Commando
with Tshombe) and left the country in February 1967, passing command to
24-year-old South African George Schroder. Mobutu disbanded and repatriated 5 Commando a few months later.

Denard and Schramme were the last men standing. Schramme could barely
tolerate being in the same room as the Frenchman, his dislike having grown
into hatred after one of his friends died in mysterious circumstances during
an argument with Denard. All that kept the pair together was the knowledge
that Mobutu intended to disband both mercenary groups to create a purely
Congolese army. They had to act soon.

But something had gone badly wrong. Two months earlier, Tshombe had
been kidnapped at gunpoint on a flight from Madrid.


The Hawker Siddeley 125 business jet touched down in Algiers. Journalists
assumed that the Algerians were behind the hijacking but Captain David Taylor
remembered how confused the local authorities had been when Bodenan led
the passengers off the plane at gunpoint. The Algerians held everyone for several months, torturing some, before expelling all the prisoners except Tshombe
and Bodenan.

It was rumoured that the Frenchman was working for the SDECE or even
the CIA, both agencies close to the new Mobutu regime and hostile to the

idea of Tshombe retaking power. Bodenan had connections with the French police and had served only ten years in prison for murdering two of his business partners. On his release in 1966, he had morphed suspiciously quickly into an international businessman, flying around the Mediterranean and doing deals with people close to Tshombe.

The former Katangese president had been lured onto Bodenan's private flight to Ibiza with the promise of a business deal that would make him rich enough to fund the overthrow of Mobutu. He ended up in a North African prison cell.

Schramme and Denard went ahead with the rebellion anyway when Mobutu ordered Battalion Léopard to give up its weapons in August 1967. Schramme moved on Stanleyville and sent Congolese government troops fleeing. Denard supported him.

But without Tshombe's presence, the coup had no direction and Schramme's men wandered aimlessly around north-east Congo routing government troops but failing to make lasting gains. Denard was wounded and evacuated himself with many of his men over the border to Rwanda, an act Schramme regarded as betrayal, although the 6 Commando leader's head wound was serious enough to temporarily paralyse his right side.

When he had recovered, Denard attempted to invade southern Congo from Portuguese Angola. His French government contacts gave him no support, waiting to see how things worked out. The Portuguese played the same game and refused to provide vehicles, so Denard invaded by bicycle, one of the stranger military actions in his career. It was a failure and left Schramme alone to face the fury of Mobutu and his American backers.

'You are murderers,' the Belgian bitterly radioed Denard's HQ.[10]

Battalion Léopard fought its way eastwards towards Lake Tanganyika. There it captured the town of Bukavu, once an upscale holiday destination, and dug in. Schramme's men were now a cross-section of the Congo's wars including Belgians, ex-Katangese soldiers, ANC deserters, former Balubakat, members of Denard's 6 Commando, a few veterans of Hoare's 5 Commando who had chosen to stay on when their comrades left and dogs of war born everywhere from South Africa to Hungary. Some were fighting for glory, some for Katanga, others for white colonialism in Africa. A few even believed they could still get rich. Bukavu was their last stand.

Mobutu's ANC occupied the hills around the town. Advising them were American CIA operatives and Israeli army officers. In the skies over Bukavu, pilots who had been allies of the mercenaries only weeks before now dropped bombs on the town. The Belgian government observed the siege from over the border in Rwanda. Even Jerry Puren, who had left the country with Tshombe in 1966, flew in to join the mercenaries, his plane ditching in Lake Tanganyika.

Schramme's men were 1,000 against 10,000 opposing soldiers. They held out for twelve weeks of increasingly desperate fighting then, with the battle, the war and the cause irretrievably lost, slipped across the border to Rwanda in the last days of October 1967.

It rained the day they left, turning roads to mud. Civilians mixed with the mercenary column, leaving the country many called home for the last time. A French news cameraman filmed a little girl in a plastic raincoat dragging her teddy bear behind her in the mud. In Rwanda, Belgian soldiers disarmed the mercenaries and interned them in a prison camp. They would stay there for the best part of a year before being repatriated. Mobutu had won. The independence wars were over.

Tshombe remained in Algerian solitary confinement, his health deteriorating, living off bread and olives, reports of torture printed in the foreign press. Mobutu wanted him extradited but relations with Algeria, previously good enough to support conspiracy theories about the hijacking, had fallen apart by the late 1960s. The Algerians hung on to their uninvited guest and in 1969 moved him to a villa in the hills overlooking Algiers. On 30 June, the Algerian government reported he had died in bed of a heart attack.

Tshombe's death ended a final attempt by Jean Schramme to overthrow Mobutu. The settler had returned to Belgium a hero in 1967 but was charged with murder the following year when it emerged he had shot dead a man in the Congo who threatened to reveal his coup plan to Léopoldville.

After skipping out on his trial, Jean Schramme hid in a remote villa in Portugal. A British mercenary discovered him there test firing machine guns. The Portuguese government thought it could use Schramme to overthrow Mobutu and put Tshombe back in power. Mike Hoare was also approached and Hubert Julian may have been involved in plans for a raid on Tshombe's prison villa in Algiers. After Tshombe's death and under pressure from the CIA, Portugal abandoned the plan.

Schramme went off to Brazil and spent the next twenty years roaming South America, allegedly helping the Bolivian secret services at one point, before returning to his roots as a farmer near Mato Grosso. He married a local woman and started a family. In 1983, Belgium tried to gain his extradition. Schramme spent a few months in a Brasilia jail before the government decided not to send him back due to his dual citizenship. He got twenty years' hard labour in absentia and returned to his Mato Grosso farm, dying there in 1988.

Bodenan, Tshombe's kidnapper, was expelled to Switzerland three and half months after Tshombe's death. He lived there until 1973 (there were rumours that he had earned 10 million francs for the kidnapping) until Zurich kicked him out. He was subsequently imprisoned in Belgium for unrelated crimes: the statute of limitations on his role in the hijacking had run out. In 1982, Brussels extradited him to Madrid to face charges over the kidnapping of the two Spanish bodyguards on the flight. He got twenty years.


Biafra was the next mercenary payday after the Congo. Nigeria's southern region declared independence in May 1967, hoping to prop up its economy with oil money. Pictures of starving Biafran children made the international community more sympathetic to this secession.

Bob Denard shipped in arms, Roger Faulques organised mercenaries and Jean Zumbach abandoned a profitable business selling second-hand aeroplanes to organise the Biafran Air Force. John Trevelyn got involved. Mike Hoare approached both sides about creating a mercenary force but was turned down. Veterans of 5 Commando could be found on both sides of the fighting.

The secession ended on 15 January 1970 and Biafra was absorbed back into Nigeria. Trevelyn headed to America and a profitable life in business. Faulques dropped out of the mercenary racket for retirement in France. He died in 2011, fifteen years after Roger Trinquier, who had spent his last decades as a civilian, writing his memoirs and tending his garden. After a brief involvement with German mercenary Rolf Steiner's adventures in Sudan, Zumbach also quit the war game and headed back to Gisèle and Paris. He sold aeroplanes until the late 1970s when he surprised former comrades by forming a business venture with a Major Lokuciewski, a former RAF pilot now loyal to the communists in Warsaw. The pair exported Polish army surplus to various pro-Soviet governments in the Third World. The Służba Bezpieczeństwa (Polish security service) was also involved. In 1986 Zumbach died of cancer in Paris. Disillusioned former friends preferred to claim he had been murdered by agents from behind the Iron Curtain.

Mike Hoare returned to being an accountant but made numerous efforts to rejoin the mercenary life. In the early 1970s, the *Daily Mirror* accused him of recruiting soldiers for the war in Vietnam during a stay in Singapore. In 1974, the South African secret service warned him off involvement in Southern Rhodesia. Then the newspapers claimed he would fight in Mozambique against FRELIMO. That also failed to happen. In 1976, Hoare was approached to find 150 mercenaries for Angola with a budget of $10 million but the deal fell through. He wrote books about his Congo adventures and worked as an advisor to the 1979 mercenary movie *The Wild Geese*.

Soon after, he tried a coup in the Seychelles, accompanied by Jerry Puren. After Bukavu, the South African had returned to Durban with Julia, started up a car repossession business and become a father again. But the flame of adventure still burned and he joined Hoare's coup attempt. It went wrong and led to a firefight, a plane hijacking and jail for both men. The fall out ended their friendship. Puren wrote up his memoirs as *Mercenary Commander* when he got out, then died soon after it was published in 1986. Hoare never forgave him for some critical comments in the book.

Denard stayed on the mercenary road. A failed 1977 coup in Benin is remembered abroad today only because it led to the arrest of British writer Bruce Chatwin, wrongly suspected of being one of Denard's men. There were other adventures in Chad and Kurdistan, some sanction busting between Gabon and Rhodesia, rumours of assassinations carried out for money. Through it all, he had the support of important men in the French government, notably Jacques Foccart, de Gaulle's eyes on Africa. In 1978, Denard overthrew a government he had helped install three years earlier in the Comoros Islands off the east coast of Africa. He liked the place so much he stayed on as 'Colonel Said Mustapha M'hadju', Minister of Defence. Denard converted to Islam, picked up several wives and effectively ran the islands for seventeen years before one coup too many provoked Paris into sending in the troops. He died in October 2007 at 78, after years of retirement in South Africa and France.

Time thinned out other Katanga faces. Philippa Schuyler died as a war correspondent in Vietnam on 9 May 1967, when her helicopter ditched into the sea near Da Nang. Hubert Julian died on 19 February 1983 at the age of 86, after many years of smuggling, arms dealing and bad publicity. John Roberts, the South Kasaï mercenary, disappeared from public view after briefing Tory MPs on the secession at the House of Commons. Richard Browne of the Compagnie Internationale got into the mining business in South Africa and Scotland, remarried and died in 1992.

Jean Thiriart died the same year on a trip to Moscow. He had spent the previous decades trying to promote pan-European communitarianism through groups like Jeune Europe. His mix of left and right inspired everyone from Russian fascists to Renato Curcio, founder of Italian leftist terror group the Brigate Rosse (Red Brigades).

On the United Nations side, Conor Cruise O'Brien died in 2008 after decades as an intellectual agitator in academia and Irish politics. His 1962 memoir *To Katanga and Back*, a masterclass in rococo prose, annoyed many in the UN by blaming Hammarskjöld and Khiari for Operation Morthor, and ducking any personal responsibility. Swedish UN man Tommy Nilsson went home in May 1963 but the following year signed up again to police Cyprus. After that, it was back to the Malmö police and a career keeping the streets of Sweden safe. He was clear-eyed about how his fellow Swedes viewed the secession:

It's my opinion that the Katanga-case wasn't of great interest in Sweden. I don't think that many knew anything about Katanga, where it was located, what the trouble down there consisted of and depended on and why Swedish troops were there. At this time, most of the Swedes swam in their own little duck-pond. The only ones who had some interest in it and followed it were parents, wives, children and other relatives to the soldiers. Of course, when the fights were going on and the newspapers headlines were written in big, black letters, some more woke up, not all, but the day after it was forgotten again.[11]

Belgian soldier Guy Weber died in 2002, leaving behind a number of books and no regrets. Fouga pilot Pierre Magain returned home and ended up owning a chain of laundrettes. He regarded Katanga as ancient history and could not understand why anyone cared enough about it to interview him. Christian Tavernier stayed loyal to Mobutu through the mercenary revolt. He was rewarded with a job as a military advisor, which he combined with publishing ventures in Europe. Enemies claimed he was an agent for the Belgian secret services.

Charles Masy served in 5 Commando, taking part in Mike Hoare's disastrous attack on Albertville and later in the liberation of Stanleyville. Then there was some action in Yemen before he returned to Brussels to open Bar Simba.

'Everyone comes here,' said Masy. 'Generals sit down and drink with privates. That's the way it is.'[12]

Bar Simba shut down years ago. Today, former colonists who might have appreciated a Simba beer stay at home and flick through albums of black and white photographs. They like to show off pictures of Baudouin I driving through Léopoldville. The colonists cross themselves as they remember Baudouin's death in 1993. They make coffee and talk about life in the colonies. On the way to the door they might stroke a dusty black monkey skin hanging on the wall over a shelf filled deep with African tchotchkes. Memories are all they have left.

Mobutu remained dictator of the Congo for thirty-two years, most of them swimming in blood and corruption. He had widespread international support. America's President Kennedy died in Dallas at the hands of a disgruntled Marxist-Leninist in November 1963 (although many liked to believe some-one else pulled the trigger) but subsequent administrations continued to back Mobutu. Larry Devlin remained close by, first as an agency man and later representing the de Beers diamond cartel. His 2007 memoir *Chief of Station, Congo*, published the year before he died, is less candid than it appears.

Mobutu treated his enemies with both ruthlessness and charity. Godefroid Munongo had been a minister in Tshombe's Congolese government. In October 1964, he became governor of Katanga province, then from April 1965 governor of South Katanga, after the provinces were sliced even more thinly. He was arrested when Mobutu came to power and imprisoned on an island in the mouth of the River Congo until his pardon in August 1968.

Munongo was luckier than Évariste Kimba, who served briefly as prime minister after Tshombe's removal. In June 1966, Mobutu publically hanged Kimba in Léopoldville, alleging a coup plot.

Munongo spent the next eight years quietly, until his brother, chief of the Bayeke, died and he became Mwenda VI, fifth successor to Msiri's throne. The remainder of his life was spent as royalty. In 1992, he announced that he would tell the truth about the death of Patrice Lumumba. His statement was scheduled for 5 p.m. on 28 May. That lunchtime, Mwenda VI died of a heart attack.

He passed away in the last years of Mobutu's Congo, the country renamed 'Zaire' in 1971 as part of a process of Africanisation which included renaming Léopoldville as Kinshasa and Elisabethville as Lubumbashi. In 1997, Laurent Kabila, the former Balubakat and Simba commander, invaded and seized power. Christian Tavernier led a group of mostly Serb mercenaries that failed to stop Kabila, but the Belgian escaped with his life. Zaire became the Democratic Republic of the Congo and conflict returned as African nations jostled to support or depose the new leader. So many countries sent troops that the conflict became known as 'Africa's World War'. Kabila died in 2001 and the Congo wars ended two years later. The country has still not recovered. Guerrillas and foreign soldiers, mostly exiled Rwandans, stalk the eastern jungles raping and murdering.

Albert Kalonji watched it all happen from his exile in Paris. The *Mulopwe* looked more like a malignant raisin with every passing year and preferred to rewrite history than return to his homeland.

'We were not manipulated by the Belgians,' he said. 'We were nationalists opposed to the concentration of power in Léopoldville, in short, federalists for the good of the Congo.'[13]

There are still secessionists and federalists in Katanga, where the Tshombe years lie like sediment in the collective memory. Some men collect memorabilia from the secession, like engraved plates and tattered flags, and dream of the day Katanga will be independent again. They claim that Tshombe tried to build a bridge between tribal Africa and the modern state, between white and black; that Katanga only became a victim of the Cold War because world superpowers needed the secession crushed to earn the admiration of Afro-Asian postcolonial countries; that those postcolonial countries wanted Katanga finished more from fear of home-grown secessionist movements than any moral objections to the province's independence.

Outside the Congo, the secession occasionally flicks its tail above the waves in popular culture. In 1962, Christian Souris, a Belgian journalist who worked as an information officer and fought against the first Baluba revolts, published *Les héros sont affreux* under the pseudonym Christian Lanciney, a novel based on truth. Other novels, including Wilbur Smith's 1966 *Last Train from Katanga*, touch on the subject. The protagonist of Frederick Forsythe's 1971 novel *The Day of the Jackal*, about a plot to assassinate de Gaulle, is a veteran of Katanga. Belgium is his hunting ground for weapons and fake passports.

In 1968, Pino Carusa, an Italian singer popular in Rome's cabaret world, recorded *Il Mercenario di Lucera* (The Mercenary from Lucera), a cynical soldier's lament whose protagonist is a Katanga veteran. The same year, a group of working-class French taking part in the occupation of the Sorbonne campus in Paris called themselves 'Les Katangais', trying to persuade journalists that they had been mercenaries, although none were old enough. Two years later, the 'Katanghesi' was the name adopted by leftist streetfighters of Milan's Movimento Studentesco (Student Movement) during clashes with the Italian police. The Vietnam War had pushed Katanga so far from popular memory that neither group realised the secession had been a right-wing phenomenon. No one in communist Poland cared much either. Its Silesia region was seen as so autonomous under local leader Edward Gierek in the 1960s that it was known as 'the Polish Katanga'.[14]

Only a few non-fiction books have been written about the secession since the 1960s and hardly any in recent years. The most prominent was 1999's *The Assassination of Lumumba* by left-wing Flemish sociologist Ludo de Witte. It accused the Belgian government of killing Lumumba, building a case from suspicious telexes and government memos. Brussels launched an official investigation in 2001, which disproved some of de Witte's accusations but accepted that Belgium had failed in its moral duty to stop the Katangese killing Lumumba. It found no evidence that the Belgian government had ordered the assassination. Some believed the conclusion; others did not.

The investigation brought historical debris to the surface in its wake. A documentary television crew tracked down Gérard Soete to talk about what happened to Lumumba's corpse. After the fall of Katanga, the Flamand had switched sides and worked as a policeman under Mobutu, before returning to Bruges to become a schoolteacher and writer. As the cameras rolled, Soete revealed he still kept Lumumba's teeth in a wooden box. He died the year after his interview, in 2000.

Dag Hammarskjöld's death is equally controversial. In 2011, British academic Susan Williams wrote *Who Killed Hammarskjöld?*, a comprehensive survey of conspiracy theories surrounding the crash: confessions of dying mercenaries, overlooked black Rhodesian eyewitnesses, even a playing card snagged in

Hammarskjöld's shirt pocket. Despite her research, many refuse to believe that the Swede's death was anything but an accident. Aviation experts point out that 65 per cent of all aeroplane crashes in the 1960s were caused by crew error.[15] But the book convinced UN investigators to recommend a new inquiry in 2013, hoping to shake loose any missing pieces of the puzzle. Nothing definitive emerged.

No one is interested in investigating Tshombe's death, although it also involves conspiracies, Western secret services and rumours of assassination. He is dismissed as a puppet of white imperialism and capitalism, hanging on strings pulled from Brussels. Tshombe did not behave the way the world wanted postcolonial Africans to behave. No one seems to care how or why he died.

# NOTES

*Katanga Confidential*

1 'Assassination: Colonial Style –
Patrice Lumumba, an African
Tragedy', CBC Documentary, 2007.

2 'Congo: Boom in the Jungle', *Time*,
16 May 1955.

3 'Brussels' Bar Simba', *Soldier of
Fortune*, August 1987.

4 Roberts, John, *My Congo Adventure*
(Jarrolds, 1963), p. 77.

5 'Assassination: Colonial Style', CBC.

*1 A Slice of African Cake*
Background for the Congo under
Léopold II and subsequent Belgian
colonialism comes from Colin Legum's
*Congo Disaster* (Penguin, 1961) and *The
Congo: Plunder and Resistance* by David
Renton, David Seddon and Leo Zeilig
(Zed Books, 2007).

1 'Congo: Freedom at Last', *Time*,
30 June 1960.

2 www.nationalarchives.gov.uk/
news/421.htm.

3 Tyler, Rev. Josiah, *Livingstone Lost and
Found* (Mutual Publishing Company,
1873), p. 329.

4 Renton, Seddon and Zeilig, *The
Congo: Plunder and Resistance*, p. 18.

5 Legum, *Congo Disaster*, p. 21.

6 Nzongola-Ntalaja, Georges, *The
Congo from Leopold to Kabila* (Zed
Books, 2004), p. 16.

7 Forbath, Peter, *The River Congo: The
Discovery, Explorations and Exploitation
of the World's Most Dramatic Rivers*
(Harper & Row, 1977), p. 374.

8 Gondola, Ch. Didier, *The History of
the Congo* (Greenwood Publishing
Group, 2002), p. 50.

9 www.urome.be/en/econgchiff.htm.

10 Farr, Michael, *Tintin: The Complete
Companion* (John Murray, 2001), p. 22.

11 Green, Lawrence G., 'Africa's "Heart
of Darkness" Today', *The Living Age*,
1 August 1929.

12 Waldron, D'Lynn, extract from
*The Secret in the Heart of Darkness:
The Sabotaged Independence of the
Belgian Congo* (www.dlwaldron.com/
Luluabourg.html).

13 Renton, Seddon and Zeilig, *The
Congo: Plunder and Resistance*, p. 61.

14 O'Brien, Connor Cruise, *To Katanga
and Back* (Simon & Schuster, 1962),
p. 160.

15 O'Donoghue, David, ed., *The Irish
Army in the Congo 1960–64* (Irish
Academic Press, 2006), p. 11.

16 Gibbs, David N., *The Political Economy
of Third World Intervention* (University
of Chicago Press, 1991), p. 60.

17 *Le Potentiel*, 20 February 2006.

18 Coleman, James S., and Carl G.
Rosberg, Jr., *Political Parties and
National Integration in Tropical Africa*
(University of California Press, 1964),
p. 565.

*2 Keys to the Congo*
Patrice Lumumba's role in the Congo's independence is detailed in Legum's *Congo Disaster* and Renton, Seddon and Zeilig's *The Congo: Plunder and Resistance*. Ian Scott's *Tumbled House: The Congo at Independence* (Oxford University Press, 1969) provides a first-hand account of Léopoldville around the time of the independence celebrations.

1 www.africanrhetoric.org/pdf/L%20%20%20Lumumba%20-%20The%20Congo%20Independence%20Speech.pdf.
2 Ibid.
3 Ibid.
4 'Marred, M. Lumumba's offensive speech in King's presence', *Guardian*, 1 July 1960.
5 Ibid.
6 Shillington, Kevin, *Encyclopaedia of African History: Volume 1* (CRC Press, 2005), p. 529.
7 Kalonji, Albert, *Congo 1960, la secession du Sud-Kasaï: la vérité du Mulopwe* (L'Harmattan, 2011), p. 38, n. 14.
8 www.dlwaldron.com/deWittLumumba.html.
9 Scott, *Tumbled House*, p. 10.
10 O'Donoghue, *The Irish Army in the Congo*, p. 27.
11 Vansina, Jan, *Living with Africa* (University of Wisconsin Press, 1994), p. 75.
12 Moraes, Frank, *The Importance of Being Black: An Asian Looks at Africa* (Macmillan, 1965), p. 181.
13 Colvin, Ian, *The Rise and Fall of Moïse Tshombe* (Leslie Frewin, 1968), p. 37.
14 Gibbs, *Political Economy of Third World Intervention*, p. 74.
15 Lumumba – JPRS:4629 (US Joint Publications Research Service, 1961).
16 Trinquier, Roger, *Le temps perdu* (Albin Michel, 1978), p. 381.
17 'Arthur C. Clarke's Mysterious World', episode 11, Yorkshire Television, 1980.
18 'Marred, M. Lumumba's offensive speech in King's presence'.
19 Ibid.

*3 The Piano Player*
Information on Philippa Schuyler comes from Kathryn Talalay's biography, *Composition in Black and White: The Tragic Saga of Harlem's Biracial Prodigy* (Oxford University Press, 1995), and Schuyler's own *Who Killed the Congo?* (Devin-Adair, 1962). 'La crise congolaise de juillet 1960 et le sexe de la décolonisation' by Pedro Monaville (*Sextant* magazine, no. 25, 2008) gives an overview of the post-independence rapes and murders. Schuyler's *Who Killed the Congo?* and Sandy Gall's *Don't Worry about the Money Now* (New English Library, 1983) describe interviews with victims.

1 Schuyler, *Who Killed the Congo?*, p. 10.
2 Ibid., p. 11.
3 Gregory, Dick, 'And I Ain't Just Whistling Dixie', *Ebony* (August 1971), p. 149.
4 Talalay, *Composition in Black and White*, p. 24.
5 Ibid., p. 13.
6 Ibid., p. 79.
7 Ibid., p. 162.
8 Schuyler, *Who Killed the Congo?*, p. 170.
9 O'Donoghue, *The Irish Army in the Congo*, p. 98.
10 Schuyler, *Who Killed the Congo?*, p. 5.
11 Scott, *Tumbled House*, p. 46.
12 Willame, Jean-Claude, *Patrimonialism and Political Change in the Congo* (Stanford University Press, 1972), p. 64.
13 Ibid., p. 63.
14 Legum, *Congo Disaster*, p. 111.
15 Gall, *Don't Worry about the Money Now*, p. 118.
16 Fontaine, André, *History of the Cold War* (Vintage, 1970), p. 368.
17 Legum, *Congo Disaster*, p. 109.
18 Gall, *Don't Worry about the Money Now*, p. 117.

19 Mummendey, Dietrich, *Beyond the Reach of Reason: The Congo Story 1960–1965* (Sora Mummendey, 1997), p. 7.

20 Schuyler, *Who Killed the Congo?*, p. 16.

21 Legum, *Congo Disaster*, p. 125.

22 Davister, Pierre, 'Au pays de l'horreur', *Pourquoi Pas?*, 22 July 1960, p. 9.

23 Vansina, *Living with Africa*, p. 86.

24 Fontaine, *History of the Cold War*, p. 370.

25 Mummendey, *Beyond the Reach of Reason*, p. 7.

26 'Who Killed Lumumba? A transcript of BBC Correspondent aired on the 21st October 2000 written and presented by David Akerman', (www.raceandhistory.com/historicalviews/Lumumbascript.html).

27 Behr, Edward, *Anyone Here Been Raped and Speaks English?* (Viking Press, 1978), p. 136.

28 Schuyler, *Who Killed the Congo?*, p. 188.

## 4 Emperor Msiri's Ghost

The main sources for the events in Katanga are Jules Gérard-Libois' *Katanga Secession* (University of Wisconsin, 1966), Ian Colvin's *The Rise and Fall of Moïse Tshombe* and Smith Hempstone's *Rebels, Mercenaries and Dividends: The Katanga Story* (Praeger, 1962). Information about Roger Jaspar comes from Marie Nicolaï's *Ici Radio Katanga* (Éditions J.M. Collet, 1987).

1 Nicolaï, *Ici Radio Katanga*, p. 19.

2 Gérard-Libois, *The Katanga Secession*, p. 277.

3 Colvin, *The Rise and Fall of Moïse Tshombe*, p. 66.

4 Nicolaï, *Ici Radio Katanga*

5 Hempstone, *Rebels, Dividends and Mercenaries*, p. 19.

6 Harrison, *Dark Trophies* (Oxford, Berghahn Books, 2012), p. 70.

7 Scott, *Tumbled House*, p. 58.

8 Trinquier, Colonel Roger, Jacques Duchemin and Jacques le Bailly, *Notre guerre au Katanga* (Paris: La Pensée Moderne, 1963), p. 8.

9 Gérard-Libois, *Katanga Secession*, p. 87.

10 O'Donoghue, *The Irish Army in the Congo*, p. 101.

11 Ibid., p. 120.

12 Löfgren, Claes J.B., *Fredsknekarna: FN-Svenskarna I Kongo 1960–64* (T. Fischer & Co., 1990), p. 39.

13 O'Brien, *To Katanga and Back*, p. 119.

14 Löfgren, *Fredsknekarna*, p. 37.

15 Gall, *Don't Worry about the Money Now*, p. 128.

16 Löfgren, *Fredsknekarna*, p. 39.

17 US Documents (Department of State, Central Files, 770G.00/7–1160).

18 Nicolaï, *Ici Radio Katanga*, p. 20.

19 Ibid., p. 23.

## 5 L'Affaire du Sud-Kasaï

The main sources for the events in Kasaï are John Roberts' *My Congo Adventure*, Albert Kalonji's *Congo 1960* and *Freedom and Anarchy* by Eric S. Packham (Nova, 1996). Events elsewhere in Katanga and the Congo are covered in Gérard-Libois' *Katanga Secession* and various United Nations documents, notably the 'Second Progress Report to the Secretary General from his Special Representative in the Congo, Ambassador Rajeshwar Dayal' (S/4557).

1 Roberts, *My Congo Adventure*, p. 48.

2 De Vos, Luc, Emmanuel Gérard, Jules Gérard-Libois and Philippe Raxhorn, *Les secrets de l'affaire Lumumba* (Éditions Racine, 2005), p. 620.

3 Weber, Guy, *Comme je les ai connus* (L. Bourdeaux-Capelle, 1991), p. 94.

4 Information from J.P. Sonck, September 2012.

5 Legum, *Congo Disaster*, p. 159.

6 Boehme, Oliver, 'The Involvement of the Belgian Central Bank in the Katanga Secession 1960–63', *African Economic History*, no. 33 (2005).

7 Hempstone, *Rebels, Dividends and Mercenaries*, p. 109.

8 'UN Rushes Assurances to Katanga', *Red Bank Register*, 4 August 1960.

9 Colvin, *The Rise and Fall of Moïse Tshombe*, p. 50.

10 Roberts, *My Congo Adventure*, p. 9.

11 Schuyler, *Who Killed the Congo?*, p. 148.

12 Waldron, D'Lynn, extract from *The Secret in the Heart of Darkness: The Sabotaged Independence of the Belgian Congo* (www.dlwaldron.com/Luluabourg.html).

13 Gall, *Don't Worry about the Money Now*, p. 130.

14 Ibid., p. 133.

15 Colvin, *The Rise and Fall of Moïse Tshombe*, p. 33.

16 Kalonji, *Congo 1960*, p. 117.

17 Roberts, *My Congo Adventure*, p. 90.

18 Ibid., p. 105.

## 6 Assignment – Léopoldville

Information about Lumumba's fall from power and surrounding events comes from Devlin's *Chief of Station, Congo* (PublicAffairs, 2007), *Les secrets de l'affaire Lumumba* by de Vos, Gérard, Gérard-Libois and Raxhon, and de Witte's *The Assassination of Lumumba* (Verso, 2001). Details on the United Nations and the constitutional crisis are taken from UN document 'Second Progress Report to the Secretary General from his Special Representative in the Congo, Ambassador Rajeshwar Dayal' (S/4557).

1 Beeston, Richard, *Looking for Trouble: The Life and Times of a Foreign Correspondent* (Tauris, 2006), p. 57.

2 Devlin, *Chief of Station, Congo*, p. 50.

3 Ibid., p. 54.

4 Ibid., p. 62.

5 Urquhart, Brian, *Ralph Bunche: An American Odyssey* (W.W. Norton, 1993), p. 332.

6 'A licence to kill? Oh heavens, no!', *Daily Telegraph*, 24 April 2003.

7 Ibid.

8 Colvin, *The Rise and Fall of Moïse Tshombe*, p. 35.

9 Devlin, *Chief of Station, Congo*, p. 88.

10 Colvin, *The Rise and Fall of Moïse Tshombe*, p. 38.

11 *Transcript of The Congo Crisis, 1960–1961: A Critical Oral History Conference*, The Woodrow Wilson International Center for Scholars, 23–24 September 2004.

12 Ambrose, Stephen E. and Richard H. Immerman, *Ike's Spies: Eisenhower and the Espionage Establishment* (University Press of Mississippi), p. 295.

13 Moraes, *The Importance of Being Black*, p. 200.

14 Devlin, *Chief of Station, Congo*, p. 103.

15 Behr, *Anyone Here Been Raped and Speaks English?*, p. 143.

## 7 We Are the United Nations

Sources for United Nations activities in Katanga include O'Donoghue's *The Irish Army in the Congo*, a series of email interviews with Tommy Nilsson in 2011 and Roberts' *My Congo Adventure*.

1 www.tuamherald.ie/plus/roundup/articles/2014/03/28/4022789-from-galway-to-the-congo--into-the-heart-of-darkness--part-3.

2 O'Donoghue, *The Irish Army in the Congo*, p. 180.

3 Ibid., p. 66.

4 Ibid., p. 78.

5 Prenderville, Tom, 'Congo Hell Cannibals Killed My Comrades … And Ate Every One; Irish Soldier who Survived Jungle Horror … and Still Waits for Medal', *The People*, 30 May 2004.

6 Ibid.

7 O'Donoghue, *The Irish Army in the Congo*, p. 81.

8 Tommy Nilsson, email 2011.

9 Ibid.

10 Weber, *Comme je les ai connus*, p. 112.

11 O'Donoghue, *The Irish Army in the Congo*, p. 52.

12 Roberts, *My Congo Adventure*, p. 145.

13 Ibid., p. 157.

14 Ibid., p. 184.

15 Tommy Nilsson, email 2011.

## 8 Les Affreux

The story of Belgian mercenary recruitment is told in *Le visage des affreux* (Éditions Labor, 2005) by Roman Pasteger. Additional information about Jean Thiriart comes from Kevin Coogan's *Dreamer of the Day: Francis Parker Yockey & the Postwar Fascist International* (Autonomedia, 1999) and Martin Lee's *The Beast Reawakens* (Little, Brown, 1997). *De l'avant à l'après-guerre. L'extrême droit en Belgique francophone* by Francis Balace et al. (De Boeck Supérior, 1994) contains details about Cadba.

1 Laroche, Fabrice, *Salan devant l'opinion* (Éditions Saint-Just, 1963), p. 65.

2 Balace et al., *De l'avant à l'après-guerre*, p. 134.

3 Balace et al., *De l'avant à l'après-guerre*, p. 138.

4 Pasteger, *Le visage des affreux*, p. 12.

5 Ibid., p. 13.

6 Ibid., p. 14.

7 Bourseiller, Christophe, *Extrême-droite: l'enquête* (F. Bourrin, 1991), p. 114.

8 Laurent, Frédéric, *L'Orchestre noir* (Stock, 1978), p. 101.

9 Pasteger, *Le visage des affreux*, p. 25.

10 Ibid., p. 58.

11 O'Donoghue, *The Irish Army in the Congo*, p. 51.

## 9 The Rhodesian Connection

Information about John Trevelyn's adventures in Katanga comes from a series of email interviews conducted in 2011–12. Rhodesia's dealings with Katanga are dealt with in Matthew Hughes's article 'Fighting for White Rule in Africa: The Central African Federation, Katanga, and the Congo Crisis, 1958–65', which appeared in *International History Review* (September 2003), pp. 505–756.

1 John Trevelyn, email 2011–12.

2 Ibid.

3 'The Exodus from Katanga – Congo Refugees', The North Road: Northern Rhodesians Worldwide message board archive (www.greatnorthroad.org/bboard/archives.php?period=200708).

4 St Jorre, John de, 'Looking for mercenaries (and some pen-portraits of those we found)', *Transition*, vol. 6, no. 33 (1967).

5 John Trevelyn, email 2011–12.

6 *Encyclopedia of the Jewish Diaspora: Origins, Experiences, and Culture: Volume 1*, ed. Mark Avrum Ehrlich (ABC-CLIO, 2009), p. 519.

7 Hughes, 'Fighting for White Rule in Africa'.

8 Gall, *Don't Worry about the Money Now*, p. 32.

9 John Trevelyn, email 2011–12.

10 Ibid.

11 'Names in the News', *Shih-chieh Chih-shih*, April/May 1961.

12 Mazov, Sergei, 'Soviet Aid to the Gizenga Government in the Former Belgian Congo (1960–61) as Reflected in Russian Archives,' *Cold War History*, vol. 7, no. 3 (August 2007), p. 433.

13 John Trevelyn, email 2011–12.

## 10 Pissing Blood in Katanga

Information about Lumumba's death comes primarily from *Les secrets de l'affaire Lumumba* by de Vos, Gérard, Gérard-Libois and Raxhon. Further details appear in the United Nations document 'Report to the Secretary General from His Special

Representative Regarding Mr. Patrice Lumumba' (S/4688/Add.1), Devlin's *Chief of Station, Congo* and de Witte's *The Assassination of Lumumba.*

1 *Transcript of the Congo Crisis, 1960–1961: A Critical Oral History Conference* (The Woodrow Wilson International Center for Scholars, 23–24 September 2004).
2 Cox, Richard, 'The Strong Man of Katanga', *The Reporter*, 30 April 1961.
3 De Witte, *The Assassination of Lumumba*, p. 97.
4 Trinquier, *Le temps perdu*, p. 381.
5 De Vos, Gérard, Gérard-Libois and Raxhorn, *Les secrets de l'affaire Lumumba*, p. 446.
6 De Witte, *The Assassination of Lumumba*, p. 142.
7 Doyle, David W., *True Men and Traitors* (John Wiley & Sons, 2001), p. 140.

## 11 The Counter-Revolutionaries
The story of Trinquier's involvement can be found in his autobiography, *Le temps perdu* and *Notre guerre au Katanga* by Trinquier, Duchemin and le Bailly. Additional details are from Roman Pasteger's *Le visage des affreux.*

1 Hempstone, *Rebels, Mercenaries and Dividends*, p. 133.
2 Kurzman, Dan, 'Katanga was not Crushed', *The Reporter*, 9 November 1961.
3 Trinquier, *Le temps perdu*, p. 368.
4 Ibid.
5 Ibid., p. 373.
6 Ibid., p. 374.
7 Ibid., p. 380.
8 Ibid., p. 381.
9 Ibid., p. 382.
10 Vandewalle, Frédéric, *Une tenebreuse affaire ou Roger Trinquier au Katanga* (Éditions de Tamtam Ommegang, 1979), p. 88.

11 Leguil-Bayart, Jean-François, *Global Subjects: A Political Critique of Globalization* (Polity, 2008), p. 145.
12 Mummendey, *Beyond the Reach of Reason*, p. 45.
13 Moraes, *The Importance of Being Black*, p. 202.
14 Mummendey, *Beyond the Reach of Reason*, p. 48.
15 UN Document (S/4688/Add.2).

## 12 Sold up the River
The history of the Compagnie Internationale is sourced from an email interview with Interviewee A, a former member of the unit (March 2011), and comments by the same member in the article 'First Recruiter for the Congo' on Terry Aspinall's Mercenary website (www.terryaspinall.com/03merc/congo/first-recruiter.html). Additional information comes from the 'UN Report to the Secretary General From His Acting Special Representative in the Congo Concerning the Interrogation of Thirty Mercenaries Apprehended in Kabalo on 7 April 1961' (S/4790), Jerry Puren's *Mercenary Commander* (Galago, 1986), the *Glasgow Herald* of 10 April 1961, the *Leader-Post* of 11 April 1961, articles in the *Rand Daily Mail* from the spring of 1961 and Eddy Hoedt's 'Marscompagnieën in Afrika: Het Eskadron Der Gidsen In De Katangese Secessie' on his Eddy's History Corner website (advalorum. weebly.com/het-eskadron-der-gidsen-in-de-katangese-secessie.html). Trinquier's activities are covered in his *Le temps perdu* and Trinquier, Duchemin and le Bailly's *Notre guerre au Katanga.* The primary source for 4 Commando's activities is *The Road to Kalamata: A Congo Mercenary's Personal Memoir* by its commander Mike Hoare (Lexington Books, 1989). Leif Hellström provided additional information in October 2012.

1 Hoskyns, Catherine, *The Congo since Independence, January 1960–December 1961* (Oxford University Press, 1965), p. 388.

2 UN Document (S/4691/Add.2).

3 UN document (Interview with a Katanga mercenary by Anne Ashe of the BBC, 19 January 1962 – S-0875-0003-06-00001 Items in Peace Keeping Operations, United Nations Operations in the Congo – Katanga – Tshombe).

4 Pasteger, *Le visage des affreux*, p. 119.

5 Trinquier, Duchemin and le Bailly, *Notre guerre au Katanga*, p. 97.

6 Ibid.

7 Aspinall, 'Congo 1960/68: The First Recruiter for the Congo', Soldiers of Fortune: Mercenary Wars (www.terryaspinall.com/03merc/congo/first-recruiter.html).

8 Interviewee A, email, 5 March 2011.

9 'Mercenaries Back in S.A. after Katanga Adventure', *Rand Daily Mail*, April 1961.

10 Aspinall, 'Congo 1960/68: The First Recruiter for the Congo', Soldiers of Fortune: Mercenary Wars (www.terryaspinall.com/03merc/congo/first-recruiter.html).

11 'Mercenaries Back in S.A. after Katanga Adventure'.

12 UN Document (S/4790).

13 O'Brien, *To Katanga and Back*, p. 197.

14 Interviewee A, email, 5 March 2011.

15 John Trevelyn, email, 2011–12

16 Pasteger, *Le visage des affreux*, p. 141.

17 Ibid., p. 136.

18 Saideman, Stephen, *The Ties That Divide: Ethnic Politics, Foreign Policy and International Conflict* (Columbia University Press, 2001), p. 44.

19 O'Brien, *To Katanga and Back*, p. 100.

## 13 Cocktails with Crèvecœur

Information on Conor Cruise O'Brien comes from his memoir *To Katanga and Back*. Mercenary figures are from *Le visage des affreux*. Mike Hoare quotes come from *The Road to Kalamata* and a letter written to Interviewee A of the Compagnie Internationale on 28 August 1961.

1 O'Brien, *To Katanga and Back*, p. 104.

2 Jordan, Anthony J., *To Laugh or To Weep: A Biography of Conor Cruise O'Brien* (Blackwater Press, 1994), p. 83.

3 O'Brien, *To Katanga and Back*, p. 66.

4 Kurzman, 'Katanga was not Crushed'.

5 Colvin, *The Rise and Fall of Moïse Tshombe*, p. 57.

6 Hempstone, *Rebels, Mercenaries and Dividends*, p. 139.

7 Hunter, Fred and Donanne, 'Travels in Africa: Coquilhatville, Congo, 1963', 19 November 2010 (www.travelsinafrica.com/2010/11/travels-in-africa-coquilhatville-congo-1963/).

8 Colvin, *The Rise and Fall of Moïse Tshombe*, p. 59.

9 Mummendey, *Beyond the Reach of Reason*, p. 96.

10 O'Brien, *To Katanga and Back*, p. 110.

11 Hoare, *The Road to Kalamata*, p. 81.

12 Kurzman, 'Katanga was not Crushed'.

13 Cox, 'The Strong Man of Katanga'.

14 Kurzman, 'Katanga was not Crushed'.

15 Löfgren, *Fredsknekarna*, p. 39.

16 Colvin, *The Rise and Fall of Moïse Tshombe*, p. 62.

17 Gérard-Libois, *Katanga Secession*, p. 204.

18 O'Brien, *To Katanga and Back*, p. 134.

19 Kurzman, 'Katanga was not Crushed'.

20 Moraes, *The Importance of Being Black*, p. 212.

21 Hoare, *The Road to Kalamata*, p. 57.

22 O'Brien, *To Katanga and Back*, p. 202.

23 Mike Hoare Letter to Interviewee A, 28 August 1961.

24 Ibid.

## 14 Rumpunch

United Nations document (S/4940) and *To Katanga and Back* show Conor

Cruise O'Brien's side of Operation Rumpunch. The main source for Bob Denard's life is his autobiography, *Corsair de la République* (Fixot, 1999) and the biography *Bob Denard: le roi de fortune* by Pierre Lunel (Éditions No. 1, 1991).

1 Chomé, Jules, *Tshombe et l'escroquerie katangaise* (Éditions de la Fondation Jos. Jacquemotte, 1966), p. 354.
2 Ibid.
3 UN Document (Interview with a Katanga mercenary by Anne Ashe of the BBC, 19 January 1962 – S-0875-0003-06-00001 Items in Peace Keeping Operations, United Nations Operations in the Congo – Katanga – Tshombe).
4 Denard, *Corsair de la République* (extracts available at www.orbspatrianostra.com/ops/ops-katanga.html/1).
5 Ibid.
6 Ibid.
7 'Congo: Stillness over Katanga', *Time*, 8 September 1961.
8 O'Brien, *To Katanga and Back*, p. 218.
9 UN Document (S/4940/Add.1).
10 John Trevelyn, email 2011–12.
11 Ibid.
12 Gérard-Libois, *Katanga Secession*, p. 165.
13 UN Document (S/5053/Add.12).
14 Colvin, *The Rise and Fall of Moïse Tshombe*, p. 90.
15 Victor Rosez, email July 2012.
16 'Canadian Officer Routs Young Mob', *The Ottawa Citizen*, 7 September 1961.
17 UK National Archives (5 September 1961 – CAB/195/20).
18 O'Brien, *To Katanga and Back*, p. 246.

## 15. *I am Prepared to Die Fighting in My Own Home*

The September fighting is described in the daily addendum to the 'Report of the Officer-in-Charge of the United Nations Operation in the Congo to the Secretary-General, Relating to

the Implementation of Paragraph A-2 of the Security Council Resolution of 21 February 1961' (S/4940/Add.2-8). Further information comes from 'Historia Spécial no. 406: Les Mercenaires 1960–1980' (Libraire Jules Tallandier, 1980), *Time* 22 September 1961, the Red Bank Register for the period and information in an email from Victor Rosez, July 2012.

1 Tommy Nilsson, email 2011.
2 Colvin, *The Rise and Fall of Moïse Tshombe*, p. 80.
3 Victor Rosez, email July 2012.
4 Ibid.
5 O'Brien, *To Katanga and Back*, p. 272.
6 'The Congo: War in Katanga', *Time*, 22 September 1961.
7 Reigel, Ralph, and John O'Mahoney, *Missing in Action: The 50 Year Search for Ireland's Missing Soldier* (Mercier Press, 2011), p. 104.
8 Ibid., p. 159.
9 Boulden, Jane, *Peace Enforcement: The United Nations Experience in Congo, Somalia, and Bosnia* (Greenwood Publishing Group, 2001), p. 36.
10 O'Donoghue, *The Irish Army in the Congo*, p. 105.
11 Ibid., p. 116.
12 Nicolaï, *Ici Radio Katanga*, p. 190.
13 O'Brien, *To Katanga and Back*, p. 254.
14 Gall, *Don't Worry about the Money Now*, p. 162.
15 'Historia Spécial no. 406: Les Mercenaires', p. 30.

## 16 *Katanga against the World*

The main sources here include the 'Report of the Officer-in-Charge of the United Nations Operation in the Congo to the Secretary-General, Relating to the Implementation of Paragraph A-2 of the Security Council Resolution of 21 February 1961' (S/4940/Add.2-8) and Nicolaï's *Ici Radio Katanga*. Information on Avikat comes from 'L'aviation militaire katangaise 1960–1963', *Les vieilles tiges de Belgique*, no. 3, July/August/September 1997. Leif Hellström provided information about Pierre Magain in October 2012.

1 O'Donoghue, *The Irish Army in the Congo*, p. 117.
2 Hempstone, *Rebels, Mercenaries and Dividends*, p. 165.
3 Hughes, 'Fighting for White Rule in Africa'.
4 Nicolaï, *Ici Radio Katanga*, p. 195.
5 Ibid., p. 198.
6 Reigel and O'Mahoney, *Missing in Action*, p. 129.
7 Lunel, *Bob Denard: le roi de fortune*, p. 170.
8 Nicolaï, *Ici Radio Katanga*, p. 201.
9 Shay, Reg, *The Penny-a-line Man* (Athena, 2006), p. 161.
10 Denard, *Corsair de la République* (extracts available at www.orbspatrianostra.com/ops/ops-katanga.html/7).
11 'Congo: The Heart of Darkness', *Time*, 22 December 1961.
12 Kurzman, 'Katanga was not Crushed'.
13 Binda, Alexandre, *The Saints: The Rhodesian Light Infantry* (30 Degree South Publishers, 2007), p. 28.
14 Reigel and O'Mahoney, *Missing in Action*, p. 164.
15 Mahoney, Richard D., *JFK's Ordeal in Africa* (Oxford University Press, 1983), p. 100.
16 Shay, *The Penny-a-line Man*, p. 160.
17 Lunel, *Bob Denard: le roi de fortune*, p. 170.
18 Gall, *Don't Worry about the Money Now*, p. 170.
19 Victor Rosez, email July 2012.

## 17 The Last Flight of the Albertina

Information on the 18 September 1961 crash comes from 'UN Report of the Commission of Investigation into the Conditions and Circumstances Resulting in the Tragic Death of Mr Dag Hammarskjold and of Members of the Party Accompanying Him, 24 April 1962' (A/5069); Bengt Rösiö's article 'The Ndola Crash and the Death of Dag Hammarskjöld', *Journal of Modern African Studies*, vol. 31, no. 4 (December 1993), pp. 661–71, and Rösiö's 'The Ndola Disaster' and 'End Notes to the Ndola Disaster' manuscripts (both 1992), accessed at the University of Gothenburg's website (https://gul.gu.se); Brian Urquhart's *Hammarskjöld* (New York: Alfred A. Knopf, 1972); Susan Williams' *Who Killed Hammarskjöld? The UN, the Cold War and White Supremacy in Africa* (Hurst, 2011).

1 'Ready to Fight', *Daytona Beach Morning Journal*, 21 September 1961.
2 Puren, *Mercenary Commander*, p. 17.
3 'The Congo: War in Katanga', *Time*, 22 September 1961.
4 Williams, *Who Killed Hammarskjöld?*, p. 588.
5 O'Brien, Conor Cruise, *Memoir: My Life and Themes* (Poolbeg, 1998), p. 259.
6 Puren, *Mercenary Commander*, p. 43.
7 Ibid., p. 46.
8 Binda, *The Saints: The Rhodesian Light Infantry*, p. 27.
9 'The Pride – Rhodesian Light Infantry Regimental Association', *Australasia Branch Newsletter*, January 2008.
10 Gall, *Don't Worry about The Money Now*, p. 151.
11 John Trevelyn, email 2011–2012.
12 'Belgian Troops Freed in Congo', *Glasgow Herald*, 26 June 1961.
13 O'Brien, *To Katanga and Back*, p. 207.
14 Puren, *Mercenary Commander*, p. 59.
15 Rösiö, 'The Ndola Disaster', p. 2.
16 UN Document (A/5069), p. 58.
17 Rösiö, 'The Ndola Disaster', p. 23.
18 John Trevelyn, email 2011–12.
19 Rösiö, 'End Notes to the Ndola Disaster', p. 14.

20 Fröhlich, Manuel, 'The Unknown
   Assignation: Dag Hammarskjöld in
   the Papers of George Ivan Smith',
   *Critical Currents*, no. 2 (March 2008).


## *18* Un Africain Blanc

The main source for Jean Schramme's
life is his Congo memoir *Le Battalion
Léopard: souvenirs d'un africain blanc*
(Robert Lafont, 1969) with additional
information from Anthony Mockler's
*The New Mercenaries* (Corgi, 1986).
The UN document 'Foreign Military
Personnel Reliably Reported to
ONUC to Have Been at Large in
Katanga as from January 1962' (S/5053/
Add.12/Annex I) corrects some of
Schramme's exaggerations.


1 Schramme, *Le Battalion Léopard*, p. 56.
2 Ibid., p. 65.
3 Ibid., p. 72.
4 UN Document: Foreign Military
   Personnel Reliably Reported to
   ONUC to Have Been at Large
   in Katanga as from January 1962
   (S/5053/Add.12 Annex I).
5 Schramme, *Le Batallion Léopard*, p. 76.
6 Gall, *Don't Worry about the Money
   Now*, p. 158.
7 'A Letter from the Publisher: Sep. 29,
   1961', *Time*, 29 September 1961.
8 Murphy, Philip, *Closer Association: 1945–
   1958* (Stationery Office, 2005), p. xci.
9 'The Congo: War in Katanga', *Time*,
   22 September 1961.
10 'The Congo: Full Circle', *Time*,
   29 September 1961.
11 Mummendey, *Beyond the Reach of
   Reason*, p. 70.
12 'Congo: The Heart of Darkness',
   *Time*, 22 December 1961.
13 Gérard-Libois, *Katanga Secession*, p. 224.
14 Nolutshungu, Samuel Clement,
   *South Africa in Africa: A Study in
   Ideology and Foreign Policy* (Africana
   Pub. Co., 1975), p. 87.
15 Victor Rosez, email July 2012.

16 'Mercenaries in Katanga are a
   Strange Mixture', *Spokane Daily
   Chronicle*, 29 September 1961.
17 *Africa Today*, vol. 9–11.
18 Schramme, *Le Battalion Léopard*, p. 83.
19 UN Document (S/4940/Add.II –
   Annex I).
20 Mummendey, *Beyond the Reach of
   Reason*, p. 139.
21 UN Congo Advisory Committee
   Meeting at 11.00am Friday 17
   November 1961 (S-0875-0001-01-
   00001). (The new Secretary General
   had only a single name: Thant.
   Pantanaw U Thant translates as
   Mr Thant from Pantanow.)
22 Hempstone, *Rebels, Mercenaries and
   Dividends*, p. 49.
23 US Document (Department of State,
   Central Files, 770G.00/2–2462).
24 Sitkowski, Andrzej, *UN Peacekeeping:
   Myth and Reality* (Praeger, 2006), p. 73.
25 Mummendey, *Beyond the Reach of
   Reason*, p. 80.


## *19* The Work of American Gangsters

Information on the December 1961
fighting comes from the four-part
'Report of the Officer-In-Charge of
the United Nations Operation in the
Congo concerning the situation in
Elisabethville' (S/4940/Add.16-19), as
well as contemporary newspapers and
magazines, notably *Time* and the *Red
Bank Register*. Smith Hempstone's *Rebels,
Mercenaries and Dividends* describes the
war from the Katangese side.


1 'Congo: Battle for Katanga', *Time*,
   15 December 1961.
2 UN Document (S/4940/Add.16).
3 'Captain Courage', Bharat Rakshak
   (www.bharat-rakshak.com/
   LAND-FORCES/History/1948-
   62/259-Captain-Courage.html).
4 'Congo: Battle for Katanga', *Time*,
   15 December 1961.
5 Puren, *Mercenary Commander*, p. 89.

6 Ibid.

7 UN Document (S/4940/Add.18).

8 O'Donoghue, *The Irish Army in the Congo*, pp. 101–02.

9 UK National Archive (7 December 1961 – CAB/195/20).

10 'Congo: The Heart of Darkness', *Time*, 22 December 1961.

11 Victor Rosez, email June 2012.

12 'Congo: The Heart of Darkness', *Time*, 22 December 1961.

13 Puren, *Mercenary Commander*, p. 92.

14 'Congo: Battle for Katanga', *Time*, 15 December 1961.

15 'Congo: The Heart of Darkness', *Time*, 22 December 1961.

16 Ibid.

17 Denard, *Corsair de la République* (extracts at www.orbspatrianostra. com/ops/ops-katanga.html/10).

18 *Red Bank Register*, 7 December 1961.

19 Ibid., 11 December 1961.

20 Saideman, *The Ties That Divide*, p. 44.

## 20 Clear Victory

Sources include 'UN Report on Developments in Katanga Following the Kitona Talks, 9 January 1962' (S-0888-0006-04-00001), 'The United Nations and the Congo White Paper, January 1962' (S-0875-0004-11-00001), as well the sources used for Chapter 18.

1 Hempstone, *Rebels, Mercenaries and Dividends*, p. 198.

2 UN Document: Foreign Military Personnel Reliably Reported to ONUC to Have Been at Large in Katanga as from January 1962 (S/5053/Add.12/Annex I).

3 'Congo: The Heart of Darkness', *Time*, 22 December 1961.

4 Struye et al., *Forty-Six Angry Men: The 46 civilian doctors of Elisabethville denounce U.N. violations in Katanga of its own charter, the universal declaration of human rights, the Geneva conventions* (American Opinion, 1962), passim.

5 *Katanga Libre*, 10 December 1961.

6 Victor Rosez, email July 2012.

7 Lunel, *Bob Denard: le roi de fortune*, p. 185.

8 Schramme, *Le Batallion 'Léopard*, p. 91.

9 'Congo: Battle for Katanga', *Time*, 15 December 1961.

10 Mockaitis, Thomas R., *Peace Operations and Intrastate Conflict: The Sword or the Olive Branch?* (Greenwood Publishing Group, 1999), p. 34.

11 Dobbins, James, Seth G. Jones, Keith Crane, Andrew Rathmell, Brett Steele, Richard Teltschik and Anga Timilsina, *The UN's Role in Nation-Building: From The Congo to Iraq* (Rand Corporation, 2005), p. 17.

12 UN Report on Developments in Katanga Following the Kitona Talks, 9 January 1962 (S-0888-0006-04-00001), p. 49.

13 Puren, *Mercenary Commander*, p. 125.

14 The United Nations and the Congo White Paper, January 1962 (S-0875-0004-11-00001), p. 80.

15 United Nations Operations in the Congo - Analysis on the Situation at Elisabethville, 14 December 1961 (S-0875-0004-07-00001), p. 5.

16 *Time*, 29 December 1961.

17 UN Document (S/5038).

18 UN Kongolo Commission (FCOPS3031), p. 15.

19 UN Document (62-02161).

20 UN Document (Clear Cable L.288).

## 21 Mr Brown from Poland

The best source on Zumbach's life is his autobiography *On Wings of War: My Life as a Pilot Adventurer* (Corgi, 1977), originally published in French as *Mister Brown: aventures dans le ciel* (Opera Mundi, 1973). Leif Hellström provided additional information in November 2012, as did Daniel Kowalczuk in February 2015.

1 Zumbach, *On Wings of War*, p. 37.
2 Ibid., p. 86.
3 Ibid., p. 126.
4 Ibid., p. 168.
5 Boehme, 'Involvement of the Belgian Central Bank'.
6 *Time*, 19 January 1962.
7 Mazov, 'Soviet Aid to the Gizenga Government'.
8 UN Reports on Developments Relating to Mr Antoine Gizenga, 20 January 1962 (S-0888-0006-04-00001), p. 39.
9 'Fascist Adventure Ended without Glory', *Le Peuple*, 30 January 1962.

## 22 The Black Eagle

Hubert Fauntleroy Julian is the subject of John Peer Nugent's biography *The Black Eagle* (Bantam, 1972). Additional information comes from contemporary articles in *Jet* magazine and article 'The Black Eagle of Harlem' in the online History of Flight section of *Air & Space Magazine* (1 January 2009).

1 Julian, 'The Black Eagle of Harlem'.
2 Ibid.
3 *The Speeches of Malcolm X at Harvard*, ed. Archie Epps (William Morrow & Co., 1968), p. 167.
4 Mjagkij, Nina, *Organizing Black America: An Encyclopedia of African American Associations* (Taylor & Francis, 2001).
5 *Negro World*, October 1962.
6 Gérard-Libois, *Katanga Secession*, p. 181.
7 Talalay, *Composition in Black and White*, p. 223.
8 Scheider, Gregory, *Cadres for Conservatism: Young Americans for Freedom and the Rise of the Contemporary Right* (NYU Press, 1999), p. 52.
9 Nugent, *The Black Eagle*, p. 69.
10 Ibid., p. 115.
11 Ibid., p. 175.

## 23 Occupation: Warlord

The main sources for this chapter are *Katanga Secession* by Jules Gérard-Libois, Schramme's *Battalion Léopard*, Denard's *Corsair de la République* and Lunel's *Bob Denard: le roi de fortune*.

1 Schramme, *Le Battalion Léopard*, p. 97.
2 Ibid., p. 96.
3 Ibid., p. 99.
4 Symes, Peter J., *Bank Notes of Katanga* (privately published, 1998).
5 'The Administration: An Abuse of Power', *Time*, 28 December 1962.
6 'Katanga Controversy', *The Heights*, vol. XLIII, no. 18 (6 April 1962).
7 Balace et al., *De l'avant à l'après-guerre*, p. 139, n. 39.
8 Pasteger, *Le visage des affreux*, p. 191.
9 Gérard-Libois, *Katanga Secession*, p. 266.
10 Clarke, S.J.G., *The Congo Mercenary: A History and Analysis* (The South African Institute of International Affairs, 1968), p. 32.
11 'Who are the Mercenaries?', *Time*, 22 December 1961.
12 Ibid.
13 Ibid.
14 Germani, Hans, *White Soldiers in Black Africa* (Nasionale Boekhandel Bpk, 1967), p. 12.
15 Gérard-Libois, *Katanga Secession*, p. 241.
16 US Document (Department of State, Central Files, 770G.00/11–2862).
17 Gérard-Libois, *Katanga Secession*, p. 267.
18 US Document (Department of State, Central Files, 110.12–McG/9–2962).
19 Gérard-Libois, *Katanga Secession*, p. 265.
20 US Document (Department of State, Central Files, 770G.00/6–2562).
21 Schramme, *Le Battalion Léopard*, p. 119.

## 24 The Flying Horror

The main sources here are Zumbach's *On Wings of War*, Nugent's *The Black Eagle* and Puren's *Mercenary Commander*.

1 Nugent, *The Black Eagle*, p. 180.
2 Turp, Robert, *Gunrunner: The Confessions of an Arms Dealer* (W.H. Allen, 1972), p. 10.
3 'Julian, Tongue-Lashed by Ghanaian, Quits Congo', *Jet*, 6 September 1962.
4 *Le Soir*, 14 September 1962.
5 Puren, *Mercenary Commander*, p. 128.
6 Ibid., p. 134.
7 Ibid., p. 141.
8 Zumbach, *On Wings of War*, p. 203.
9 Turp, *Gunrunner*, p. 71.
10 Ibid., p. 115.
11 Zumbach, *On Wings of War*, p. 211.
12 Ibid., p. 212.
13 Ibid., p. 210.
14 Ibid., p. 217.
15 Kalonji, *Congo 1960*, p. 137.
16 US Document (Department of State, Central Files, 770G.00/11–2862).

## 25 Christmas in Elisabethville

The story of Katanga's last months comes from UN Document (S/5053/add.15), Puren's *Mercenary Commander*, interviews with Tommy Nilsson and Victor Rosez, *Time* magazine, and assorted UN and US documents. Leif Hellström's *The Instant Air Force* (VDM Verlag Dr. Muller Aktiengesellschaft & Co. KG, 2008) has the full story of the CIA's Cuban pilots in the Congo.

1 'The Congo: Round 3?', *Time*, 4 January 1963.
2 Tommy Nilsson, email 2011.
3 UN Document (G-1936).
4 US Document (Department of State 95/01/13 Foreign Relations, 1961–63, vol. XX, Congo Crisis, p. 346).
5 Puren, *Mercenary Commander*, p. 145.
6 Ibid., p. 148.
7 Colvin, *The Rise and Fall of Moïse Tshombe*, p. 128.
8 Mummendey, *Beyond the Reach of Reason*, p. 85.
9 'The Congo: Round 3?', *Time*, 4 January 1963.

10 Mummendey, *Beyond the Reach of Reason*, p. 86.
11 'The Congo: Round 3?', *Time*, 4 January 1963.
12 UN Document (62-30765).
13 Victor Rosez, email 2012.
14 Puren, *Mercenary Commander*, p. 153.
15 Ibid., p. 154.
16 'The Congo: Round 3?', *Time* (4 January 1963).

## 26 Katanga '63

Information on the secession's final days comes from UN Document (S/5053/add.15), Puren's *Mercenary Commander*, Lunel's *Bob Denard: le roi de fortune*, Schramme's *Battalion Léopard*, *Time* magazine and other UN documents.

1 'The Congo: The UN Drives Implacably Ahead', *Time*, 11 January 1963.
2 The Association for Diplomatic Studies and Training Foreign Affairs Oral History Project, Ambassador Jonathan Dean interviewed by Charles Stuart Kennedy. Initial interview date: 8 July 1997.
3 UN Document (S/5053/Add.15).
4 Lunel, *Bob Denard: le roi de fortune*, p. 199.
5 UN Document (ONUC 66 OPI 1162).
6 'Sitting on a Powder Keg', *The Knickerbocker News*, January 1963.
7 Schramme, *Le Battalion Léopard*, p. 121.
8 Ibid., p. 125.
9 UN Document (G-166).
10 Puren, *Mercenary Commander*, p. 158.
11 Ibid.
12 Tommy Nilsson, email 2011.
13 Puren, *Mercenary Commander*, p. 160.
14 UN Document (Bunche from Gardiner: ELLE0227).
15 Dobbins et al., *The UN's Role in Nation-Building*, p. 233.
16 Clarke, *The Congo Mercenary*, p. 33, n. 50.

17 'The Congo: Tshombe's Twilight',
   *Time*, 25 January 1963.
18 UN Document (G-225).

## 27 Vers L'Avenir

Information on Tshombe's kidnapping
comes from *The Abduction and Death
of Moïse Tshombe: The End of a Hope
for the Congo* by Burkard Baron von
Müllenheim-Rechberg (Worldview
Publishing, 2001) and an article
published in *Life* magazine on 14
July 1967. Other sources include
Mockler's *New Mercenaries* and
interviews conducted with Khanti
Patel at his London home on 26
June 2010 and with Brian McCabe
via Skype on 17 April the same year.
Further information comes from
ex-mercenaries who wish to remain
anonymous.

 1 Müllenheim-Rechberg, *The Abduction
   and Death of Moïse Tshombe*, p. 12.
 2 'The Congo: Bare Cupboard', *Time*,
   8 February 1963.
 3 Moraes, *The Importance of Being Black*,
   p. 230.

 4 Butcher, Tim, *Blood River: A Journey
   into Africa's Broken Heart* (Vintage
   2008), p. 173.
 5 Tshombe, Moïse, *My Fifteen Months
   in Government* (University of Plano,
   1967), p. 35.
 6 Patel, taped interview, 26 June 2010.
 7 McCabe, Skype interview, 17 April
   2010.
 8 'NBC News Specials: Congo: Victim
   of Independence', 3 April 1966
   (www.nbcuniversalarchives.com/
   nbcuni/clip/51A06131_s01.do).
 9 Tshombe, *My Fifteen Months in
   Government*, p. 117.
10 Mockler, *The New Mercenaries*, p. 110.
11 Nilsson email interview, 2011.
12 'Brussels' Bar Simba' (Soldier of
   Fortune, August 1987).
13 congovox.blogspot.com/2011/02/
   albert-kalonji-ditunga-se-confie.
   html.
14 Davies, Norman, *God's Playground:
   A History of Poland in Two Volumes*
   (Columbia University Press, 2005),
   p. 459.
15 Planecrashinfo.com (www.
   planecrashinfo.com/cause.htm).

# SELECT BIBLIOGRAPHY

Behr, Edward, *Anyone Here Been Raped and Speaks English?* (Viking Press, 1978).

Colvin, Ian, *The Rise and Fall of Moïse Tshombe* (Leslie Frewin, 1968).

De Vos, Luc, Emmanuel Gérard, Jules Gérard-Libois, and Philippe Raxhorn, *Les secrets de l'affaire Lumumba* (Éditions Racine, 2005).

De Witte, Ludo, *The Assassination of Lumumba* (Verso, 2001).

Denard, Bob, *Corsair de la République* (Fixot, 1999).

Devlin, Larry, *Chief of Station, Congo* (PublicAffairs, 2007).

Dugauquier, D.P., *Congo Cauldron* (Jarrolds, 1961).

Gall, Sandy, *Don't Worry about the Money Now* (New English Library, 1984).

Gérard-Libois, Jules, *Katanga Secession* (University of Wisconsin Press, 1966).

Hempstone, Smith, *Rebels, Mercenaries and Dividends: The Katanga Story* (Praeger, 1962).

Hoare, Mike, *The Road to Kalamata: A Congo Mercenary's Personal Memoir* (Paladin Press, 2008).

Lawson, Richard, *Strange Soldiering* (Hodder and Stoughton, 1963).

Legum, Colin, *Congo Disaster* (Penguin, 1961).

Lunel, Pierre, *Bob Denard: le roi de fortune* (Éditions No. 1, 1991).

Mockler, Anthony, *The New Mercenaries* (Corgi, 1986).

Moraes, Frank, *The Importance of Being Black: An Asian Looks at Africa* (Macmillan, 1965).

Müllenheim-Rechberg, Burkard Baron von, *The Abduction and Death of Moïse Tshombe: The End of a Hope for the Congo* (Worldview Publishing, 2001).

Mulopwe, Albert Kalonji Ditunga, *Congo 1960, la sécession du Sud-Kasaï: la vérité du Mulopwe* (L'Harmattan, 2005).

Mummendey, Dietrich, *Beyond the Reach of Reason: The Congo Story 1960–1965* (Sora Mummendey, 1997).

Nicolaï, Marie, *Ici Radio Katanga … 1960–61* (J.M. Collet, 1987).

Nugent, John Peer, *The Black Eagle* (Bantam, 1972).

O'Brien, Conor Cruise, *The Road to Katanga* (Simon & Schuster, 1962).

O'Donoghue, David, *The Irish Army in the Congo 1960–1964: The Far Battalions* (Irish Academic Press, 2006).

Packham, Eric S., *Freedom and Anarchy* (Nova, 1996).

Pasteger, Romain, *Le visage des affreux* (Éditions Labor, 2005).

Patruno, Michele, *Quando E' L'ONU A Combattere* (Photocity, 2011).

Péan, Pierre, *Le mystérieux Docteur Martin* (Libraire Arthème Fayard, 1993).

Puren, Jerry, and Brian Pottinger, *Mercenary Commander* (Galago, 1986).

Reigel, Ralph, and John O'Mahoney, *Missing in Action: The 50 Year Search for Ireland's Missing Soldier* (Mercier Press, 2010).

Renton, David, David Seddon, and Leo Zeilig, *The Congo: Plunder and Resistance* (Zed Books, 2007).

Roberts, John, *My Congo Adventure* (Jarrolds, 1963).

Schramme, Colonel Jean, *Le Batallion Léopard: souvenirs d'un africain blanc* (Robert Lafont, 1969).

Schuyler, Philippa, *Who Killed the Congo?* (Devin-Adair, 1962).

Scott, Ian, *Tumbled House: The Congo at Independence* (Oxford University Press, 1969).

Talalay, Kathryn, *Composition in Black and White: The Life of Philippa Schuyler* (Oxford University Press, 1995).

Trinquier, Colonel Roger, *Le temps perdu* (Albin Michel, 1978).

Trinquier, Colonel Roger, Jacques Duchemin, and Jacques le Bailly, *Notre guerre au Katanga* (Éditions de la Pensée Moderne, 1963).

Tshombe, Moïse, *My Fifteen Months in Government* (University of Plano, 1967).

Turp, Major Robert, *Gunrunner: The Confessions of an Arms Dealer* (W.H. Allen, 1972).

Valahu, Mugur, *The Katanga Circus: A Detailed Account of Three UN Wars* (R. Speller, 1964).

Vandewalle, Frédéric, *Une ténébreuse affaire ou Roger Trinquier au Katanga* (Éditions de Tamtam Ommegang, 1979).

Weber, Guy, *Comme je les ai connus* (L. Bourdeaux-Cappelle, 1991).

Weber, Guy, *Le Katanga de Moïse Tshombe ou le drame de la loyauté* (L. Musin, 1983).

Williams, Susan, *Who Killed Hammarskjöld?* (Hurst & Co., 2011).

Zumbach, Jean, *On Wings of War: My Life as a Pilot Adventurer* (Corgi, 1977).

# INDEX